THE APPROA

SECOND PART

Alinari

ARPINUM, birthplace of Cicero, the great Roman orator

THE APPROACH TO LATIN

BY

JAMES PATERSON, M.A.

FORMERLY HEADMASTER, HILLHEAD HIGH SCHOOL, GLASGOW

AND

EDWIN G. MACNAUGHTON, M.A.

FORMERLY RECTOR, HAMILTON ACADEMY

SECOND PART

OLIVER AND BOYD

EDINBURGH

OLIVER & BOYD
Robert Stevenson House
1–3 Baxter's Place, Leith Walk, Edinburgh EH1 3BB
A Division of Longman Group Limited

ISBN 0 05 000293 7

FIRST PUBLISHED 1939
NEW EDITION 1969
TWENTY-FIFTH IMPRESSION 1980

Printed in Hong Kong by
Wing Tai Cheung Printing Co. Ltd.

PREFACE

THIS book continues *The Approach to Latin, First Part,* which has had a most gratifying reception from teachers of Latin. It covers the work of the second year, bringing the pupil to that point beyond which his interests are best served by separate books for translation, grammar and composition.

The book maintains the methods and ideals of its predecessor. Every effort has been made to render the transition from the first to the present part easy and natural. At the same time we have kept in view the possibility of using the present volume independently of its predecessor. For the newcomer to our course, the set of preliminary exercises will bridge any gap that may exist between his knowledge and that assumed in the first exercise of this book.

Grammar is again kept down to a minimum ; but that minimum is clearly set out, very gradually unfolded, and, it is hoped, adequately and interestingly exercised. The Subjunctive is introduced early and exercised in the simplest possible way to facilitate thorough grasp of forms before intricacies of syntax are encountered. In the treatment of the syntax, prominence is given to the great cardinal constructions which form the backbone of the second year's work, and care has been taken not to obscure the issues by admitting a mass of minor usages.

In vocabulary, some 700 words are added to the 600 given in the first book. Special vocabularies are again provided.

In the 45 exercises of the book the A sections are usually continuous passages. It is hoped that these will prove interesting in themselves and that collectively they will give the pupil an abiding impression of some of the dramatic moments in Republican history, of the Roman character at its best, and of the general course of Rome's rise to greatness. Each passage is written expressly for the place where it stands, without anticipation of grammar, vocabulary or syntax—unless, of course, the teacher prefers to do an A exercise *before* the formal learning of the attendant grammar and special vocabulary. To this method the book lends itself perfectly well.

It is necessary to emphasise that the average second year class is not expected to work through the whole book. For such a class the A and B exercises provide an adequate course. The C exercises which occur at intervals are for classes or pupils of special ability.

Importance is attached to the word-studies and other interest-material. Though the treatment of these is suggestive rather than exhaustive, it is hoped that time will be found to use them as a means of conveying some sense of the content and significance of the Roman civilisation.

Again we owe much to friends. Dr McGlynn has contributed the Appendices and scrutinised the Latin of the book; Mr R. G. M. McDougall, of Woodside Secondary School, Glasgow, has read the book through in typescript; Mr R. G. McCallum of the High School of Glasgow has rendered signal service in the reading of the proofs.

J. P.
E. G. M.

CONTENTS

Passive verb → cause of action a thing — use abl.

— for person a or ab + abl.

PRELIMINARY EXERCISES

A

N.B. The little boys were frightened by the soldiers,

Parvī puerī ā mīlitibus territī sunt.

The little boys were frightened by the soldiers' weapons,

Parvī puerī tēlīs mīlitum territī sunt.

1. (*a*) Bonī discipulī rīsū magistrum salūtant.
   (*b*) Sed ignāvī puerī ab hōc magistrō saepe castīgantur.
       Vōce igitur eius terrentur.
   (*c*) Trucī vultū magister eōs discipulōs exspectat.
   (*d*) Sērō enim in lūdum intrābunt. Diū in cubīlibus mānsērunt.
   (*e*) Stultitiae igitur poenās dabunt. Crās nōn sērō ad lūdum domō venient.

2. The mountains are beautiful. I love the mountains but my friend loves the sea.
3. To-day we shall walk to the sea. We shall be delighted by the sailors' stories.
4. Father will soon come home. Nothing has been prepared for him.
5. That building has been destroyed by fire.
6. Gifts will be given to the best pupils by their parents.
7. We shall not walk through the field; for we are frightened by the horns of the oxen.
8. Our native land has often been defended by the fleet.
9. The dog has been dragged from the water by the little boy.
10. Your plan has been adopted by all the farmers.

P. 8 ? quis
P. 251)

B

N.B. Some common interrogative words are—

quis ?	who ?	**ubi ?**	where ? (i.e. in what place ?)
quem ?	whom ?	**quō ?**	where . . . to ? (i.e. to what place ?)
quid ?	what ?	**unde ?**	where . . . from ? (i.e. from what place ?)
cūr ?	why ?	**quid novī est ?**	what news is there ?
quandō ?	when ?	*(gen. sing)*	

1. (*a*) Cūr diū in cubīlī manēs, Mārce ?   Tempus fugit.
   mi – voc,
   s, masc   (*b*) Ubi iam habitās, mī amīce ?   Iam in Galliā habitō.
   (*c*) Quid novī est, mī fīlī ?   Quid hodiē in lūdō fēcistī ?
   (*d*) Quem videō ?   Quis ad vīllam nostram festīnat ?
       Mehercule, Mārcus est !
   (*e*) Quandō, pater, in campō ambulābimus ?   Post cēnam,
       mī fīlī, ad campum festīnābimus.
   (*f*) Quō festīnātis, puerī, et unde vēnistis ?
   (*g*) Ā campō, magister, domum festīnāmus.   Sērō enim est.
       Māter nostra īrāta erit.

2. When will you give me back my ball, master ?
3. Whom do I see in the street ?   Upon my word, it is the new master !
4. Why does the old man not hear my voice ?
5. He does not hear because he is engrossed in his book.
6. Why did the foolish boy throw the ball into the water ?
7. " To-morrow," said the idle boy, " we shall discuss work."
8. Forgetful of danger the old men have remained outside the walls.
9. Where has your friend come from ?   His horse is tired, and his clothes are dirty.
10. The unhappy citizens had buried much gold in the fields.

C

N.B. *Statement :* **Pater iam domum vēnit,** Father has now
come home.

Question : **Paterne iam domum vēnit?** Has
father now come home ?

THOSE ROMANS

PATER : Domumne vēnistī, mī fīlī ? Quid hodiē in lūdō audīvistī ?

FĪLIUS : Domum vēnī, mī pater ; sed dēfessus sum. Hodiē
enim dē Rōmānīs et dē bellīs eōrum agēbāmus.

PATER : Magna quidem et nōbilis gēns Rōmāna erat.

FĪLIUS : Ita vērō, pater, sed quid dīcis ? Semperne bellum
gerēbant Rōmānī ?

PATER : Minimē vērō, mī fīlī. Saepe enim—

FĪLIUS : Nihil nōs nisi dē bellīs Rōmānōrum audīmus. Cum
vīcīnīs gentibus, cum Poenīs, cum Graecīs, cum Gallīs, cum
Britannīs, cum multīs aliīs bella gerēbant. Omnēs superāvērunt. Cūr nōn ab hostibus ipsī superātī sunt ? Rōmānōs
enim nōn amō.

PATER : Sed, mī fīlī—

FĪLIUS : Ita vērō, pater ; tū semper Rōmānōs laudās. Ego
tamen bella nōn amō ; pācem laudō. Quid prō pāce
Rōmānī umquam fēcērunt ? Quandō agrōs colēbant,
oppida aedificiīs et templīs pulchrīs ōrnābant ?

PATER : Pācem, mī fīlī, Rōmānī semper amābant, semper
laudābant, multīs gentibus dedērunt. Ubi barbarōs enim
superāvērunt, lēgēs iīs dedērunt, pulchrās urbēs aedificā-
vērunt, iūstitiam et scientiam docuērunt. Per montēs, per
silvās, in omnēs partēs viās optimās fēcērunt. Multīs in
terrīs hodiē etiam viās et pontēs eōrum vidēmus. Quid iam
dīcis, mī fīlī ? Semperne bellum Rōmānī gerēbant ?

FĪLIUS : Minimē vērō, mī pater. Mox dē pāce Rōmānā plūra
mihi nārrābis. Ōlim et ego fortāsse gentem Rōmānam
laudābō.

D

N.B. Some useful exclamatory words are—

ecce ! lo ! look ! behold !	**mehercule !** upon my word !
ēheu ! alas !	**vae tibi !** woe to you !
edepol ! upon my word !	**age, agite !** come !
goodness gracious !	**quam !** what ! how !

1. (a) Ubi est canis meus ? Nusquam eum videō. Quō fūgit ? Ecce, cum aliīs canibus parvus canis tuus lūdit.

   (b) Cūr īrāta es, mea māter ? Cūr ? Ecce, frātrēs tuī in pulvere lūdunt. Quam sordidae novae togae sunt ! Edepol, poenās mihi dabunt !

   (c) Mīlitēs, " Ēheu ! ", inquiunt, " diū labōrāvimus ; nihil tamen invēnimus. Pretium labōris nūllum habēmus."

   (d) Imperātor, " Vae tibi, sceleste homō," inquit, " ubi est scūtum tuum ? Ubi signum collocāvistī ? Edepol poenās dabis ignāviae."

   (e) Mārcus, " Agite, puerī," inquit, " hodiē ā lūdō fugiēmus ; ad campum festīnābimus et pilā lūdēmus. Hodiē magnus erit magistrī dolor ; crās magnus erit noster."

2. Where have the children fled to ?
3. Look, they are playing on the bank of the river.
4. In that little temple the maidens guard the eternal fire of the goddess.
5. The poet fled from the battle without his shield.
6. " Alas," said the shepherd, " who will carry this mass of gold ? "
7. We do not fear wounds and death.
8. We love honour and justice.
9. When father came home nothing had been prepared for him.
10. How angry he was ! The slaves all feared his anger.

E

Rules of Time : _when_
1. Time *at* or *within which* is expressed by the Ablative, e.g. :
   We shall come on the third day, **Tertiō diē veniēmus.**
   We shall come in three days, **Tribus diēbus veniēmus.**
2. Time *throughout which* is expressed by the Accusative, e.g.
   We shall remain for three days, **Trēs diēs manēbimus.**

1. (*a*) Quid novī est, Mārce ? Quandō ad urbem veniēs ?
   (*b*) Quīnque diēbus ad urbem veniam ; sed nōn multōs diēs in eā manēbō ; diē enim decimō ad Siciliam nāvigābō.
   (*c*) Multōsne diēs in eā īnsulā, Mārce, manēbis ?
   (*d*) Minimē vērō, mī amīce. Paucōs diēs manēbō ; festīnābō tamen ad multās urbēs ; frūmentum comparābō et ad urbem mittam ; dē Cicerōne, amīcō nostrō, homine optimō, multa audiam.
   (*e*) Quam fēlīx es, Mārce ! Ego semper in urbe maneō, semper labōrō ; nōn dēlectat mē haec vīta.

2. Why is the wife of Marcus anxious ?
3. Her husband is in Sicily ; he has already remained many days in the island.
4. In a few days he will come home just as the consul has ordered.
5. The old man is rich but he is just.
6. Therefore he will procure corn for the poor citizens.
7. Why is that old man dragging the little boy to his parents ?
8. The old man was sitting on a seat. The wicked boy threw dust at (**in** *with Acc.*) him.
9. For many hours we discussed your plan.
10. You have worked enough to-day, boys. In one hour I shall send you home.

F

1. The reflexive pronouns in Latin are :

mē, myself; **tē,** yourself; **sē,** himself, herself, itself; **nōs,** ourselves; **vōs,** yourselves; **sē,** themselves.

These are used when the action of the verb is *reflected* (i.e. bent) back upon the doer, e.g. :

Mīles scūtō sē servābat, The soldier protected himself with his shield.

2. To be distinguished from the above is the emphasising pronoun or adjective, **ipse, ipsa, ipsum,** e.g. :

Ipse tē vīdī, I myself saw you.

Note.—A useful way of deciding the proper translation of " -self " is to see if the word can be omitted without destroying the sense. If it can, the proper Latin word is some part of *ipse, -a, -um.* Test this method on the examples given above.

1. (*a*) Cūr ille senex tam miser est ?   Cūr semper labōrat, semper sē culpat ? Cūr numquam cum amīcīs, sīcut aliī senēs, in Campō ambulat ?

   (*b*) Ille senex ūnum fīlium habēbat. Amābat quidem fīlium ; pater tamen dūrus erat. Fīlium semper castīgābat. Is tandem īrā patris dēfessus domō fūgit, trāns mare nāvigāvit. Iam mīles est. Pater igitur, " Ēheu ! " inquit, " fīlium iterum numquam vidēbō. Mē tamen, nōn eum culpō. Quam miser sum ! Semper labōrābō ; numquam rīdēbō. Stultitiae meae ipse poenās dabō."

2. We ourselves shall never despair of victory.

3. Wise men often laugh at themselves.

4. The soldier will protect himself with his shield.

5. When shall we build ourselves a house ?

6. We ourselves do not know the way. Who will lead us to the farm ?

7. The wicked general has killed the very priests (i.e. the priests themselves) in the temple.

8. The centurion himself was ignorant of the general's instructions.

9. At that very hour I was engrossed in my book.

G

Note the following carefully :

> **Mēcum,** with me ; **tēcum,** with you ; **sēcum,** with himself, herself, itself, themselves ; **nōbīscum,** with us ; **vōbīscum,** with you (*pl.*).

But—

> When the pronouns do not refer to the subject of the sentence, with him, with her, with it, with them, must be translated **cum eō, cum eā, cum eō, cum eīs.**

1. (*a*) Agite, puerī, quid hodiē faciēmus ? Sciō (*I know*). Vōs mēcum trāns flūmen ad Campum Mārtium festīnābitis ; in Campō pilā lūdēmus ; corpora exercēbimus. Deinde domum ad cēnam mēcum veniētis. Post cēnam pater meus, nisi dēfessus erit, per Forum nōbīscum ambulābit. Fortāsse ad arcem nōs dūcet.

   (*b*) Ubi est pila mea ? Ēheu ! nusquam est. Herī eam in flūmen, in altam (*deep*) aquam coniēcit Sextus, frāter meus, puer pessimus. Sed poenās nōbīs dabit. Pilam enim et ipse habet optimam. Eā in Campō lūdēmus. Mox domum ā lūdō Sextus veniet. Pilam nōn inveniet. Quam īrātus erit !

2. Whom will you take (i.e. *lead*) with you to the city, father ?
3. First, I shall hurry home ; then, after dinner, I shall walk to the citadel with you.
4. Look, Marcus is sitting on that seat. Who is sitting with him ?
5. Upon my word, it is Sextus. They will come home with us.
6. Meanwhile I shall hurry home and prepare the dinner.
7. Why are you angry, mother ? Do you blame me ?
8. Yes indeed, my son ; you love games, but never read your books.
9. Who will play with us to-day ?
10. I shall not play with you ; for Marcus is playing with me.

I

DIRECT QUESTIONS

1. In Latin as in English, a question may be asked by means of an Interrogative Pronoun, Adjective or Adverb.

The Interrogative Pronoun **quis ?, quis ?** (or **quae ?**), **quid ?**, who ?, what ?, is declined as follows :

No.	Case	Masculine	Feminine	Neuter	Meaning
Singular	*Nom.*	quis ?	quis ? *or* quae ?	quid ?	who ?, what ?
	Acc.	quem ?	quam ?	quid ?	whom ?, what ?
	Gen.	cuius ?	cuius ?	cuius ?	whose ?, of what ?
	Dat.	cui ?	cui ?	cui ?	to, for whom ? *or* what ?
	Abl.	quō ?	quā ?	quō ?	by, with, from whom ? *or* what ?
Plural	*Nom.*	quī ?	quae ?	quae ?	who ?, what ?
	Acc.	quōs ?	quās ?	quae ?	whom ?, what ?
	Gen.	quōrum ?	quārum ?	quōrum ?	whose ?, of what ?
	Dat.	quibus ?	quibus ?	quibus ?	to, for whom ? *or* what ?
	Abl.	quibus ?	quibus ?	quibus ?	by, with, from whom ? *or* what ?

2. The Interrogative Adjective **quī ?, quae ?, quod ?**, what ?, which ?, is declined like the above, except that Nominative and Accusative Singular are :

Nom. **quī ?   quae ?   quod ?**
Acc. **quem ?   quam ?   quod ?**

3. Further Interrogative Adjectives and Adverbs are :

quantus, -a, -um ?, how great ? **quālis, -is, -e ?**, what kind of ?, of what kind ? **quot ?** (*indeclinable*), how many ? **cūr ?**, why ? **quandō ?**, when ? **ubi ?**, where ? **unde ?**, whence ?, where . . . from ? **quō ?**, whither ?, where . . . to? **quotiēns ?**, how often ? **quam ?**, how ? **quamdiū ?**, how long ?

EXERCISE 1

A

1. Cūr, pater, cīvēs in forum conveniunt ? Quid petunt ? Quis eōs vocāvit ?
2. Mehercule, cīvēs īrātī sunt. Viās enim īnfēstō agmine latrōnēs occupant.
3. Cīvēs, " Quamdiū," inquiunt, " latrōnēs in hāc cīvitāte erunt ? Quis eōs in vincula coniciet ? "
4. Ecce, cōnsul in forum festīnat. Quid dīcet ? Quā ōrātiōne animōs cīvium cōnfirmābit ?
5. Cōnsul exclāmat, " Cūr convēnistis ? Hodiē tempus nōn satis idōneum est. Crās iterum conveniētis. Tum dē latrōnibus agēmus."
6. Age, mea uxor, rem parvam ā tē petō. Vocābimusne hodiē ad cēnam paucōs amīcōs ?
7. Ita vērō, mī vir ; sed quot erunt ? Quantam cēnam parābō ?
8. Quam bona uxor es ! Grātiās tibi agō. Sī ego trēs amīcōs, tū frātrēs duōs vocābis, quot habēbimus ?
9. Mī vir, rem rogās facillimam ; duo enim et trēs quīnque sunt.
10. Quōrum canēs in agrō nostrō videō ? Cuius est canis ille magnus et niger ?

B

1. For whom are you preparing dinner, mother ?
2. Shall we go to the city to-day, father ?
3. No, my son ; the time is not suitable. To-morrow we shall discuss that matter.
4. Whose horse are you leading to the water, Syrus ?
5. It is my master's horse. What sort of man is your master ? He is a very good man.

6. How often have you seen the games, Marcus?
7. My father always takes (i.e. leads) me with him to the games.
8. Who are you, men? What are you seeking?
9. Why have the maidens fled to the woods?
10. The unhappy maidens are thoroughly frightened.
11. For the wicked robbers have attacked their homes and killed their parents.
12. Whom have you invited to dinner to-day, father?
13. I have invited three friends. But what are you seeking, my son? Shall we invite your friend Sextus?
14. How big is your house, Marcus? Is it bigger than ours?
15. How high is that wall? It is higher than your house, my friend.

ROMAN HISTORY

THE REPUBLIC

You will find in this book a number of reading lessons which gradually unfold an outline of the history of Rome down to the establishment of the Empire. The wise traveller, when about to enter new territory, equips himself with a map. For our excursion into Roman history such a map is provided in the chart opposite. Let us consider what it has to teach us.

We begin with 753 B.C., in which year, according to Roman tradition, the city was founded by Romulus, of the princely race of Alba Longa, and a descendant of the Trojan hero Aeneas about whom you read last year. Between 753 B.C. and 510 B.C. lies the period of the kings. Roman tradition gives the names of seven kings and adds many details concerning the reign of each; but it must be realised that those accounts are legend, not sober history. What is certain is that for long Rome was ruled by kings, and that kingship ultimately gave way to a republican form of government.

The Republic extends from 510 B.C. to 31 B.C. We notice first a series of wars ending with the conquest of Italy in 275 B.C.

Century	Vital Dates	Periods and Notes
	B.C. 753	Descendants of Aeneas rule Alba Longa
700 B.C.		THE PERIOD OF THE KINGS — Romulus – founds city 753 B.C.
		Numa – founds state religion
		Tullus Hostilius – warrior king
600 B.C.		Aneus Martius – extends Roman power
		Tarquinius Priscus – great builder
		Servius Tullius – reorganises people
		Tarquinius Superbus – tyrant; expelled 510 B.C.
500 B.C.	B.C. 510	THE PERIOD OF THE REPUBLIC — Long series of wars ending with defeat of Pyrrhus 275 B.C. leaves Rome mistress of Italy
400 B.C.		
300 B.C.		
200 B.C.	B.C. 275 / B.C. 264 / B.C. 241 / B.C. 218 / B.C. 202	First Carthaginian War 264-241 B.C.
		Second Carthaginian War 218-202 B.C.
100 B.C.	B.C. 133	Rome becomes mistress of the Mediterranean world 202-133 B.C.
		A century of revolution and civil wars. Sulla and Marius: Caesar and Pompey: Octavius and Antony. Octavius master of Roman world, 31 B.C. Founds empire, and receives name Augustus.
	B.C. 31	THE EMPIRE

ROMAN HISTORY, 753–31 B.C.

Alba Longa now Castel Gandolfo, in Alban Hill
S.E. of Rome.

Those wars began with the efforts of the kings to regain Rome—the wars in which figure Horatius, Scaevola and Cloelia of whom you read last year. Then came wars with more and more distant Italian states. Those campaigns produced heroes like Cincinnatus, Coriolanus and Camillus. Near the end of those wars came Rome's first encounter with an enemy from overseas, the Greek king Pyrrhus. In the course of this year's work you will find that during most of the period 510 B.C. to 275 B.C. there was in Rome itself a struggle between two classes of citizens, the Patricians and Plebeians. This struggle ended in the Plebeians obtaining political equality with the Patricians and in the practical disappearance of any real distinction between the classes.

Soon came the great wars against the African power, Carthage, 264 B.C. to 202 B.C. The overthrow of Carthage led to Rome's conquest of the Mediterranean world. The sudden rise to empire produced changes in Roman life which led to revolution, civil war and the fall of the Republic. Later on we shall have to look more closely at the events of the last century of the Republic. For the present let us fix the main lines of the story thus far :

(1) The Monarchy, 753–510 B.C.

(2) The Republic, 510–31 B.C., comprising—

    (*a*) Period of internal strife and, simultaneously, of expansion of Roman power in Italy, 510–275 B.C.

    (*b*) Period of great wars with Carthage, 264–202 B.C.

    (*c*) Period of expansion and conquest around Mediterranean, 202–133 B.C.

    (*d*) Period of civil wars and disorder, ending with establishment of the Empire, 133–31 B.C.

II

DIRECT QUESTIONS—*continued*

4. In Latin a statement is converted into a question by adding
-**nĕ** to the first word, e.g. :

STATEMENT	QUESTION
Mīlitem laudō, I praise the soldier.	**Mīlitemne laudō ?** Do I praise the soldier ?

The most emphatic word in the sentence is placed first, and
has -**ne** attached to it, e.g. :

Hodiēne mīles vēnit ? Did the soldier come *to-day* ?
Mīlesne hodiē vēnit ? Did *the soldier* come to-day ?

If no one word seems more emphatic than the rest, put the
verb first, and attach -**ne** to it, e.g. :

Has the boy a book ?   **Habetne puer librum ?**

5. A question which suggests the answer " Yes " is introduced by
nōnne, e.g. :

Is the farmer not working ?
Surely the farmer is working ? } **Nōnne agricola labōrat ?**
The farmer is working, isn't
he ?

6. A question which suggests the answer "No " is introduced
by **num,** e.g. :

Surely the farmer is not working ? } **Num agricola labōrat ?**
The farmer is not working, is he ?

7. Alternative questions are asked in Latin by placing **utrum**
before the first part, **an** before the second, e.g. :

Is he working or fighting ?   **Utrum labōrat an pugnat ?**
Did he come or not ?   **Utrum vēnit an nōn ?**

Notes.—(1) " OR NOT " forming second part of alternative direct
questions is always **an nōn** (frequently written as one
word **annōn**).

(2) " OR " coupling the two parts of an alternative question is
always **an** ; coupling alternative *words* or *statements* it
is **aut.**

(3) Distinguish **utrum . . . an,** (whether) . . . or,
and **aut . . . aut,** either . . . or, e.g. :

Utrum hostēs an amīcī sunt ? Are they enemies or friends ?
Aut hostēs aut amīcī sunt. They are either enemies or friends.

EXERCISE 2

A

THE REIGN OF ROMULUS. I

[*According to tradition,* ROMULUS *founded Rome in* 753 *B.C.
Our reading lesson tells of the stratagems by which he
procured men for his new city and then wives for his
men.*]

Rōmulus, ubi novam urbem condidit, eam ex nōmine
suō Rōmam vocāvit. Magna quidem urbs erat ; sed paucōs
cīvēs habēbat. In Monte Capitōlīnō lūcus erat ; hunc
Rōmulus asȳlum fēcit. Mox in id asȳlum multitūdō
latrōnum pāstōrumque ē vīcīnīs agrīs festīnāvit. Omnēs in
cīvitātem acceptī sunt. Tum Rōmulus, quod ipse popul-
usque uxōrēs nōn habēbant, lēgātōs ad vīcīnās gentēs
mīsit. Lēgātī societātem cōnūbiumque petēbant. Ēheu !
nusquam benignē audītī sunt. Multī enim exclāmābant,
" Quid ? Quālia petitis, Rōmānī ? Quō fīliās nostrās
vocātis ? Num latrōnibus eās hominibusque scelestīs
dabimus ? Minimē vērō. Vōs, tamen, cūr nōn fēminīs
asȳlum facitis ? Sīc enim uxōrēs comparābitis idōneās."

Rōmulus īrātus est ; īrātī sunt et omnēs cīvēs. Iuvenēs

igitur ad Rōmulum festīnant, et, " Quid facimus, Rōmule ?" *loc.*
inquiunt. " Quamdiū domī sedēbimus ? Quandō nōs *casa*
contrā vīcīnās gentēs dūcēs ? Tum enim aut fīliās suās
nōbīs dabunt, aut agrōs eōrum hominum vāstābimus,
urbēs dēlēbimus." Sed Rōmulus, " Utrum bellō," inquit,
" an cōnsiliō hanc urbem aedificāvī ? Utrum bellō an
cōnsiliō cīvēs huic urbī comparāvī ? Cōnsiliō, nōn bellō,
uxōrēs comparābimus." Tum magnōs lūdōs Rōmulus
parāvit. Vīcīnās gentēs ad hoc spectāculum vocāvit.
Multī hominēs convēnērunt ; vēnit et ingēns multitūdō
Sabīnōrum cum līberīs et uxōribus. Benignē sunt acceptī ;
per novam urbem ductī sunt. Templa, aedificia, moenia
vidēbant ; omnia laudābant. Tandem spectāculī tempus
vēnit. Ubi mentēs Sabīnōrum cum oculīs in lūdōs dēfīxae
sunt, tum Rōmulus iuvenibus suīs signum dedit. Illī in
multitūdinem impetum faciunt. Virginēs ab eīs capiuntur
et in urbem trahuntur. Parentēs virginum fugiunt perterritī.

B

1. (a) Salvē, mī amīce ! Quid agis ? Unde vēnistī ? Quam
fēlīx sum quod tē vīdī ! Sed quid dīcis ? Nōnne *(that*
domum mēcum ad cēnam veniēs ?

(b) Cūius vōcem audiō ? Sextumne videō, amīcum meum ?
Euge, Sextus est ! Quid ? Ad cēnamne mē vocās ?
Veniam, et maximō cum gaudiō.

(c) Iam domum nostram, Mārce, vidēs. Ecce, Lūcia, uxor
mea, ad iānuam stat ; nōs exspectat. Sed quid videō ?
Num trīstis es, mea uxor ?

(d) Minimē vērō, mī vir. Nōn trīstis sed īrāta sum.

(e) Quid ? Īrātane es, mea vīta ? Cūr ? Num ego causa
īrae sum ?

(f) Minimē vērō. Causa Syrus est, servus pessimus. Quam
bonam cēnam scelestus homō dēlēvit ! Edepol,
incēnsa sunt omnia.

(g) Tē, igitur, Sexte, et uxōrem tuam mēcum domum ad cēnam dūcam. Agite, quandō parātī eritis ? Mox sērō erit.

2. Surely you are not terrified, Marcus ?
3. Did you see the games, Sextus ? Yes, indeed ; it was a most beautiful spectacle.
4. How kindly Marcus's father received us ! Shall we not invite him to our house ?
5. Shall we seek the alliance of the Romans or of the Sabines ?
6. Will father come home to-day or not ? He will come in a few days.
7. We shall invite either the children or their parents to the games.
8. Surely you are not angry, master ? Have we not read the book ?
9. I shall ask the boys about the Roman kings.
10. Marcus, who founded Rome ?
11. Shall we travel to the city to-day or not ?
12. You are the boys' father, are you not ?
13. Have the children not come home ? Father will be angry.
14. Where is our dog, mother ? Has it hurried to school with Marcus ?
15. Good day, Marcus ! How do you do ? What's new in the city ?

WORD STUDY

From the interrogative words with which you have been busy, can you select the parents of our English words *quality* and *quantity* ? Why is the answer to a division sum called the *quotient* ?

Now derive and establish the meaning of *invocation, society, spectacular, petition, vicinity, benignant.* If you take up any tale of the Scottish Covenanters, you will probably find their meetings frequently called *conventicles.* From which of our recent Latin words is this derived ?

III

THE PRESENT IMPERATIVE

8. The forms of the Present Imperative, Active and Passive, of the four Regular Conjugations are as follows :

CONJUGATION	PERS. & NO.	ACTIVE	PASSIVE
1 **(amāre)**	2 *Sing.* 2 *Plur.*	**amā** love **amāte** ,,	**amāre** be loved **amāminī** ,, ,,
2 **(monēre)**	2 *Sing.* 2 *Plur.*	**monē** advise **monēte** ,,	**monēre** be advised **monēminī** ,, ,,
3 **(regere)**	2 *Sing.* 2 *Plur.*	**rege** rule **regite** ,,	**regere** be ruled **regiminī** ,, ,,
4 **(audīre)**	2 *Sing.* 2 *Plur.*	**audī** hear **audīte** ,,	**audīre** be heard **audīminī** ,, ,,

Notes.—(1) Verbs of the Third Conjugation in **-iō** drop **i** in forming the Present Imperative. Thus the Imperatives of **capiō** are :—

cape, capite   capere, capiminī.

(2) The Present Imperatives Active of **dīcō** I say, **dūcō** I lead, **faciō** I do, I make, are :—

dīc, dīcite ; dūc, dūcite ; fac, facite.

(3) The Present Imperatives of **sum** are :—

es, este.

(4) Observe that in all conjugations the 2nd Sing. Pres. Imperative Passive has the same form as the Present Infinitive Active.

EXERCISE 3

A positive command addressed to the second person is expressed by the Present Imperative, e.g. :

Labōrā, agricola. Work, farmer.
Labōrāte, agricolae. Work, farmers.

A negative command or prohibition is expressed by **nōlī** (*sing.*), **nōlīte** (*plur.*), followed by the Present Infinitive, e.g. :

Nōlī labōrāre, agricola. Don't work, farmer.
Nōlīte labōrāre, agricolae. Don't work, farmers.

(**Nōlī, nōlīte,** are Present Imperatives of **nōlō,** I am unwilling, I refuse.)

A

THE REIGN OF ROMULUS. II

[*The seizure of the Sabine maidens is followed by war.* TARPEIA's *treachery. The intervention of the captured maidens brings peace.*]

Sabīnī cum īnfēstō exercitū agrōs Rōmānōrum vāstābant. Mox ipsam urbem obsidēbant. Tum Tatiō, ducī Sabīnōrum, ex mīlitibus ūnus, " Vidēsne ? " inquit, " Puella ex urbe venit. Quae est ? Quid petit ? " Tatius, " Mox audiēmus." inquit, " Festīnāte, virī ; capite illam virginem et ad mē dūcite." Ubi ducta est, " Rōmāna," inquit, " puella sum. Tarpeiam mē cīvēs vocant. Tarpeius, pater meus, arcem dēfendit. Aquam petō extrā moenia." Tum Tatius, " Audī, Tarpeia," inquit, " sī nōs in arcem dūxeris, ingentia dōna tibi dabimus." Et Tarpeia, (mēns enim ēius cum oculīs in armillās Sabīnōrum ānulōsque dēfīxa est), " Quid ? " inquit, " Num ea dabitis quae in sinistrīs manibus habētis ? " Sed Tatius, " Et ea," inquit, " accipiēs." Tum virgō, patris et patriae immemor, hostēs in arcem dūxit.

Anderson

THE TARPEIAN ROCK

Over this cliff, which takes its name from Tarpeia, criminals were hurled
to their death.

Tandem, ubi arx iam occupāta ā Sabīnīs est, Tarpeia vēnit ; dōna petit. Sed statim Sabīnī, " Vae tibi, virgō scelesta ! " inquiunt, " Accipe quae in manibus sinistrīs habēmus ! " Tum scūta (habuērunt enim et ea in manibus sinistrīs) in Tarpeiam coniēcērunt. Pondere scūtōrum necāta est : ita poenās dedit illa prōditiōnis.

Ubi Rōmānī cum Sabīnīs iam proelium commīsērunt, ipsae fēminae Sabīnae vēnērunt, et " Dirimite īnfēstās aciēs," inquiunt, " dirimite īram. Num patrēs nostrī cum virīs nostrīs bellum gerent ? Num socerī generōs necābunt, et generī sanguine socerōrum sē maculābunt ? Nōlīte pugnāre. In nōs vertite īram ; in nōs tēla conicite : nōs enim, nōs causa bellī, nōs causa vulnerum et mortis virīs parentibusque sumus."

Rēs omnēs movet : ducēs conveniunt ; dē condiciōnibus agunt. Mox pāx cīvibus reddita est ; cīvitātem ūnam ex duābus faciunt.

B

1. (a) Festīnāte, puerī ! Sī sērō domum vēnerimus, nūlla cēna dabitur.
   (b) Magister, " Monēminī ā mē," inquit, " puerī ; sī man-dāta mea iterum neglēxeritis, poenās īgnāviae dabitis."
   (c) Quid agis, Mārce ? Mane paucās hōrās mēcum ; nōn sērō est.
   (d) Nōlī id petere, Sexte ; iam enim ad forum festīnō.
   (e) Vae tibi, sceleste puer ! Nōlī in miserum senem pulverem conicere.
2. (a) Ā patre, puerī, monēminī ; hodiē domī manēte.
   (b) Nōlīte dēspērāre, mīlitēs ; auxilium ā sociīs petēmus ; crās fortāsse hostēs superābimus.
   (c) Mēnsam parā, mea fīlia ; mox enim pater tuus domum veniet.

(*d*) Nōlīte, patrēs, īram in mē vertere ; numquam ego cīvium sanguine manūs maculāvī.

(*e*) Accipite, cīvēs, hās condiciōnēs ; meliōrēs ab hostibus numquam dabuntur.

3. To-day hurry home ; meet again to-morrow morning (*crās māne*).

4. See, Lucia ! what beautiful rings there are in that shop !

5. Do not turn your anger, Senators, upon thè wretched girl.

6. She has already paid the penalty for her treachery.

7. Do not break off the alliance, citizens.

8. Surely sons-in-law will not stain their hands with the blood of fathers-in-law ?

9. Hurry to school, Sextus. Don't neglect the master's instructions.

10. Don't invite my father-in-law to dinner, wife.

11. For I shall not receive him kindly.

12. Surely the citizens will accept these conditions ?

13. Shall we kill those men or throw them into prison ?

14. Surely they will pay the penalty for their treachery ?

15. How do you do, Marcus ? You are not hurrying to the games, are you ?

WORD STUDY

What is an advertisement ? A notice in the newspapers or a poster on the hoardings ? Well, these are certainly examples of advertisement, but to reach the essential meaning of the word, let us use our Latin. Derived from **ad** and **vertō,** an *advertisement*, whatever its form, is just a method of turning people toward our wares or ourselves.

If you ever stood on the edge of a high cliff, you may have felt your head " turn round." The ordinary name of that highly unpleasant sensation is dizziness ; but a doctor might term it *vertigo*, a word the derivation and meaning of which your Latin makes plain.

2

What are *sanguine* hopes ? What is a *sanguine* disposition ? A little thought will show you that the word means cheerful, confident, optimistic. A very interesting story lies behind the development of that meaning. Originally the word meant full of blood. Then it came to be applied especially to full-blooded, brisk, confident, energetic, optimistic people ; and finally to hopes, plans, and expectations of an optimistic nature.

Our English word *sinister* has an interesting history. In origin it is just the Latin word **sinister** meaning left. However, as the left was considered an unlucky side for signs and omens, *sinister* soon came to mean unlucky. Then it went on to mean evil, malicious, bad-intentioned, which are the ordinary meanings of the word to-day.

Now for a few problems for you to solve. Derive and explain—*reverse, inverse, version, pound, ponderous, imponderable, preponderant, ponder, immaculate.*

SOME FAMOUS SAYINGS

(a) *The Ideal of Fitness.*

Mēns sāna in corpore sānō, A healthy mind in a healthy body.

(b) *A Good Conscience.*

Mēns sibi cōnscia rēctī, A mind conscious of its rectitude.

(c) *Don't Panic.*

Aequam mementō rēbus in ārduīs servāre mentem, Remember to keep a calm mind in difficulties.

IV

THE RELATIVE PRONOUN

9. The declension of **quī, quae, quod,** who, which.

No.	Case	Masculine	Feminine	Neuter	Meaning
Singular	*Nom.*	quī	quae	quod	who, which
	Acc.	quem	quam	quod	whom, which
	Gen.	cuius	cuius	cuius	whose, of whom, of which
	Dat.	cui	cui	cui	to, for whom *or* which
	Abl.	quō	quā	quō	by, with, from whom *or* which
Plural	*Nom.*	quī	quae	quae	who, which
	Acc.	quōs	quās	quae	whom, which
	Gen.	quōrum	quārum	quōrum	whose, of whom, of which
	Dat.	quibus	quibus	quibus	to, for whom *or* which
	Abl.	quibus	quibus	quibus	by, with, from whom *or* which

Notes.—(1) The relative pronoun agrees with its antecedent in NUMBER and GENDER. Its CASE is determined by its function in its own clause. Consider the following sentences :—

(*a*) I have seen the boy who did this, **Puerum vīdī quī hoc fēcit.**
Here the relative pronoun is masculine singular to agree with the gender and number of the antecedent **Puerum ;** but it is in the nominative case because it is subject of **fēcit.**

(*b*) The boy whom you praised has come, **Puer, quem laudāvistī, vēnit.**
Here the relative pronoun is masculine singular to agree with antecedent **Puer ;** but accusative because object of **laudāvistī.**

(2) Before translating a relative pronoun into Latin, decide its number, gender and case. The antecedent will tell you the number and gender required ; the case is shown by analysis of the relative clause.

EXERCISE 4

Note.—" To leave," meaning " to depart from," is translated not by **relinquere,** which means " to leave behind," " to abandon," but by **discēdere,** to depart, to go away from, with **ā** or **ab** and the ablative, e.g. :

I shall leave the city, **Ab urbe discēdam.**

But before **domō,** from home, and before names of cities no preposition is used, e.g. :

I shall leave home, **Domō discēdam.**
I shall leave Rome, **Rōmā discēdam.**

A

1. Magister puerum quī sērō ad lūdum vēnit, castīgāvit.
2. Mehercule, puer quem magister herī castīgāvit, hodiē domō nōn discessit.
3. Ēheu! ānulus meus quem hodiē māne in mēnsā relīquī, nusquam est.
4. Eius urbis aedificia quae saepe ā poētīs laudāta sunt, ā mīlitibus incēnsa sunt.
5. Canēs ferōcissimōs timeō, quōs ille agricola habet.
6. Ego, Mārce, quī tē saepe laudāvī, hodiē tē culpō.
7. Tūne quī herī ad urbem vēnistī, hodiē discēdēs ?
8. Nōs quī portās custōdīmus, eās hostibus numquam aperiēmus.
9. Ingēns pondus aurī quod ā cīvibus sepultum erat, ā mīlite Rōmānō inventum est.
10. Portae huius templī quae multōs annōs apertae erant, iam clausae sunt.

B

1. The robbers who frightened the citizens have been thrown into prison.
2. We shall guard the state which we love.

3. Who has seen the she-bear which frightened Marcus ?
4. We have heard about the war which was waged for ten years.
5. Will you give me the ring which you have in your left hand ?
6. We all praise the laws which Caesar gave to the citizens.
7. The city which was founded by Romulus was enlarged by Numa.
8. My brother who came home in the morning remained for a short time.
9. " Hurry, boys ! " exclaimed the master who was awaiting us at the door.
10. I was thinking about the book which I had left at home.
11. Why have the doors of the temple been closed ?
12. The young man who came to our house has left his toga.
13. The beasts which live in those woods are very fierce.
14. Marcus had never heard about the maidens who guard the everlasting fire.
15. The gods whom we worship will guard our state.

C

Two Men and a Bear

Per silvam iter faciēbant duo iuvenēs, Mārcus et Septimus. Mārcus vērō perterritus est ; sed Septimus, " Quid timēs ? " inquit, " Num ignāvus homō tēcum ambulat ? Sī perīculum erit, num ego tē relinquam ? Quid ? Nōnne amīcus certus in rē incertā cernitur ? [1] Sī ego tē dēfendam, quī latrōnēs, quae ferae tē terrēbunt ? " Mox tamen vīdērunt iuvenēs ursam ingentem. Fŭgit Septimus ; sed Mārcus fugae immemor (mēns enim eius cum oculīs in ursam dēfīxa est), " Quō fugis, Septime ? " inquit, " Ēheu ! unde auxilium comparābō ? Ō mē miserum ! Quandō parentēs, līberōs, uxōrem vidēbō ? "

Intereā vōcem Mārcī ursa audit, et ad eum festīnat. Propter

---

[1] A well-known Latin proverb, the equivalent of our *A friend in need is a friend indeed.*

AMICUS CERTUS IN RE INCERTA CERNITUR

terrōrem relinquit animus Mārcum. Stat ursa, novā rē attonita ;
oculōs in corpus Mārcī dēfīgit ; diū manet, sed tandem, ubi
nūllum signum vītae videt, Mārcum relinquit, in silvam discēdit.
Tum vērō, ubi nūllum iam perīculum est, věnit Septimus, et
rīsū, "Mehercule, Mārce," inquit, "longam tibi fābulam ursa
nārrābat !" Et Mārcus, "Ita vērō," inquit, "Multa enim et
ūtilia mihi dīxit ; omnium tamen hoc maximum fuit.
' Audīsne, iuvenis ? ' inquit, ' sī umquam posthāc cum illō tam
īgnāvō sociō in hanc silvam intrāveris, tum ego tē necābō.' "

Note.—**animus relinquit M.,** M. faints. **posthāc,** hereafter.

V

THE RELATIVE PRONOUN—*continued*

10. Remember that—

The Relative Pronoun agrees with its antecedent in *Number* and *Gender* ; its *Case* is determined by its function in its own clause.

Let us consider some further applications of this rule.

(*a*) I have seen the boy whose father did this, **Puerum vīdī cuius pater hoc fēcit.**

Here the relative **cuius** is masc. sing. agreeing with the antecedent **Puerum,** but genitive as possessing **pater.**

Note.—A useful working rule for the present is that " whose " is always GENITIVE.

(*b*) I have seen the boy to whom you gave this, **Puerum vīdī cui hoc dedistī.**

Here the relative **cui** is masc. sing. agreeing with antecedent **Puerum,** but dative as indirect object of **dedistī.**

(*c*) I have seen the boy by whom this was said, **Puerum vīdī ā quō hoc dictum est.**

Here the relative **quō** is masc. sing. agreeing with antecedent **Puerum,** but abl. as denoting agent. Note presence of preposition.

By whom is **ā quō, ā quā, ā quibus**⎫ according to number and
By which is **quō, quā, quibus** ⎭ gender of antecedent.

Notes.—(1) When the ablative of the relative is accompanied by the preposition **cum,** we may say *either* **cum quō, cum quā, cum quibus,** *or,* **quōcum, quācum, quibuscum.**

(2) The relative takes the *person* of its antecedent, e.g. :
We who came, did this. **Nōs, quī vēnimus, hoc fēcimus.**
Here the relative is first pers. pl., and is therefore followed by a first pers. pl. verb.

(3) The relative must never be omitted in Latin, though English frequently leaves it out, e.g. :
I saw the boy you praised, *must be in Latin,* **Puerum vīdī quem laudāvistī.**

(4) Pay careful attention to the phrases **is quī,** the man who, he who ; **ea quae,** the woman who, she who ; **id quod,** the thing which, that which.

In these phrases the antecedent **is, ea, id** is sometimes omitted, e.g. :

> **Quod tū laudās, ego culpō,** I blame what (=that which) you praise.

Commonly, also, the antecedent **is, ea, id** is placed *after* the relative clause and *with* the main clause, e.g.

> **Quod tū laudās, id ego culpō.**

EXERCISE 5

1. In Latin **et** is not followed by a negative. Thus, instead of *et non*, we say **neque** *or* **nec.** Similarly—

instead of *et nūllus*, we use **neque ūllus,** " and no ; "

„ *et numquam*, we use **neque umquam,** " and never ; "

„ *et nusquam*, we use **neque usquam,** " and nowhere."

2. For "both . . . and " we use **et . . . et ;**

„ "neither . . . nor " „ **neque . . . neque,** *or* **nec . . . nec.**

A

THE REIGN OF NUMA

[After the miraculous disappearance of ROMULUS, NUMA POMPILIUS *becomes king. He cherishes peace, and organises the state religion.]*

Ubi Rōmulus, iam senex labōribusque dēfessus, cīvibus ōlim in Campō Martiō mandāta dabat, dēnsā nūbe cēlātus est, magnāque tempestāte perterritī cīvēs fūgērunt. Neque posteā Rōmulus umquam vīsus est. Rēs nova cīvēs movēbat ; rēgem omnēs dēflēbant. Patrēs tamen, " Nōlīte timēre." inquiunt, "Dirimite īram. Neque īrae neque timōris ūlla causa est. Ē terrā, enim, in caelum Rōmulus discessit. Deī fīlius, ipse iam deus est ā quō haec cīvitās semper dēfendētur. Quirīnum eum vocāte ; sīcut deum colite." Laudāvērunt cīvēs cōnsilium patrum ; deum Quirīnum maximō semper honōre colēbant.

Deinde rēx erat Numa Pompilius, vir optimus et iūstissimus, quī cōnsiliō deae Ēgeriae (ita enim ipse dīcēbat) lēgēs plūrimās ūtilēsque cīvibus dedit. Bellum quidem nūllum gessit, sed pāce cīvitātem auxit nōn minus quam bellō Rōmulus.

Maxima semper in deōrum cultū prūdentia Numae erat. Exclāmābat enim saepe, " Quid ? num condita est urbs Rōma sine deōrum auxiliō ? Num fēlīx dīvesque patria erit, nisi deōs colēmus ? Minimē vērō. Neque enim aedificium sine fundāmentō, neque cīvitās sine deōrum cultū diū stābit." Āram igitur Vestae cōnsecrāvit in quā ignis ārdēbat quem Virginēs Vestālēs, fīliae virōrum nōbilissimōrum, semper custōdiēbant. Iovis sacerdōtem creāvit cui vestīmenta pulcherrima sellamque curūlem dedit. Ubi templa iam plūrima Numa aedificāvit, duābus portīs templum Iānī ōrnāvit quae pācem semper bellumque indicābant. Eās enim Rōmānī aperiēbant, ubi bellum gerēbātur ; nōn, nisi ubi pāx reddita est, clausae sunt.

Sīc multōs annōs Numa cīvēs regēbat. Propter iūstitiam prūdentiamque nōn minus ā vīcīnīs gentibus quam ā cīvibus suīs amābātur.

B

1. (*a*) Translate :

  Rēx dē quō ; mīlitēs quibuscum ; sacerdōs cui ; dē deīs quōs ; poētae quōrum fābulās audīvimus ; is cui ; ea quam vīdī ; ea quae scrīpserāmus ; magistrōrum ā quibus ; is cuius sermōne mōtī sumus.

 (*b*) Complete each of the following by inserting the correct form of the relative :

  (1) Dominum vidēmus—īram servī timēbant.
  (2) Is in sellā sedet—dōnum herī dedī.
  (3) Rēx—laudāmus urbem pāce auxit.
  (4) Tibi—prūdentiā servātī sumus, grātiās agimus.

(*c*) — Translate.

(c) Cuius deae parvum templum in forō videō ?

(d) Vestae templum est, cuius in ārā ignis semper ārdet.

(e) Is ā quō haec urbs condita est, posteā deus fuit.

(f) Quis ille fuit ā quō tam benignē acceptī sumus ?

(g) Numquam ego tē relinquam quī mē semper adiūvistī.

2. The men who have been elected consuls will defend the state.

3. The men with whom we travelled will stay with us.

4. Surely you have often heard about the gods whom the Romans worshipped ?

5. Tell me about the god by whom fire was given to men.

6. By what plan shall we avoid the war which we fear ?

7. The worship of the gods will never be neglected by good men.

8. What do you say, Gallus ? Surely you have not neglected the instructions which I gave you ?

9. On account of his justice and wisdom, both the Romans and the Sabines loved Numa.

10. Neither Romulus nor Numa ever stained his hands with the blood of citizens.

11. How foolish Marcus is ! The new house which he has built has no foundations. Upon my word, it won't stand long (**diū**) !

12. Be advised by me, Septimus. Don't invite Sextus to the games. He always stays at home and never comes to the city.

THE ROMAN RELIGION

Many great scholars have spent years in the study of the religion of ancient Rome. Their labours have unfolded for us a wonderful and fascinating story. In the first place they have shown that the history of Roman religion goes back to a remote antiquity, far beyond the age at which King Numa was supposed to live. Secondly, it has been shown that in its

Alinari

VULCAN AND THE CYCLOPES AT WORK IN THEIR FORGE BENEATH MOUNT ETNA

earliest stages the Roman religion thought not so much of gods as of vague supernatural powers which had to be kept favourable to men by the recital of certain prayers and the performance of a number of rites and sacrifices. Gradually, many of those powers came to be named, and several of them thought of as persons. Then, when Rome came into contact with Greece, a great many of her divinities were identified with the gods and goddesses of Greece ; they were given the features and characteristics which the Greeks had long bestowed on their divine beings, and the many wonderful and beautiful stories which the Greeks told about their gods were attached to their supposed Roman counterparts. Here is a list of a few of the great Roman divinities—a list which will not only help you to understand many things in Latin but will be of great service to you in reading many passages in English poetry :

Jupiter : god of the sky, the father of gods and men ; the patron of Rome, where he had his temple on the Capitol ; he sent the rain and the thunder ; his weapons were the thunderbolts forged for him by the Cyclopes, giants who toiled in the depths of the earth under Mount Etna in Sicily.

Juno : the wife of Jupiter, goddess of marriage.

Minerva : the goddess of wisdom and the arts.

Neptune : the god of the sea.

Vulcan : the lame god of fire and metal-working.

Mars : the god of war.

Mercury : the messenger of the gods.

Diana : the goddess of the moon ; goddess of hunting.

Ceres : the goddess of agriculture.

Venus : the goddess of love and beauty.

Besides these there were many other gods and goddesses, such as the **Lārēs** and **Penātēs,** gods of the household ; **Vesta,** the goddess of the hearth. In her temple at Rome the sacred fire was kept constantly burning and was tended by a group of maidens drawn from the noblest families and called the Vestal virgins.

ghosts of the dead but orig. gods of farm-land.

gods of store-cupboard

VI

FURTHER ADJECTIVES AND PRONOUNS

11. Ĭdem, eădem, ĭdem, the same, is declined thus :

SINGULAR

	MASC.	FEM.	NEUTER
Nom.	ĭdem	eădem	ĭdem
Acc.	eundem	eandem	ĭdem
Gen.	eiusdem	eiusdem	eiusdem
Dat.	eīdem	eīdem	eīdem
Abl.	eōdem	eādem	eōdem

PLURAL

	MASC.	FEM.	NEUTER
Nom.	eīdem	eaedem	eădem
Acc.	eōsdem	eāsdem	eădem
Gen.	eōrundem	eārundem	eōrundem
Dat.	īsdem	īsdem	īsdem
Abl.	īsdem	īsdem	īsdem

Note.—In dative and abl. plural the forms **iīsdem** and **eīsdem** are also found.

12. Alius, alia, aliud, other, another, is declined thus :

SINGULAR

	MASC.	FEM.	NEUTER
Nom.	alius	alia	aliud
Acc.	alium	aliam	aliud
Gen.	alīus	alīus	alīus
Dat.	aliī	aliī	aliī
Abl.	aliō	aliā	aliō

The plural is perfectly regular.

13. There are several words whose genitive singular of all genders ends in **-īus**, while the dative singular, all genders, ends in **-ī**. Of such note : **ūnus, ūna, ūnum,** one ; **sōlus, sōla, sōlum,** alone ; **tōtus, tōta, tōtum,** whole, entire ; **ūllus, ūlla, ūllum,** any ; **uter, utra, utrum,** which (*of two*) ? ; **alter, altera, alterum,** the other (*of two*) ; **neuter, neutra, neutrum,** neither (*of two*) ; **nūllus, nūlla, nūllum,** no, none.

14. The following phrases are to be noted :
   (a) **aliī . . . aliī,** some . . . others.
   (b) **aliī alia dīcunt,** some say one thing, some another.
   (c) **alter . . . alter,** the one . . . the other.

EXERCISE 6

A

1. (a) Give the correct word for " same " to agree with : sacerdōtibus ; operum ; ārās ; cōnūbiī ; societās ; fīliās ; poētās ; scūta ; rosa ; agricola ; templum ; agrīs ; sermō ; virginum ; imperātōrum ; bellum.

   (b) Translate :
      puerī sōlī ; puerō sōlī ; puerī sōlīus ; ūnī fīliae ; alius cōnsul ; alter cōnsul ; nūllus exercitus ; nūllīus exercitūs ; neutrīus virginis ; nūllus mīles vēnit ; neque ūllus mīles vēnerat.

   (c) Translate :
      Alter ab alterō servātus est ; aliī alia amant ; alia aliōs terrent ; aliīs alia dabuntur ; alter alterī hōc dedit.

2. Hodiē neque in Campō ambulābō neque ab urbe discēdam ; magnō enim in opere tōtus sum.

3. Quī illī puerī sunt quī in eādem sellā sedent ?

4. Sextus et Mārcus sunt, pater. Alter puer doctissimus est ; alterīus mēns saepe in lūdōs dēfīxa est.
5. Ego paulisper in tabernā manēbō ; intereā tū nōlī ā forō discēdere.
6. Propter māchinās quibus moenia dēfenduntur haec urbs nōn capta est.
7. Mihi sōlī, quī amīcus ēius semper fuī, cōgitātiōnēs suās nārrāvit.
8. Magister noster quī ōlim mīles fuit eāsdem semper dē bellō fābulās nōbīs nārrat. Edepol, mīrābilēs fābulae sunt !

B

1. Give Latin for :

   Neither you (s.) nor I ; either you (s.) or I ; of another army ; for no citizen ; I saw the same ring ; the other consul will wage the war ; some are playing, others are working ; of the same states.

2. By means of a relative pronoun change each of the following pairs of sentences into a single sentence and translate into Latin :

   (a) Orbilius is a learned man. Orbilius is engrossed in his thoughts.
   (b) I shall tell a wonderful story to you. You alone are my friend.
   (c) Sextus has a book in his left hand. He is sitting on the seat.

3. The Romans gave good laws to the states which they conquered.
4. Some said one thing, others another ; all blamed the folly of the general.
5. These boys don't live in the same street, do they ?
6. When Catiline (*Catilīna, -ae*, m.) entered the senate house, no senator greeted him.

7. Which slave opened the door this morning ? Bring (i.e. *lead*) him to me.
8. Train your men to-day, centurions ; to-morrow we shall join battle with the enemy.
9. Which consul (N.B. *there were only two consuls in office at a time*) has neglected the old man's advice ?
10. To the one girl we shall give a ring, to the other a ball.
11. Don't be afraid, boys ; there are neither any bears nor any robbers in this wood.
12. Good morning, Sextus. How do you do ? Whom have you brought with you from the city ? Is it Marcus, your son-in-law ?

C

A GREAT SCIENTIST

[*In your Science lessons you may have heard of the Principle of* ARCHIMEDES. *Here we read how he helped to defend Syracuse against the Romans, and, on the capture of the town, met his death while engrossed in a mathematical problem.*]

In secundō bellō Pūnicō Sicilia societātem quae cum Rōmānīs fuerat dirēmit et prō Carthāginiēnsibus pugnāvit. Marcellus, igitur, cōnsul Rōmānus, cum īnfēstō exercitū Syrācūsās, urbem Siciliae nōbilissimam, oppugnāvit. Diū urbem Marcellus obsidēbat ; neque eam, nisi post trēs annōs, cēpit. Erat enim eō tempore in urbe vir doctissimus, Archimēdēs, mīrābilis inventor māchinārum quibus multōs mīlitēs Rōmānōs necāvit, opera Rōmānōrum vāstābat, nāvēs eōrum plūrimās dēlēvit. Tandem, ubi maximō impetū Rōmānī urbem cēpērunt, Marcellus (prūdentiā enim Archimēdis dēlectātus est), mīlitibus quī iam in urbem intrābant, " Servāte Archimēdem," inquit, " et ad mē dūcite." Sedēbat intereā domī Archimēdēs, tōtīus bellī

THE DEATH OF ARCHIMEDES

immemor; mēns ēius cum oculīs in fōrmās dēfīxa est quās in pulvere dēscrīpserat, neque dē victōriā Rōmānōrum audīverat. Tōtus erat in rē mathematicā. Tandem domum ēius intrāvit mīles quī trucī vultū, "Quis tū es?" inquit. "Num tū ille Archimēdēs es ā quō tam diū urbs dēfēnsa est?" Alter nihil respondit; mīlitem neque audīvit neque vīdit; tōtus enim in fōrmīs suīs et cōgitātiōnibus erat. Sed mīles, īrātus quod nihil Archimēdēs responderat, gladiō eum necāvit. Mortem ēius Marcellus dēflēvit, et omnī honōre corpus sepelīvit.

Note.—

inventor, -ōris, *m.*, inventor, discoverer.

fōrma, -ae, *f.*, figure, diagram.

dēscrībō, -ere, -scrīpsī, -scrīptum, draw, describe.

mathematicus, -a, -um, mathematical.

VII

COMPARISON

15. Remember that—

The word *than* after a comparative adjective is expressed in Latin by **quam.** Words joined by **quam** are in the same case, e.g. : **Agricola fortior quam poēta est,** The farmer is braver than the poet.

Special attention should be paid to sentences of the type—Our camp is larger than that of Caesar.

In such sentences, *that* or *those* is not translated. The Latin is—

Castra nostra māiōra sunt quam Caesaris, *literally,* Our camp is larger than Caesar's—which is, of course, a perfectly usual English expression.

16. When two nouns or pronouns are directly compared by means of a comparative adjective, **quam** may be omitted and the second noun or pronoun put in the ablative (Ablative of Comparison), e.g. :

Quis doctior est illō ? Who is more learned than he ? **Puerum meliōrem Marcō numquam vīdī,** I have never seen a better boy than Marcus.

Observe most carefully that this construction can only be used when two persons or things are directly compared, i.e. instead of **quam** with a nominative or **quam** with an accusative, but not instead of **quam** with any other case.

Note.—The Latin Comparative as well as meaning **-er,** *or* **more . . .,** can mean **rather . . ., somewhat . . ., too . . .,** e.g. :

Iuvenis trīstior erat, The youth was rather (*or* somewhat, *or* too) sad. Similarly, the Superlative, as well as meaning **-est,** *or* **most . . .,** can mean **very . . ., exceedingly . . .,** e.g. :

Opus difficillimum erat, The task was exceedingly difficult.

EXERCISE 7

A

THREE ROMAN KINGS

[*Scene: a Roman schoolroom. A review of Roman history leads the master to say something of the third, fourth and fifth kings of Rome.*]

MAGISTER : Age, Sexte, quis prīmus rēx fuit Rōmānōrum ? *Come!*

SEXTUS (*to himself*) : Ō mē miserum ! Ego sōlus nesciō ; ecce, tamen, mē prīmum rogat.

MAGISTER : Quid est, Sexte ? Quamdiū respōnsum exspect-ābimus ? Cūr nōn statim dīcis quod rogō ?

SEXTUS : Mehercule, magister, nesciō. Sed—manē paul-isper. Num Remus erat ?

MAGISTER : Quid ? Remumne dīcis ? Vae tibi, sceleste ! Puerum tē stultiōrem vīdī numquam. Quotiēns ego tibi, ō puer stultissime, nōmen prīmī rēgis dīxī ? Sed dē tē satis. Mārce, quid tū dīcis ? Quis hanc urbem condidit, cīvēsque prīmus regēbat ?

MĀRCUS (*very nervously*) : Ne-ne-nesciō.

MAGISTER : Mehercule, in eādem nāvī estis, tū et Sextus. Sed, ō bonī puerī, poenās īgnāviae vestrae idōneās mihi dabitis hodiē. Intereā Quīntum audiēmus. Quid tū dīcis, Quīnte ?

QUĪNTUS : Rōmulus fuit.

MAGISTER : Ita vērō. Posteā quis rēx fuit ? Dīc, Septime.

SEPTIMUS : Numa Pompilius, vir iūstitiā prūdentiāque īnsignis. Deōs colēbat ; pācem amābat ; pāce cīvi-tātem ille auxit nōn minus quam bellō Rōmulus.

Anderson

THE CLOACA MAXIMA WHERE IT ENTERS THE TIBER

MAGISTER : Euge, Septime ! Respōnsum dedistī optimum.
Iam audīte, omnēs. Quis tertius rēx erat ? Cūr tacē-
tis ? Num īgnōrātis ? Dīc, Tite.

TITUS : Numquam audīvimus. Multa quidem dē prīmo et
secundō rēge nōs docuistī ; nihil tamen dē aliīs.

MAGISTER : Post mortem Numae Tullus Hostīlius rēx
creātus est, vir ipsō Rōmulō ferōcior. Statim enim
Albam Longam oppugnāvit et magnō impetū cēpit.
Urbem, ubi capta est, dēlēvit et cīvēs Rōmam
dūxit.

TITUS : Sīc ruīnīs Albae Longae Rōma aucta est.

MAGISTER : Deinde bellum Tullus cum Sabīnīs gessit, neque
umquam ūlla quiēs ab armīs cīvibus dabātur.

Tɪᴛᴜs : Nōnne bellō iam dēfessī cīvēs Rōmānī erant ? Sed dē quārtō rēge quid nārrās ? Utrum pācem dedit ille cīvitātī an bellum cum vīcīnīs gentibus gessit ?

Mᴀɢɪsᴛᴇʀ : Quārtus rēx Ancus Mārtius fuit, Numae Pompiliī nepōs, vir avī similis. Bellum enim cum Latīnīs gessit et eōs superāvit. Oppida eōrum multa dēlēvit ; cīvēs Rōmam dūxit. Deinde cīvitātem auxit ; novum mūrum aedificāvit ; Pontem Sublicium in Tiberī fēcit.

Bridge of Piles

Sᴇᴘᴛɪᴍᴜs : Sed quīntus rēx ? quid ille fēcit ? quis fuit ?

Mᴀɢɪsᴛᴇʀ : Lūcius Tarquinius Prīscus quī bellum cum Sabīnīs gessit eōsque vīcit et fīliō, puerō tredecim annōrum, quod in proeliō hostem necāvit, togam praetextam et bullam dedit. Ex eō tempore haec puerōrum Rōmānōrum īnsignia sunt. Neque post bellum quiēs data est ab eō cīvitātī. Operibus enim ingentibus cīvēs exercēbat ; novum mūrum et is aedificāvit, urbisque loca humillima Cloācā Maximā siccāvit.

B

1. Translate the following sentences into English ; then rewrite each in Latin using the ablative of comparison instead of **quam** :

   (*a*) Discipulum doctiōrem quam tuum nepōtem numquam vīdī.

   (*b*) Canis meus māior est quam tuus ; sed tuus ferōcior est quam meus.

   (*c*) Onus meum gravius est quam tuum ; sed tuum māius est quam meum.

   (*d*) Cūr tacēs, Sexte ? Edepol discipulum stultiōrem quam tē numquam vīdī.

2. Translate each of the following into English ; then rewrite each in Latin using **quam** instead of ablative of comparison :

(a) Canem tuō māiōrem numquam vīderam.
(b) Vīdistīne umquam spectāculum hōc mīrābilius ?
(c) Ānulus meus tuā armillā pulchrior est.
(d) Hīc centuriō illō mīlite fortior est.

3. Why are you silent, boys ? I am asking you a very easy thing.
4. Is not your house larger than that of your brother ?
5. The Romans had often conquered fiercer enemies than the Greeks.
6. Give me back the ball which I gave you yesterday.
7. I have never heard more beautiful stories than those of this poet.
8. That book was written by a more learned man than Orbilius.
9. Many distinguished men have been taught by that master.
10. Who is more wretched than I ? Will you (*pl.*) not help me ?
11. No one had ever made more wonderful engines than Archimedes.
12. The new master tells us better stories than your grandfather.
13. Marcus is very lucky ; he has now the emblems of a consul.
14. Surely you have not seen a more beautiful toga than Marcus's ?
15. Good-day, Marcus. Where have you come from ? Have you seen the two men with whom we travelled (*iter facere*) to the city yesterday ?

WORD STUDY

No doubt you know what is meant by an *auction* sale ; but to-day, as a result of your recent Latin lessons, you can understand just why it came to receive that name. To-day also, you can say quite readily what an *alternative* is, and whence and why the *alternating current* received its name. *Aperture* you can recognise as a word of Latin origin meaning an opening ; and you should have no difficulty in stating what *fundamental* means. Can you give a word of non-Latin origin which means the same as *vicinity* ? Finally, what is the real meaning of *neuter* gender ?

VIII

COMPARISON OF ADVERBS

17. The Comparative of an adverb is formed by changing **-ior** of the comparative adjective into **-ius** ; the Superlative by changing **-us** of the superlative adjective into **-ē**, e.g. :

stultē, foolishly	**stultius**	**stultissimē**
pulchrē, beautifully	**pulchrius**	**pulcherrimē**
celeriter, quickly	**celerius**	**celerrimē**
facile, easily	**facilius**	**facillimē**

The following are irregular :

bene, well	**melius**	**optimē**
male, badly	**pēius**	**pessimē**
magnopere, greatly	**magis**	**maximē**
multum, much	**plūs**	**plūrimum**
paulum, little	**minus**	**minimē**
diū, for long	**diūtius**	**diūtissimē**
saepe, often	**saepius**	**saepissimē**

Note.—(1) **Quam** with a superlative adjective or adverb means *as . . . as possible*, e.g. : **quam maximus**, as large as possible ; **quam celerrimē**, as quickly as possible.

(2) A comparative adjective or adverb is frequently qualified by **multō**, (*by*) much ; **paulō**, (*by*) a little ; **aliquantō**, considerably (*literally*, by a considerable amount), e.g. : **multō māior**, much greater ; **paulō celerius**, a little more quickly ; **aliquantō melius**, considerably better.

EXERCISE 8

A

From Slave Boy to King

[*In the palace of* Tarquinius Priscus *a miracle befell a slave boy. The result was the boy's elevation to princely rank and succession to the throne.*]

Erat in rēgiā Tarquiniī Prīscī inter servōs puer quīdam nōmine Servius Tullius, cuī, ubi dormiēbat, caput ōlim ārdēre vidēbātur ; quod ad spectāculum servī omnēs convēnērunt. Oculōs in flammās dēfīgunt. Aliī tacent, novā rē perterritī ; aliī, " Contendite." inquiunt, " Aquam petite. Puerum celerrimē servāte." Rēx et rēgīna clāmōrēs audiunt ; ad puerum festīnant. Stant paulisper attonitī ; deinde rēgīna, " Quid timētis ? " inquit. " Nōlīte puerum dēflēre. Ecce, bene dormit. Neque eum excitābimus neque movēbimus. Edepol, maximōs illae flammae honōrēs in- dicant, neque sine deōrum cōnsiliō missae sunt." Tandem suā sponte puer oculōs aperuit ; flammae statim discēs- sērunt. Tum rēgī rēgīna, " Hic puer," inquit, " ōlim cīvi- tātem magnopere augēbit ; rēgiam in perīculīs fortissimē cūstōdiet. Age, statim eum līberā, et maximōs eī dā honōrēs."

Puer igitur līberātus est ; bullā togāque praetextā ōrnātus est. Omnia docētur quae rēgis fīliō idōnea sunt. Ubi iuvenis erat, rēgis fīliam dūxit. Post mortem socerī ipse rēx creātus est. Multōs annōs Servius Tullius bene et sapienter cīvēs rēxit ; mors tamen ēius misera fuit. Habē- bat enim duās fīliās, alteram ferōcem, alteram mītem. Erant et duo fīliī Tarquiniī Prīscī quōrum alter mītis, alter ferōx erat. Mītis Tarquinius ferōcem Tulliam, ferōx

Tarquinius mītem Tulliam dūxit. Ēheu! brevī tempore mītēs ā ferōcibus necantur; ferōx Tarquinius ferōcem Tulliam dūcit. Deinde cōnsiliō uxōris Lūcius Tarquinius (sīc ferōx ille appellātus est) rēgnum petit; socerum crūdēliter necat. Videt rem Tullia; prīma virum rēgem salūtat. Tum—ō scelus!—pietātis immemor super ipsum corpus patris currum agit.

Ex eō tempore vīcus in quō id Tullia fēcit Scelerātus ā cīvibus appellātus est.

B

1. (*a*) Age, Sexte, quid Rōmulus fēcit? Respondē quam celerrimē.
   (*b*) Celeriter respondēbō; rem enim rogās facillimam. Rōmulus, vir pietāte īnsignis, hanc urbem condidit.
   (*c*) Et tū, Marce, respondē mihi nōn minus celeriter. Quid dē Rōmānīs antīquīs dīcimus? Utrum magis propter pietātem an propter virtūtem īnsignēs erant?
   (*d*) Edepol, magister, nesciō. Aliī enim pietāte, virtūte aliī īnsignēs erant.
   (*e*) Ita vērō, Marce; bene respondistī.

2. Give Latin for:

   As often as possible; for a considerably longer time; a little less; as much as possible; very badly; much oftener.

3. Well done, Marcus! You write much better than your brother.

4. How do you do, Valerius? On which bank of the river will you drive your chariot?

5. This morning I slept as long as possible.

6. A certain man whom I do not like is waiting for me in the street.

7. Do not waken your father ; he has not slept for long.
8. Rouse the slaves as quickly as possible.
9. For to-day I shall drive my chariot to the city.
10. Is your master often angry, Syrus ? No, he is a very mild man.
11. Don't frighten the boys, master. They will come as quickly as possible of their own accord.
12. The boys will not work much to-day ; for to-day Marcus's brother will marry the master's daughter.

C

Solve the following crossword puzzle :

CLUES ACROSS

1. Your science master will have something to say about him.
8. Abl. sing. of a personal pronoun.
10. Perhaps you know ; I don't.
13. If you're doing this, you won't solve this puzzle.
14. A wife (*abl.*).
16. In this year the Greeks took Troy.
18. A nominative pl. of **locus**.
20. The Bible says that if you do this you will find.
21. A reflexive pronoun.
22. Prefix the first letter of 21, append the second letter of 1 across, and the result will be sinister.
24. Besiege !
28. You will have been.
30. Gen. sing. of 18.
32. Imperative pl. of 28.
33. A relation by marriage.
35. Add **patria** and you have a famous phrase.

36. Abl. sing. of a fifth declension noun.
37. With these the Sabines tempted Tarpeia.
39. To, towards.
41. Both deep and high.
44. So.
46. Present Indicative of 20.
47. Accus. sing. of **sus, suis,** *c.*, a pig.
48. Accus. sing. of personal pronoun.
49. You give.
53. This is *the same,* but it is different from anything else in this puzzle.
56. Present Infinitive ending of 1st conj.
57. With a book.
58. 1 across met his fate while engrossed in some of these.
59. An acc. pl. ending, and also a Roman coin.

CLUES DOWN

1. The Sabines wore these as well as 37 across.
2. A king.
3. This does not look like a Latin word but it is.
4. Only.
5. What you might exclaim if you met 28 down on a dark night.
6. I shall teach.
7. He will be.
8. Gen. sing. of a personal pronoun.
9. Many a dog would be happy with this.
11. By this in the end Romans and Sabines settled their differences.
12. Don't put things off until this.
15. 2nd pl. pres. ind. of 7.
17. My (*nom. pl.*).
19. A heavy one is hard to bear.
23. Singular of 15.

25. I have written.
26. Hard (*fem.*).
27. This person should not be too prominent.
28. There are few in our woods nowadays.
29. Gen. pl. of 36 across.
31. Self.
34. A disaster (*abl.*).
38. Add **facere** and you won't stand still.
40. What is this acc. doing in the 4th declension ?
42. A school (*abl.*), or a verb ?
43. He stands.
45. Definitely not good men.
47. Thus.
50. Where ?
51. Anger.
54. Abbreviation common in English.
55. Voc. sing. of 17 down.

REVISION EXERCISES

A

1. Do not depart (s.); increase (*pl.*); do you (s.) not train?; do not neglect (*pl.*); are you (s.) sleeping?; shall I rouse?; how long will you (s.) remain?; be silent, boy; be advised (*pl.*); what news is there?
2. How many boys were with you (*pl.*) in the house?
3. Surely you will not neglect your father's instructions, my son?
4. Shall we leave the city to-day or remain for a short time?
5. What wonderful engines Archimedes made!
6. Your master is very learned, is he not, Sextus?
7. Yes indeed; to-day he told us much about Archimedes.
8. Who was the man who received us so kindly?
9. Surely you (s.) will not leave the city alone? Will you not take me with you?
10. Good morning, friends! Are you hurrying to the games? Yes indeed; for the spectacle is wonderful. Why not come with us?

B

1. We whose friends you are; the maiden for whom; to the city in which; of those whom; for those whose.
2. The maiden whom he will marry is the consul's daughter.
3. We shall guard the city which we all love.
4. The boy who did not know the kings' names was scolded by the master.
5. The man whom I roused is now sleeping.
6. We were warned by a certain young man who was walking on the bank of the river.
7. My father, than whom no one is more gentle, rebuked the foolish girls.
8. The gate which I opened is now closed.

9. Are you (s.) not afraid of the wild beasts which live in that wood ?
10. The burden which I am carrying is very heavy.

C

1. In eōdem currū ; eārundem lēgum ; cūiusdam iuvenis ; eādem pietāte ; mihi sōlī ; eadem īnsignia ; eīsdem condiciōnibus ; māchina quaedam ; ipsīus socerī ; eōdem opere.
2. Quid agis, Marce ? Cūr tū sōlus tacēs ? Nōlī mē appellāre, Sexte ; tōtus enim sum in gravī quādam cōgitātiōne.
3. Mihine sōlī quī tōtum diem labōrāvī cēna nūlla est ?
4. Cūr Sextum excitāvistī quī tam bene dormiēbat ?
5. Ō mea Lūcia, unde illum tam pulchrum ānulum comparāvistī ?
6. Iuvenis quīdam nōmine Titus quī mox mē dūcet, eum mihi dedit.
7. Quam mīrābilēs māchinae sunt quās in urbe vīdimus !
8. Cūr virī nostrī contrā patrēs nostrōs pugnant ? Dirimite īnfēstās aciēs ! Nōlīte prō nōbīs manūs sanguine maculāre.
9. Quis avō meō mītior est ? Edepol, hominem mītiōrem numquam vīdī.
10. Feram illā ursā ferōciōrem numquam vīderam. Mehercule, quam celerrimē fūgī !

D

1. Hōc onus illō aliquantō gravius est ; illud opus hōc multō difficilius est ; domum paulō māiōrem tuā vīdī ; equum quam maximum mihi comparāvī ; cum eīsdem hostibus nōn iterum proelium committēmus.
2. I have never seen a more beautiful ring than yours, Lucia.
3. Why do you (pl.) not leave the house as quickly as possible ?
4. Were you (s.) not greatly terrified by the huge flames ?

5. Who was the king by whom our city was very greatly enlarged ?
6. Did Cicero leave the city of his own accord ?
7. I shall come home more quickly than you (*pl.*).
8. The master will scold the little girls whose books he found outside the door.
9. Why do you not procure a much larger house, Valerius ?
10. My house is very small, my friend ; nevertheless, it is large enough for me.

E

1. Write down and decline in the singular the Latin for : *this larger house ; the same chariot ; that wonderful story.*
2. Decline in the plural only the Latin for : *a small grandson ; a serious thought.*
3. Give the genitive singular, gender and meaning of : **socer, vir, pōns, quiēs, opus, sanguis, iġnis, pāx.**
4. Give principal parts and meaning of : **dirimō, dēfleō, colō, ġerō, reddō, custōdiō, sedeō, vertō, coniciō, neġleġō.**
5. Compare : **bonus, ferōx, maġnus, similis, diū, saepe, pulchrē, pulcher, maġnopere, multum.**
6. *Derive* : sedentary, mental, prudence, ignite, annual, accept, auxiliary, ponderous, dormitory.
7. Give Latin words for :

time	shepherd	heaven
robber	citadel	worship
suitable	gift	building
game	weight	inn
parent	alliance	palace
marriage	cloud	treason
invite	cause	honour

IX

THE VERB " TO BE "

18. The Present and Imperfect Subjunctive of **esse,** to be :

TENSE	PERS.	SINGULAR	PLURAL
PRESENT	1	sim	sīmus
	2	sīs	sītis
	3	sit	sint
IMPERFECT	1	essem	essēmus
	2	essēs	essētis
	3	esset	essent

Notes.—

(1) The various forms of the subjunctive have a variety of meanings which will be mastered gradually. For the present, note that **sim** can mean *I may be, may I be, let me be* ; and that in many types of subordinate clause it must be translated by an English present indicative, e.g. :

cum sim, since I am.

(2) Similarly with the imperfect subjunctive. **Essem** can mean *I might be, I would be, I should be* ; and in many kinds of subordinate clause must be translated by an English past indicative, e.g. :

cum essem, since I was.

(3) The imperfect subjunctive active of any Latin verb is formed by adding **-m, -s, -t,** etc., to the present infinitive active, e.g. : **amārem,** I might love ; **audīrem,** I might hear.

EXERCISE 9

Note.—An exhortation addressed to the first person is expressed by the present subjunctive, e.g. **Sīmus fortēs,** Let us be brave.
This is called the *Hortative Subjunctive.*
A command addressed to the third person is also expressed by the present subjunctive, e.g. : **sit fortis,** let him be brave.
This is called the *Jussive Subjunctive.*
The negative of such subjunctives is **nē,** e.g. :

> **Nē sīmus īgnavi,** Let us not be cowardly.
> **Nē taceat,** Let him not be silent.

A

1. Nē īgnāvī sīmus, mīlitēs ; hodiē mēcum contrā hostēs contendite ; fortāsse crās proelium committēmus.
2. Sit populus Rōmānus inter omnēs gentēs pietāte et virtūte īnsīgnis.
3. Sit pāx inter vōs, patrēs nostrī et virī !
4. Nē stultī sīmus, amīcī ; cōnsilium melius hōc nūllum inveniēmus.
5. Ōlim meō magistrō doctior sim.
6. Hodiē sit magister noster homo mītissimus ; ego enim sine librīs ad lūdum vēnī.
7. Nē sīmus cīvibus invīsī ; hanc enim cīvitātem magnopere amāmus.
8. Hodiē, mī fīlī, ad lūdum nōn festīnābis. Iuvenis enim quīdam magistrī fīliam hodiē dūcit. Contende igitur ad vīllam avī ; tōtum diem in agrīs lūde ; fēlīx sīs ; post cēnam domum festīnā.

B

1. You (*s.*) might be ; let them be ; we may be ; he might be ; I may be ; they might be ; let us be ; we shall have been ; you (*s.*) may be ; you (*pl.*) were ; let them not be.

2. In the following translate the words in italics only :

   (a) Prepare your father's bed ; perhaps *he may be tired.*

   (b) The general encouraged his men, so that *they might be brave.*

   (c) The Romans killed Caesar, lest one day *he might be king.*

   (d) We shall come home early, lest *you* (pl.) *may be anxious.*

   (e) He carried the old lady's parcel, lest *she might be tired.*

3. Why do you despair of victory, soldiers ? May you be brave !

4. May we be more learned than the girls !

5. May you alone, because of your resolution (*cōnstantia*) be our general !

6. Let him not be my master. For he is very fierce.

7. May there be no kings among the Romans !

8. Let us be free citizens in a free state.

9. He works better than the others. Therefore let him be leader.

10. May you be distinguished among the soldiers by your boldness, Titus.

C

A Brave Centurion

[*In his history of the Gallic Wars* Caesar *tells how the centurion* Publius Sextius Baculus *rose from a sick-bed to save the situation when the camp was in dire danger.*]

Erat aeger in castrīs relictus Pūblius Sextius Baculus, quem propter virtūtem quae maxima semper erat, Caesar saepe laudāvit. Is, ubi clāmōrēs barbarōrum audīvit, quī impetum magnā vī in castra faciēbant, perīculō sollicitus, ad sociōs festīnāvit. Tum, " Quid hoc est," inquit, " quod videō ? Num barbarōs īgnāvissimōs quōs iam saepe vīcimus, timētis ? Nōlīte dē victōriā, dē ipsā vītā dēspērāre. Agite, omnēs mēcum in

3

hostēs contendite." Haec ubi dīxit, ab iīs quī proximī erant, arma cēpit ; ad portam castrōrum vēnit ; in aditū stetit. Contendunt ad eum centuriōnēs cohortis ēius quae in statiōne erat. Maximā cōnstantiā proelium sustinent. Ubi vulnera iam plūrima accēpit, relinquit animus Sextium ; ā sociīs tandem ē pugnā in castra tractus est. Illīus tamen sociōrumque audāciā, aliīs quī hostium impetū perterritī erant, breve tempus datur in quō sē cōnfirmant. Deinde omnēs ad moenia contendunt ; castra fortissimē dēfendunt.

Note :

aeger, -ra, -rum, sick.
cohors, -tis, *f.*, cohort (the tenth part of a legion).
audācia, -ae, *f.*, boldness.

in statiōne esse, to be on picket duty.
relinquit animus Sextium, S. faints.

WORD STUDY

Īnsignia is a Latin word which we have taken into English without alteration. Can you recall any more ? What exactly is meant by the Law of *Gravity* ? Such a common word as *responsible* takes on a new interest when we realise that a person *responsible* for anything is simply the person who must answer for it. Can you suggest any other English words derived from respondēre ? Brevis gives us not only *brevity*, but *brief*. *Nepotism* is not by any means a common English word, but look up its meaning and note how it is derived from a Latin word which you know quite well by this time. Finally give the derivation and hence try to establish the meaning of *piety, solicitous, solicitude, solicit, adit.*

X

THE VERB " TO BE "—*continued*

19. Perfect and Pluperfect Subjunctive of **esse**, to be :

Tense	Pers.	Singular	Plural
PERFECT	1	fu-erim	fu-erīmus
	2	fu-erīs	fu-erītis
	3	fu-erit	fu-erint
PLUPERFECT	1	fu-issem	fu-issēmus
	2	fu-issēs	fu-issētis
	3	fu-isset	fu-issent

Notes.—

(1) The perfect subjunctive active of any Latin verb may be formed by adding, **-erim, -erīs, erit**, etc., to the perfect stem. Compare these endings with those of the future perfect indicative.

(2) The pluperfect subjunctive active of any Latin verb may be formed by adding **-issem, -issēs, -isset**, etc., to the perfect stem.

(3) Bear in mind what has been said about the variety of meanings of the tenses of the Latin subjunctive. The perfect subjunctive can mean *I may have* ——; and the pluperfect subjunctive can mean *I might* (or *could* or *would* or *should*) *have* ——; but in many types of subordinate clause the perfect subjunctive must be translated by the English perfect indicative, and the pluperfect subjunctive by the English pluperfect indicative, **e.g.**

> **cum fuerim,** since I have been.
> **cum fuissem,** since I had been.

EXERCISE 10

Note.—**Cum** meaning *since* .introducing a subordinate adverbial clause of reason, requires the verb of its own clause to stand in the subjunctive mood, e.g. : **cum sit,** since he is ; **cum fuissent,** since they had been.

In this construction the Latin subjunctive must be translated into English by the corresponding tense of the indicative.

Note the phrases :

> **quae cum ita sint,** since this is so, this being the case.
> **quae cum ita essent,** since this was so, this being the case, under these circumstances.

These phrases can stand only at the beginning of a sentence or clause.

A

[SEXTUS *finding his father for once at leisure demands a story about* TARQUINIUS SUPERBUS, *the last king of Rome. In response, his father tells him how the Sibylline Books were brought to Rome.*]

SEXTUS : Age, pater, cum sōlī sīmus, fābulam mihi nārrā.

VALERIUS : Sed quā dē rē, mī fīlī, fābula erit ?

SEXTUS : Dē Tarquiniō Superbō ; nōmen enim eius audīvī, et pauca dē eō magister herī nōbīs in lūdō nārrāvit. Scelestus homō fuit et ferōcissimus, quī uxōris cōnsiliō socerum crūdēlissimē necāvit et ita rēgnum occupāvit. Cum rēx dūrus et crūdēlis esset, Superbus ā cīvibus appellātus est. Nihil tamen praetereā magister dīxit.

VALERIUS : Quid ? Nōnne dē librīs Sibyllīnīs audīvistī ?

SEXTUS : Nōn audīvī, pater, sed tū nārrā, nisi molestum est.

VALERIUS : Audiēs, mī fīlī. Vēnit ōlim ad rēgiam anus quaedam. Novem sēcum librōs portābat, et Tarquiniō, " In hīs librīs," inquit, " ōrācula deōrum scrīpta sunt ;

TARQUIN AND THE SIBYL

quī, sī populus Rōmānus eōs comparāverit, maximīs in
perīculīs cōnsilium semper dabunt optimum." Tarquinius dē pretiō rogat ; anus ingēns aurī pondus
statim petit. Sed rēx, " Quid ? " inquit, " Satisne
sāna es, quae pretium tantum petis prō novem librīs
quī mihi sordidī inūtilēsque videntur ? "

SEXTUS : Ō pater ! Quid anus respondit ?

VALERIUS : Nihil illa quidem ; sed statim in ignem ex
novem librīs trēs coniēcit. Deinde rēgī, " Ecce,"
inquit, " sex librī restant. Hōs tibi dabō, sed eōdem
illō pretiō." Rīsit Tarquinius, aliīsque quī rem vidēbant,
" Mehercule," inquit, " dēlīrat haec anus." Quod ubi
illa audīvit, ex librīs trēs aliōs in flammās coniēcit.
Ubi dēlētī sunt, prō tribus quī restābant pretium
petīvit nōn minus quam quod prō omnibus petītum erat.

Quae cum ita essent, Tarquinius magnopere mōtus est.
Vultū iam sēriō animōque attentiōre dē librīs agit.
" Nōn sine causā," inquit, " tanta est anūs cōnstantia."
Quid multa ? Librōs quī nōn dēlētī erant, pretiō rēx
comparāvit nōn minōre quam quod anus prō omnibus
petīverat.

B

1. Nē suspīciō sit ; cum fortēs fuissent ; nē molestī sītis ;
   cum fēlīcēs fuerīmus ; cum nōn sāna esset ; attentiōrēs
   sīmus ; cum molestum fuisset ; nē trīstēs sint.
2. Combine each of the following pairs of sentences by changing one sentence in each pair into a **cum**-clause :

   (a) Hīc liber inūtilis est. Eum in flammās coniciēmus.
   (b) Sextus īgnāvus fuerat. Īgnāviae poenās dedit.
   (c) Senex cīvibus invīsus erat. Ab urbe discēssit.
   (d) Magister doctus est. Dē rēbus populī Rōmānī multa
       vōs docēbit.
   (e) Hoc onus gravissimum est. Dēfessus sum.

3. Translate :

   (a) Cum suspīciō prōditiōnis esset, imperātor cīvēs con-
       vocāvit.
   (b) Cum hīc equus inūtilis sit, alium comparābimus.
   (c) Cīvium mentēs cum oculīs in spectāculum dēfīxae
       erant. Quae cum ita essent, portae male custōdiē-
       bantur.
   (d) Attentī sīmus, cīvēs ; hodiē enim dē rē gravissimā
       agēmus.

4. Since we are not tired, we shall walk on the bank of the
   river.
5. Let us not be foolish, citizens ; do not leave your houses ;
   for it is dangerous.
6. Our men have been defeated across the river.

7. **Since this is** so, we shall close the gates and defend the walls.

8. Since you (*s*.) have not been troublesome to me, you will receive this big ball.

9. Since I had been at home for a long time, I had heard everything.

10. Sextus writes much better than Marcus.

11. This being the case, he will be praised by his master and parents.

12. Since you (*s*.) are engrossed in your books, I shall walk to the shops alone.

13. Since the old woman's burden is very heavy, I shall help her.

14. Prudence is much better than boldness. Since this is so, we shall not leave the camp.

15. Since the boys are tired, they will sleep for a long time.

READING THE FUTURE

Hardly anything in Roman life is more surprising to us than the way in which the Romans, before beginning a new enterprise, sought to find out whether it would succeed or not. Their method was to try to ascertain the will and attitude of the gods towards the new enterprise. They believed that the will of the gods was revealed in certain signs and omens which could be observed and interpreted by persons with the requisite knowledge. Hence we find every important public and private action regularly prefaced by the taking of omens in some form or other. No matter what was contemplated, whether a marriage, a meeting of the Senate, the foundations of a city, a declaration of war, a battle or a campaign, omens had to be sought.

The taking of omens was not left merely to individuals. The business was in the hands of a Board called the College of Augurs. These augurs had had long and elaborate training in observing signs and in interpreting what they observed.

Methods were various. Omens might be sought by watching the flight and behaviour of birds, by observing the state of the sky, and, very commonly, by studying the appearance of the bodies and particularly of the entrails of animals slain for sacrifice. Of all the parts of a victim the one which had most significance was supposed to be the liver. Its size, shape, colour, the presence or absence of spots on it—all these things had meaning for the augur.

Then there were the Sibylline Books. However these may have come to Rome in the first place, there is no doubt that they existed and were consulted. They were guarded in the temple of Jupiter on the Capitol, and were at first in the charge of two priests. Later the number was raised to ten and then finally to fifteen. At times of great emergency, when disaster had been sustained in war or there was a visitation of plague or the like, the books were consulted. The result seems generally to have been the introduction of some new god or of some new rite into the Roman religion. The consultation of the Sibylline Books went on in this way down to 83 B.C., when they perished in a great fire which destroyed the temple of Jupiter on the Capitol.

ROMAN NAMES

Except in early times a Roman had usually three names, e.g. Gaius Julius Caesar. The first, called the **praenōmen,** was a purely personal name, corresponding to our Christian name. The second, called the **nōmen,** indicated the *gens*, i.e. clan or group of families, to which the Roman belonged. The third, called **cōgnōmen,** indicated the family of which he was a member.

XI

PRESENT AND IMPERFECT SUBJUNCTIVE ACTIVE

20. The Present and Imperfect Subjunctive Active of the four regular conjugations are as follows :

Conj.	Pers.	Present		Imperfect	
		Sing.	*Plur.*	*Sing.*	*Plur.*
	1	ám-em	am-ēmus	amā-rem	amā-rēmus
1st	2	ám-ēs	am-ētis	amā-rēs	amā-rētis
	3	ám-et	ám-ent	amā-ret	amā-rent
	1	móne-am	mone-āmus	monē-rem	monē-rēmus
2nd	2	móne-ās	mone-ātis	monē-rēs	monē-rētis
	3	móne-at	móne-ant	monē-ret	monē-rent
	1	rég-am	reg-āmus	régĕ-rem	regĕ-rēmus
3rd	2	rég-ās	reg-ātis	régĕ-rēs	regĕ-rētis
	3	rég-at	rég-ant	régĕ-ret	régĕ-rent
	1	aúdi-am	audi-āmus	audī-rem	audī-rēmus
4th	2	aúdi-ās	audi-ātis	audī-rēs	audī-rētis
	3	aúdi-at	aúdi-ant	audī-ret	audī-rent

Note.—Verbs of the third conj. ending in **-iō** form their Present and Imperfect Subjunctive thus :

Pres. Subj. Active
    capiam
    capiās
    capiat
    etc.

Imperf. Subj. Active
    capĕrem
    capĕrēs
    capĕret
    etc.

EXERCISE 11

A

The First Consuls

[*The Tarquins were expelled in* 510 *B.C. Two consuls were elected as heads of the state for a year. One, being a Tarquin, was forced to resign office and leave Rome. The sons of the other, caught conspiring to restore the Tarquins, were executed by the command and before the eyes of their father.*]

Cōnsŭlēs creātī sunt Iūnius Brūtus et Lūcius Tarquinius Collātīnus, quōrum alter cīvitātī cārus, invīsus alter erat. Cīvēs enim, " Tarquiniī," inquiunt, " rēgnum semper amant. Superbus expulsus est, sed Collātīnus imperium habet. Nōmen ēius nōbīs invīsum, lībertātī perīculōsum est. Nē diūtius in urbe maneat ! Statim discēdat ! " Quae cum ita essent, Brūtus cīvēs in forum vocāvit. Ubi multitūdō convēnit, Brūtus, " Populus Rōmānus," inquit, " sollicitus est, cum rēgiam gentem, nōmen rēgium, nōn in cīvitāte sed etiam in imperiō videat. Hunc suā sponte Lūcius Tarquinius removeat metum. Expulit rēgēs : grātiās eī agimus : hōc tamen addat beneficiō suō ; removeat ex urbe rēgium nōmen. Amīcus ex urbe discēdat ; rēs eius nōn modo reddent cīvēs eī sed meō cōnsiliō magnopere augēbunt." Cum aliī eadem peterent, Collātīnus abdicāvit sē cōnsulātū et ex urbe discessit. Mox omnēs Tarquiniae gentis expulsī sunt. Tum cōnsul creātus est Pūblius Valerius cūius auxiliō Brūtus rēgēs expulerat.

Nē tum quidem quiēs cīvitātī data est. Erant enim in urbe iuvenēs quīdam, Tarquiniōrum amīcī, quī inter sē saepe, " Agite ! " inquiunt, " rēgēs in urbem nocte accipiā-mus." Ipsī Brūtī cōnsulis fīliī in societātem cōnsiliī acceptī

sunt. Convēnērunt ōlim ; tōtā dē rē agēbant. Sermōnem
eōrum ex servīs ūnus audīvit. Is cōnsulibus rem tōtam
nārrāvit. Quī ā cōnsulibus missī sunt nōn modo iuvenēs
cēpērunt sed quās ad Tarquinium scrīpserant epistolās
invēnērunt. Coniectī sunt in vincula iuvenēs ; paulō post
ad mortem ductī sunt. Cīvium oculī dēfīxī sunt in cōnsulis
līberōs quī patriae, patris, cōnsulātūs, senātūs, ipsīus
lībertātis immemorēs cōnsilium tam scelestum cēperant.
Intereā cōnsulēs vēnērunt. Brūtus, ubi fīliōs suōs vīdit,
paene superātus est dolōre ; dolōrem tamen vīcit ingēns
amor patriae. Missī sunt lictōrēs quī prīmum iuvenēs
verberāvērunt, deinde necāvērunt. Sīc poenās illī prōditiōnis dedērunt.

B

1. Combine the following pairs of sentences by using **cum**
   and subj. :
   (a) Ipse petasum nōn habeō. Tuum igitur cēpī.
   (b) Imperātor cīvibus invīsus erat. Ex urbe expulsus est.
   (c) Cīvitātem magnopere amābat. Cōnsulātū sē abdicāvit.
   (d) Iter longum est. Paulisper in hāc vīllā maneāmus.
   (e) Duōs gladiōs habeō. Alterum igitur tibi dabō.

2. Let us hasten ; since we were coming ; let them not rule ;
   may you (*pl.*) take ; let us not give ; since he was
   advising ; I might add ; they might hear ; may you (*s.*)
   be brave ; you (*s.*) might have.

3. Let us not expel the famous general from the city.

4. Since he was guarding our liberty, shall we not praise him ?

5. Let the citizens leave the forum at once, and (let them)
   assemble to-morrow.

6. Since one consul was hateful to the citizens he resigned
   his consulship.

7. Since I was writing letters to-day, I did not walk to the
   forum.

8. How do you do, grandfather ? You are not hurrying home, are you ? Let us walk to the temple of Vesta.
9. A new master has come to the town. May he teach the boys well !
10. Since Lucia had two rings, she gave one to me.
11. Since we were working, we did not see the spectacle.
12. Let us thank grandfather ; for he has sent beautiful gifts for us.

C

THE OLD EDUCATION AND THE NEW

[During the first quarter of the second century B.C., schools were fast springing up in Rome, and most citizens sent their sons to them. Some brought up their sons at home, entrusting their education to a learned slave —generally a Greek. Only a few, like CATO *in our story, clung to the ancient custom of personally teaching their sons.]*

OPPIUS : Quid hoc est quod videō ? Num Mārcus Porcius Catō, vir ille fortis et strenuus, domī sedet ōtiōsus ?

CATŌ : Domī sedeō, mī amīce, sed minimē ōtiōsus. Librum enim hunc dē populō Rōmānō magnīs litterīs scrībō Mārcō fīliō meō.

OPPIUS : Quid ? Mārcumne domī ēducās ?

CATŌ : Ita vērō. Ipse eum omnia doceō, sīcut ōlim pater meus mē docuit.

OPPIUS : Edepol, mī Catō, mōrēs semper tū laudās antīquōs ! Cum hodiē tempus fere tōtum reī pūblicae dēmus, cūr fīlium nōn mittis ad lūdum quemdam ex eīs quōs doctī hominēs iam plūrimōs in urbe īnstituērunt ? Sīc enim puer plūra discet et multō facilius ; multīs et magnīs cūrīs ipse līberāberis.

CATŌ : Mōrem nārrās pessimum et reī pūblicae perīculōsum. Quālia enim dīscunt puerī in lūdīs illīs ? Quālēs sunt ipsi magistrī ? Nōnne hominēs sunt pauperrimī, Graeculī ēsurientēs (*starveling Greeks*), quī, cum ipsī neque cōnstantiam neque virtūtem neque fidem habeant, nōn artēs virīlēs sed vitia sua docent ? Linguam Graecam puerī discunt ; tōtī sunt semper in fābulīs poētārum Graecōrum ; mōrēs intereā corrumpuntur. Quandō enim pietātem, virtūtem, patriae amōrem, laudēs populī Rōmānī audiunt ? Nisi tālia didicerint, quandō bonī cīvēs, mīlitēs fortēs, cōnsulēs prūdentēs erunt ?

Mōre igitur antīquō fīlius meus domī ēducātur. Annōs iam septem māter eum cūrābat ; nunc ego cūrō.

OPPIUS : Quid tamen eum docēs ? Quālia puer discet ?

CATŌ : Artēs virīlēs, quās ōlim parentēs omnēs in hāc cīvitāte fīliōs suōs docēbant. Habitet mēcum fīlius in fundō nostrō ; in agrīs labōret dīligenter ; flūmina natet ; equum bene regat ; hastā gladiōque pugnet ; nē hostēs, proelia, vulnera, mortem ipsam timeat. Mōrēs verbīs meīs et exemplō meō cōnfōrmet. Lēgēs discat ; deōs colat ; patriam amet. Haec ego puer didicī ; haec omnēs didicērunt quī in hāc cīvitāte praeclārī fuērunt.

Note :

ōtiōsus, -a, -um, at leisure.
ēducō, -āre, -āvī, -ātum, to bring up, educate.
fere, almost.
īnstituō, -ere, -uī, -ūtum, to set up, establish.
discō, -ere, didicī, to learn.
cūra, -ae, *f.*, care, worry.
virīlis, -is, -e, manly.
vitium, -iī, *n.*, fault, failing, vice.

lingua, -ae, *f.*, tongue, language.
corrumpō, -ere, corrūpī, corruptum, to corrupt, spoil.
cūrō, -āre, -āvī, -ātum, to look after, to care for.
dīligenter (*adv.*), hard, diligently.
natō, -āre, -āvī, -ātum, to swim.
verbum, -ī, *n.*, word.
exemplum, -ī, *n.*, example.
cōnfōrmō, -āre, -āvī, -ātum, to form, shape, model.

XII

FINAL CLAUSES

21. A final clause (so named from Latin **fīnis,** end, aim, purpose) is a subordinate adverbial clause of purpose. In Latin—

- (a) A Positive final clause is introduced by **ut,** that, in order that.
- (b) A Negative final clause is introduced by **nē,** that not, in order that . . . not, lest.
- (c) The verb of a final clause stands in the Subjunctive.
- (d) The present subjunctive must be used if the verb of the main clause is *Primary* (i.e. Present, Future, Future Perf.).
- (e) The imperfect subjunctive must be used if the main verb is *Historic* (i.e. Perfect, Imperfect, Pluperfect).

22. The infinitive can not be used in Latin, as it very commonly is in English, to express purpose.

I came to see you *must be expressed* **Vēnī ut tē vidērem.**

Notes.—(1) Imperatives are regarded as Primary. Therefore, in a final clause depending on an imperative use present subjunctive.
(2) Occasionally the so-called true perfect, or perfect with ' have,' is treated as Primary, and followed by present subj. in a dependent final clause.

EXERCISE 12

A

1. Ut studeāmus ; nē dēsistant ā labōre ; nē īgnāvī essent ; ut studia sua cūrārent ; ut equōs condūcerēmus ; ut bene discant ; nē invīsus esset cīvibus ; ut perīculum vītārēmus.
2. Quid agis, Mārce ? Cūr tam celeriter ad forum festīnās ? Num contendis ut prīmus hodiē ad Rōstra veniās ?

3. Minimē vērō, mī amīce. Contendō nē sērō ad Rōstra veniam.
4. Cīvēs enim multī iam convēnērunt ut ōrātōrem illum praeclārum audiant.
5. Quae cum ita sint, festīnā mēcum ut omnia audiās.
6. Ō mē miserum ! Domum vēnī hodiē ut ōtiōsus essem.
7. Sed quid inveniō ? Pater, " Festīnā," inquit, " Sexte, ut frātrem tuum adiuvēs, quī hodiē litterās scrībit."
8. Et māter, " Nōlī," inquit, " mī Sexte, hodiē māne diū dormīre nē sērō ad prandium veniās."
9. Et iam avus meus, " Quid, Sexte ? " inquit, " Num tē ōtiōsum videō ? Num domum vēnistī ut inūtilis nōbīs omnibus et molestus essēs ? Ō tempora ! Ō mōrēs ! Ubi ego puer eram. . . ."
10. Ō dēsiste, ave ! Quotiēns haec audīvī, " Ubi ego puer eram, māne nōn dormiēbam nē sērō ad lūdum pervenīrem ; labōrābam in lūdō ut multa discerem ; numquam ōtiōsus eram nē īgnāvum mē pater appellāret " ? Edepol, mīrābilēs puerī ōlim erant !

B

1. Lest we may be unmindful ; in order that they might study ; that you (*pl.*) may not surround ; let us learn ; I have come to learn ; let them not receive ; lest he may blame ; that they might greet us ; lest they might neglect ; let all cease from anger.
2. Let us hire teachers that our sons may study at home.
3. Let us surround our camp with a rampart and a ditch.
4. That we might come quickly to the city we hired a ship.
5. I take my ease (*ōtiōsus sum*) to-day that I may be well to-morrow.
6. Many boys come to our city to learn from our masters.
7. Cease from your anger, citizens, lest you yourselves may be punished.

8. We gave pay to the master that he might superintend (*cūrāre*) the boy's studies.
9. Let the natives (*barbarī*) cultivate the fields that they may have food.
10. Since I am at leisure, I shall walk to school to see my sons.
11. Don't walk through the wood, my friend, lest wild beasts may attack you.
12. Since we have much food in the house, we do not fear the storm.
13. Be diligent to-day, boys, that you may be at leisure to-morrow.
14. We shall hire horses to carry food from the farm.
15. Cato did not hire a teacher to educate his son.

C

Founding a School

[By the first century A.D. schools were not only numerous in Rome but were to be found in Italy and the provinces. In to-day's lesson we read how Pliny, *a distinguished Roman of the first century A.D., helped to found a school in his native town of Comum in N. Italy.]*

Nūper ubi in patriā fuī, vēnit ut mē salūtāret mūnicipis meī fīlius praetextātus. Huīc ego, " Studēsne ? " inquam. Respondit, " Studeō." " Ubi ? " " Mediōlānī." " Cūr nōn hīc ? " et pater ēius (erat enim nōbīscum et ipse ad mē dūxerat puerum), " Quod nūllōs hīc praeceptōrēs habēmus." " Cūr nūllōs ? Cūr nōn vōs, quī patrēs estis " (multī enim patrēs verba mea audiēbant), " praeceptōrēs condūxistis ut līberī in patriā manērent, sub oculīs parentum modestē vītam agerent, verbīs vestrīs et exemplō mōrēs cōnfōrmārent ? Quid ? Ubi minōre sūmptū quam domī līberī ēducantur ? Agite, pecūniam cōnferte (*contribute*), condūcite praeceptōrēs, et quod nunc in habitātiōnēs et in viātica impenditis, id addite mercēdibus ut

COMO AND LAKE COMO

It was here that Pliny founded a school.

magistrōs sapientissimōs habeātis. Ego, quī nūllōs līberōs habeō, tertiam partem pecūniae prō patriā, quasi prō fīliā aut parente, dabō. Nōn tōtam pecūniam dō, ut vōs, sī partem dederitis, dīligentēs dē rē vestrā sītis, ut ipsī studia līberōrum cūrētis, ut operam dētis omnēs nē ūllus praeceptor, nisi bonus, ā vōbīs pecūniam accipiat. Agite, cōnsiliō meō dūciminī ; cōnspīrāte ut lūdum in urbe vestrā habeatis. Nihil melius līberīs vestrīs, nihil grātius patriae dabitis. Maneant hīc quī hīc nāscuntur (*are born*), statimque patriae amōrem discant. Et operam date ut praeclārōs praeceptōrēs condūcātis. Hīc vīcīnōrum līberī studia petant. Sīcut nunc līberī vestrī Mediōlānum mittuntur, ita mox ex aliīs urbibus puerī ad urbem vestram contendant."

Note :

nūper (*adv.*), recently.
mūniceps, -ipis, *m.*, townsman.
praetextātus, -a, -um, wearing the toga praetexta.
Mediōlānum, -ī, *n.*, Milan ,
Mediōlānī, at Milan.
verbum, -ī, *n.*, word.
modestē (*adv.*), modestly.
vītam agere, to spend one's life.
exemplum, -ī, *n.*, example.

cōnfōrmō, -āre, -āvī, -ātum, to form, shape, model.
sūmptus, -ūs, *m.*, expense.
habitātiō, -iōnis, *f.*, lodging
viāticum, -ī, *n.*,travelling expenses.
impendō, -ere, -ī, impēnsum, to spend.
quasi, as if.
cōnspīrō, -āre, -āvī, -ātum, to conspire, plan together.
grātus, -a, -um, welcome.

ROMAN EDUCATION

In the earliest times Rome had no schools at all. The Roman boy received his education from his father who would teach him to ride, swim, fight in arms and work on the farm. In addition the boy would be taught the elements of reading, writing, and arithmetic, would be trained up in the old traditions of the state and of the family, would learn the proper methods of worshipping the gods, and acquire knowledge of the laws. The father would take his son with him to meetings of the Senate and to important public assemblies, thus making him familiar with the conduct of public business. In time, however, it became usual for those who could afford it to keep a tutor—often a highly educated Greek slave—to do the teaching. Later on, it was found more economical and convenient to send boys to schools outside their homes and so schools became general.

You learned something about those schools last year. They were small ; not in any way supervised by the government ; purely private ventures run for a living very often by Greek freedmen. The school might meet in the room of a house, but mostly it was held in a kind of verandah called a *pergula*, open to the street. Furniture was scanty—a chair (*cathedra*) for the master, seats (*sellae*) or benches (*subsellia*) for the pupils, perhaps a few busts of poets round the walls, and, if the school was very up-to-date, some charts and maps. Work began early—so early that in winter the boys often brought lamps with them.

Boys began to attend such schools at about the age of seven. They were regularly escorted to school by a slave called the *paedagōgus*. His task was to see that his charge or charges got into no kind of mischief on the way to and from the school. Quite often the *paedagōgus* remained with the boy all day in school. The son of a rich parent might also have a slave called the *capsarius* to carry his books and writing materials.

Fees were paid for the instruction, which was in reading, writing and arithmetic. Reading was done aloud, the boys pronouncing syllables, words and whole sentences and lines after the teacher—and often all together, so that school was quite noisy and decidedly unpopular with neighbours who wanted quiet. The books, which were in the form of rolls of papyrus, were usually works of the poets. Much was committed to memory. Writing was done on tablets coated with wax. The pen (*stilus*) was a pointed instrument suitable for tracing letters in wax. Frequently it had a blunt end which could be used for smoothing out the writing and so starting afresh. In arithmetic there was much memorising of addition and multiplication tables, and boys learned to use a counting board (*abacus*) in doing longer calculations.

Discipline was very harsh. Corporal punishment was general, and was rather approved by some parents as fostering a hard, manly spirit. For distinguished work prizes were often given, and it is interesting that the usual type of prize with the Romans as with us was a fine edition of a book.

The Roman boy had his share of holidays. He had no school on the market-day (*Nundinae-ārum*). Every eighth day was a market-day. He had holidays at all the great public games, about five days in March, frequently a long vacation in the summer, and a week at the festival of the *Saturnalia* which fell almost at our Christmas-time.

Such were the elementary schools. In time something like secondary schools grew up. These specialised in the teaching of Rhetoric. In the late republic, a Roman education might be crowned by a course of study at Athens or Rhodes. In this, the ancient equivalent of our higher University training, education was in Philosophy or advanced Rhetoric.

BREVITIES

[*The Roman poet* MARTIAL *who lived in the first century A.D. is the great master of the Epigram—a short, witty, topical or personal poem, often with a sting in its tail !*]

(a) *All Nose*

Tongiliānus habet nasum : sciō : nōn nego : sed iam
Nīl praeter nāsum Tongiliānus habet.

(b) *To an Author*

Cūr nōn mitto meōs tibi, Pontiliāne, libellōs ?
Nē mihi tū mittās, Pontiliāne, tuōs.

XIII

PERFECT AND PLUPERFECT SUBJUNCTIVE ACTIVE

23. The Perfect and Pluperfect Subjunctive Active of the four regular conjugations are as follows :

Conj.	Pers.	Perfect		Pluperfect	
		Sing.	*Plur.*	*Sing.*	*Plur.*
1st	1	amāv-erim	amāv-erīmus	amāv-issem	amāv-issēmus
	2	amāv-erīs	amāv-erītis	amāv-issēs	amāv-issētis
	3	amāv-erit	amāv-erint	amāv-isset	amāv-issent
2nd	1	monu-erim	monu-erīmus	monu-issem	monu-issēmus
	2	monu-erīs	monu-erītis	monu-issēs	monu-issētis·
	3	monu-erit	monu-erint	monu-isset	monu-issent
3rd	1	rēx-erim	rēx-erīmus	rēx-issem	rēx-issēmus
	2	rēx-erīs	rēx-erītis	rēx-issēs	rēx-issētis
	3	rēx-erit	rēx-erint	rēx-isset	rēx-issent
4th	1	audīv-erim	audīv-erīmus	audīv-issem	audīv-issēmus
	2	audīv-erīs	audīv-erītis	audīv-issēs	audīv-issētis
	3	audīv-erit	audīv-erint	audīv-isset	audīv-issent

Notes.—(1) The Perf. Subj. ·Active of any Latin verb may be formed by adding **-erim, erīs, -erit,** etc. to the Perfect stem.

(2) The Pluperf. Subj. Active is formed by adding **-issem, -issēs, -isset,** etc. to the Perfect stem.

EXERCISE 13

Note.—Negative final clauses begin with **nē.** Hence, instead of:

that no one	*we must say*			lest any one	—**nē quis,**
that nothing	,,	,,	,,	lest anything	—**nē quid,**
that no	,,	,,	,,	lest any	—**nē ūllus,**
that never	,,	,,	,,	lest ever	—**nē umquam,**
that nowhere	,,	,,	,,	lest anywhere	—**nē ūsquam.**

A

A GENERAL STRIKE

[*Rome had a privileged class of citizens, the Patricians, and an inferior class, the Plebeians. The latter had to pay taxes and serve in the army, but were debarred from holding public office and from membership of the Senate. Still, under the kings they were tolerably well treated. After the Tarquins were expelled, their lot became so hard that they went on strike, migrating in a body to the Sacred Mount, three miles from Rome. Our lesson tells how the strike was ended.*]

Lēgātus ad Montem Sacrum missus est Menēnius Agrippa, vir prūdēns et plēbī cārus. Is, ubi ductus est in castra plēbēiōrum nihil aliud quam hoc nārrāvit : " Ōlim hūmānī artūs, īrātī quod ventrem ōtiōsum vīdērunt, ' Quid hoc est ? ' inquiunt, ' Nōsne semper labōrābimus ut omnia huīc tam ignāvō petāmus, quī ipse nihil umquam facit, sed dormit semper et ōtiōsus accipit quae magnō labōre comparāmus ? Agite, cōnsilium capiāmus audācissimum ; nē manūs ad ōs cibum portent ; nē cibum ōs accipiat ; dentēs quoque ab opere suō dēsistant.' Sīc operam dabant artūs ut ventrem fame superārent. Sed ipsī mox in magnō sunt perīculō ; fame tōtum corpus ad mortem paene vēnit. Tum artūs, 'Ēheu ! ' inquiunt, ' quid facimus ? Nōn minus nōs ā ventre nutrīmur quam ā nōbīs venter. Accipit ille quidem ā nōbīs cibum : sed statim in omnēs corporis partēs reddit. Quae

cum ita sint, amīcitiam ventris petāmus ut ēius auxiliō tōtum corpus iterum valeat.' Sīcut artūs et venter, ita senātus et plēbs, quasi ūnum corpus, discordiā dēlentur, concordiā servantur."
Hāc fābulā Menēnius plēbēiōs ab īrā āvertit. Iam dē concordiā et condiciōnibus agēbant. Mox in urbem plēbs rediit (*returned*) ; creāvit tamen tribūnōs plēbis ut lībertātem suam contrā patriciōrum superbiam dēfenderet.

B

1. Cum audīverīs ; cum monuissēmus ; nē quis mē culpāret ; cum amāverītis ; nē umquam īgnāvus essem ; nē quid nōs āverteret ; cum vīcissent ; cum cinxerīmus ; cum addidisset ; ut cōnsilium capiāmus.
2. (a) Age, pater, cum ōtiōsus sīs, audī paulisper ; cūr plēbēiī ad Montem Sacrum discessērunt ?
   (b) Cūr, mī fīlī ? Edepol, multae erant causae : nē diūtius superbiam patriciōrum timērent ; ut tranquillī vītam agerent ; nē semper prō patriciīs in bellō vulnera acciperent ; ut patriciī superbiae et stultitiae poenās darent.
   (c) Grātiās tibi agō, mī pater. Cum multa dē hāc rē didicerim, aliā dē rē tē rogābō.
   (d) Minimē vērō, mī fīlī ; cum tū illud rogāverīs, ego tē hoc rogābō : cum ad Montem Sacrum plēbēiī discessissent, cūr ibi nōn manēbant ?
   (e) Rem rogās facillimam, pater ; cum homō quīdam sapientissimus bonam eīs fābulam nārrāvisset, ad urbem rediērunt (*they returned*) ut concordiā servārent rem pūblicam quae discordiā dēlēbātur.
3. I shall give pay to Syrus that he may never leave us.
4. Hang it all ! Marcus has hidden the ball that I might not find it anywhere.
5. When will you (*s.*) come to see our new home ?
6. We shall depart in the darkness that no one may see us.

7. Since we have seen a wonderful spectacle we shall hurry home.
8. Since the boys had learned much, the parents praised the teachers.
9. I shall take my dog with me that nothing may frighten me.
10. That no robbers may attack you, the soldiers will guard the road.
11. Since our men have surrounded the camp with a rampart and ditch, the enemy will be destroyed.
12. That your master may never call you lazy, my son, always work diligently.

WORD STUDY

To-day let us look for a little at some of the great Latin words which the Romans themselves seem to have loved because they expressed the noblest qualities of the Roman character.

First there is **virtūs**, which to begin with meant *manliness*, then *courage, valour, activity*, and presently *virtue* ; a close second to that great word is **cōnstantia**, *firmness, perseverance*— the attitude of the brave man in face of all the ups and downs of fortune. Often on Roman lips was the word **gravitās**. This indicates the calm, steady, serious bearing which is the outward and visible sign of a mind that knows its powers, responsibilities and purpose in life. You have frequently met **pietās**, and no doubt realise that it is rather difficult to translate, just because there is no English word that conveys all its meaning. **Pietās** denotes that blend of affection, loyalty, sheer goodness, which makes a man do his full duty to gods, parents, wife and children, and country. Three other words to remember are **indūstria**, *hard work* ; **dīligentia**, *care, thoroughness, application* ; **cōntinentia**, *self-restraint*. Observe how those seven words convey an impression of the Roman character at its best, helping us to picture the early Romans as sturdy and tireless men of action, practical, steady, hard-headed, loyal ; hard workers and hard fighters.

XIV

PRESENT AND IMPERFECT SUBJUNCTIVE PASSIVE

24. The Present and Imperfect Subjunctive Passive of the four regular conjugations are as follows :

Conj.	Pers.	Present		Imperfect	
		Sing.	*Plur.*	*Sing.*	*Plur.*
1st	1	ám-er	am-ēmur	amā-rer	amā-rēmur
	2	am-ēris	am-ēminī	amā-rēris	amā-rēminī
	3	am-ētur	am-entur	amā-rētur	amā-rentur
2nd	1	móne-ar	mone-āmur	monē-rer	monē-rēmur
	2	mone-āris	mone-āminī	monē-rēris	monē-rēminī
	3	mone-ātur	mone-antur	monē-rētur	monē-rentur
3rd	1	rég-ar	reg-āmur	régĕ-rer	regĕ-rēmur
	2	reg-āris	reg-āminī	regĕ-rēris	regĕ-rēminī
	3	reg-ātur	reg-antur	regĕ-rētur	regĕ-rentur
4th	1	aúdi-ar	audi-āmur	audī-rer	audī-rēmur
	2	audi-āris	audi-āminī	audī-rēris	audī-rēminī
	3	audi-ātur	audi-antur	audī-rētur	audī-rentur

Notes.—(1) Verbs of the 3rd conjugation ending in **-iō** form their Present and Imperf. Subj. passive thus :

Pres. Subj. Passive	*Imperf. Subj. Passive*
capiar	capĕrer
capiāris	capĕrēris
capiātur	capĕrētur
etc.	etc.

(2) Instead of **amēris, moneāris, regāris, audiāris,** the forms **amēre, moneāre, regāre, audiāre,** often occur ; and instead of **amārēris, monērēris,** etc., the forms **amārēre, monērēre,** etc.

EXERCISE 14

Notes.—(1) A Final clause containing a comparative adj. or adverb is introduced by **quō** instead of **ut**, e.g. :

Hoc fēcit quō celerius venīret, He did this that he might come more quickly.

(2) In a Final clause, " him," " her," " them," etc. is translated by the appropriate part of **sē** ; and " his," " her," " their," etc. by the appropriate part of **suus, -a, ~um,** if there is reference to subject of main verb, e.g. :

Hoc fēcit ut cōnsul sē laudāret, He did this that the consul might praise him.

A

A DICTATOR FROM THE PLOUGH

[*In times of great national danger, a special magistrate called the Dictator was often appointed. His authority was supreme in the state. He might hold office for six months, but not longer. The following tells how in 460 B.C.* CINCINNATUS *left his little farm to become Dictator and save the state.*]

Cum ab Aequīs Mĭnŭcius cōnsul et exercitus ēius in Monte Algĭdō obsidērentur, nōn minor in urbe terror erat quam sī urbem ipsam, nōn castra cōnsulis, hostēs obsidērent. Cum in alterō cōnsule nūlla spēs salūtis esset, patrēs, ut rēs pūblica servārētur, dictātōrem Quĭnctium Cincinnātum creāvērunt. Ille, spēs ūna populī Rōmānī, trāns Tiberim parvum fundum colēbat. Quī ā senātū missī sunt lēgātī, nūdum eum (labōrābat enim in agrīs) invēnērunt. Ubi eum lēgātī salūtāvērunt et ab eō salūtātī sunt, Cincinnātus Raciliae, uxōrī suae, " Ē tuguriō (*hut*)," inquit, " fer togam meam ut togātus mandāta senātūs audiam." Ubi pulverem et sūdōrem abstersit, Cincinnātus, iam togātus, dictātor salūtātus est ā lēgātīs quī dē perīculō exercitūs, dē cīvium terrōre omnia nārrāvērunt.

CINCINNATUS

Postrīdiē in forum Cincinnātus vēnit; ēius iūssū
iuvenēs in Campum Mārtium convēnērunt. Sōlis occāsū
armātī ex urbe discessērunt; mediā nocte in Algidum vēnērunt. Prīmō castra hostium in tenebrīs cinxērunt; deinde,
ubi sīgnum Cincinnātus dedit, magnō clāmōre hostēs fossā
vallōque inclūsērunt. Clāmor ā cōnsule mīlitibusque audītus
est. Arma capiunt; hostēs oppugnant; per tōtam noctem
rēs geritur. Māne hostēs, " Ēheu ! " inquiunt, " inter duōs
exercitūs Rōmānōs captī sumus ; alter nōs oppūgnat ;
alter obsidet." Cum nūlla spēs salūtis esset, hostēs sē
dictātōrī dēdidērunt. Cincinnātus mīlitēs Aequōrum
dīmīsit ; ducēs sēcum Rōmam dūxit. Maximā glōriā
urbem intrāvit, cum ducēs hostium ante currum ēius
dūcerentur, exercitus praedam ingentem portāret, cīvēs

Cincinnātum magnopere laudārent. Cincinnātus tamen neque praemia ūlla victōriae accēpit neque diū in urbe mānsit. Imperium dēposuit ; domum festīnāvit ; posteā vītam tranquillus in fundō agēbat.

B

1. (a) May they be heard ; lest we might be surrounded ; let us be advised ; in order that you (*pl.*) might be taken ; lest I may be blamed ; let the fields be cultivated.

(b) Nē hoc cōnsilium caperētur ; ut ab omnibus laudēmur ; nē umquam neglegerētur ; ut moneāmur ; quō facilius audīrēminī ; nē ā rēgibus regāmur.

2. (a) Equōs currumque, mī pater, condūcāmus quō celerius tam longum iter faciāmus.

(b) Nē sine mercēde hī hominēs dīmittantur ; dīligenter enim prō nōbīs labōrāvērunt.

(c) Quō dīligentius librum tuum legerem ad vīllam discessī ubi sōlus eram.

(d) Nē quis verba sua audīret servōs et amīcōs omnēs dīmīsit.

(e) Festīnā, Sexte, nē diūtius tē exspectēmus. Cēna iam parāta est.

(f) Manē paulisper, mea māter, quō melius sūdōrem pulveremque abstergeam. Hodiē enim cum aliīs puerīs ego et amīcī pugnābāmus in Campō.

3. Let us lead the horses home that they may not be frightened by the storm.

4. Send a letter to your grandfather, Sextus, that you may be more kindly received by him.

5. Since he has considerably more money than I, let him hire a chariot for himself.

6. Since lunch is being prepared, let us not leave the house.

7. The girls carried food with them that they might remain longer in the woods.

8. That the royal race might be removed from the city, the consul resigned from the consulship.
9. That no one might be left in the city the Gauls burned the houses.
10. Marcus has closed the door that no one may rouse him.
11. The orator praises the citizens that they may give him a reward.
12. The old woman has burned the books that the king might be more attentive.
13. The orator was silent for a long time lest any one might blame him.
14. The young men left the city next day that they might not be found by the soldiers.

C

A Limerick in Latin

In hortulō Marcus sedēbat
post cēnam, et somnus urgēbat.
    Hoc Sextus cōnspexit
    sellamque dēvexit ;
supīnus tum Marcus iacēbat !

Note :

hortulus, -ī, *m.,* little garden.
urgeō, -ēre, ursī, press hard.
cōnspiciō, -ere, -exī, -ectum, to notice.

dēvehō, -ere, -vexī, -vectum, to carry off.
supīnus, -a, -um, on his back.
iaceō, -ēre, -uī, to lie.

THE ROMAN REPUBLIC

We have seen that the Romans finally expelled their kings and set up a republic. We have now to consider how this form of government was actually worked. What precisely were those consuls, tribunes and dictators whom we have met in our reading lessons ? What were their duties and their powers ?

The essential thing about a republic is that the people elect their own rulers. After the expulsion of the kings we find the Roman citizens meeting in a political assembly at regular intervals for the purpose of electing rulers, officers of government, magistrates, as the Romans called them. To begin with, two were elected to hold office for one year. Those two heads of the government were called *consuls*. Notice how the political sagacity of the Romans reveals itself ; by making the consuls hold office for one year only, a very useful check was imposed upon their trying to make themselves kings. Another check lies in the fact that there were two consuls elected for each year. For it was possible for the one to forbid the actions of the other if he thought they endangered the welfare of the state. This power of holding up the actions of a colleague was called *veto* power, from the Latin **vetō**, I forbid. In the early republic the consuls exercised very wide authority. They were the leaders of the army in time of war ; they directed the finances of the state and they were the supreme judges in the dispensation of law and justice. In public they were attended by *lictors*, each of whom carried on his shoulder a bundle of rods and an axe, symbols of the consul's power to inflict chastisement and even the death-penalty.

As the state grew, certain changes came in. It was found that the consuls could not discharge all the duties originally entrusted to them. It was also found expedient to take away from the consuls the right of inflicting the death-penalty upon citizens, and within the city the axes were no longer included in the fasces, as the bundles of rods borne by the lictors were called. As for the new magistrates who gradually came to be elected, next in rank to the consuls themselves were the *praetors*. These were the judges of the state, presiding over the law courts. Below the praetors in rank were the *aediles* who looked after the great public games and supervised markets, streets and police organisation. Inferior to these were the *quaestors*, the financial officers of the government.

The *tribunes of the plebs* occupied a special position. Their function was really to protect plebeians against possible ill-treatment by patrician magistrates. To help them in this function, their persons were declared sacred ; no one could lay violent hands upon a tribune. Also, they were given veto power over the actions of all other magistrates.

All the magistrates mentioned so far were elected annually. At intervals of five years two magistrates were appointed who were called *censors*. Their chief duty lay in drawing up the census, i.e. a return showing the number of citizens, the amount of property owned by each, and the precise property-class to which he belonged. They also had the right of supervising the morals and conduct of citizens and could inflict degradation on any offending member of the community.

With their instinct for government, the Romans saw clearly that this system with its large number of magistrates and its sharing of authority might break down under stress of some emergency. Accordingly, in times of great national crisis we find that frequently a *dictator* was appointed. He was supreme over all other magistrates ; even the consuls were subordinate to him. But the maximum period for which he could hold office was six months, and in actual practice he was expected to lay down power as soon as the emergency which had caused his election was successfully dealt with and the state could revert to normal methods of government.

XV

PERFECT AND PLUPERFECT SUBJUNCTIVE PASSIVE

25. The Perfect and Pluperfect Subjunctive Passive of the four regular conjugations are as follows.:

Conj.	Pers.	Perfect		Pluperfect	
		Sing.	*Plur.*	*Sing.*	*Plur.*
1st	1	amātus sim	amātī sīmus	amātus essem	amātī essēmus
	2	amātus sīs	amātī sītis	amātus essēs	amātī essētis
	3	amātus sit	amātī sint	amātus esset	amātī essent
2nd	1	monitus sim	monitī sīmus	monitus essem	monitī essēmus
	2	monitus sīs	monitī sītis	monitus essēs	monitī essētis
	3	monitus sit	monitī sint	monitus esset	monitī essent
3rd	1	rēctus sim	rēctī sīmus	rēctus essem	rēctī essēmus
	2	rēctus sīs	rēctī sītis	rēctus essēs	rēctī essētis
	3	rēctus sit	rēctī sint	rēctus esset	rēctī essent
4th	1	audītus sim	audītī sīmus	audītus essem	audītī essēmus
	2	audītus sīs	audītī sītis	audītus essēs	audītī essētis
	3	audītus sit	audītī sint	audītus esset	audītī essent

Note.—The participles **amātus, monitus, rēctus, audītus,** must agree in number and gender with their subject, e.g. :

Cum amātum esset, Since it had been loved.
Cum haec audīta essent, Since these things had been heard.

EXERCISE 15

A

Rome's Day of Shame

[*For* 120 *years after the kings were expelled, Rome was occupied
with wars against other states and the struggle between
patricians and plebeians. In* 390 *B.C. came a
greater danger. A horde of Gauls swept south,
destroyed a Roman army at the Allia, and captured
and burned Rome itself.*]

Clūsīnī, cum ā Gallīs obsidērentur, auxilium ā Rōmānīs
petīvērunt. Senātus, ut Gallī āverterentur, trēs lēgātōs
mīsit quōrum ūnus nōn modo in aciē pugnāvit sed etiam
prīncipem Gallicum interfēcit. Quā rē cum Gallī sollicitī
essent, Clūsium relīquērunt ; ipsam Rōmam petiērunt.
Ad Alliam flūmen exercitum Rōmānum superāvērunt.
Rōmānī enim cum multō essent multitūdine īnferiōrēs et
ipsā speciē Gallōrum clāmōribusque perterritī essent, impetum hostium nōn sustinuērunt. Sinistrum cornū, cum
arma ā mīlitibus abiecta essent quō celerius fugerent,
tōtum est dēlētum ; ā dextrō cornū, cum procul ā flūmine
et in locō altiōre stetissent, paucī Rōmam pervēnērunt.
Nihil illī ad proelium parāvērunt ; nē portās quidem urbis
clausērunt ; in arcem et Capitōlium contendērunt urbemque
hostibus relīquērunt. Diem hūius pugnae Alliēnsem Rōmānī appellāvērunt et nefāstum (*unlucky*) semper habēbant.
Paulō ante sōlis occāsum Gallī ad urbem pervēnērunt.
Iam cīvēs omnēs aut in Capitōlium contenderant aut fugā
salūtem petēbant, praeter senēs quōsdam quī adventum
Gallōrum mortemque crūdēlem tranquillī exspectābant.
Quī magistrātūs fuerant, honōrum īnsignibus sē ōrnāvērunt
et in vestibulīs domōrum in sellīs curūlibus sedēbant ut

4

cum dīgnitāte mortem exspectārent. Mox Gallī, cum iam undique praeda peterētur, domōs intrāvērunt. Attonitī vidēbant virōs dīgnitāte deōrum simillimōs. Cum mentēs et oculī in senēs dēfīxī essent, Gallī diū stābant immōtī. Tandem ūnus barbam senis cūiusdam manū permulsit. Senex īrātus caput hominis virgā verberāvit. Gallus statim senem interfēcit ; ab eō initium caedis factum est ; cēterī in sellīs suīs omnēs necātī sunt.

B

1. Cum audīta sit ; nē interficerentur ; cum haec audīta sint ; quō celerius venīrēmus ; cum equī conductī sint ; cum permulsissent ; nē sedeāmus ; cum castra cincta essent ; cum Gallī nōn āversī essent ; cum praeda petīta esset.

2. (a) Nautae, cum tempestāte perterritī essent, ad īnsulam nōn nāvigābant.

   (b) Cum portae apertae essent, intrāvimus ut amīcum salūtārēmus.

   (c) Quō māiōrem mercēdem compārēmus, ad aliud oppidum discēdāmus.

   (d) Cum tē diū exspectāvissēmus, discessimus nē ipsī sērō ad lūdum pervenīrēmus.

   (e) Cum procul ā domibus relictī sīmus ā latrōnibus, viam īgnōrāmus.

3. Since our chief has been killed by you (*pl.*), we shall destroy your city.

4. Since father has been wakened by our shouts, he will be angry.

5. The old men were sitting motionless. They were like gods.

6. Since you (*s.*) have thrown away your shield, you will pay the penalty for (*of*) your cowardice.

7. Let us depart at once that the chief may not see us.

8. Since you have all been called together, you will hear a wonderful speech.

9. Since we had been kindly received, we gave a gift to the children.

10. Since the royal race has been removed from the city, we fear nothing.

11. Since no food has been left in the house, let us hurry to the shop.

12. Marcus hastens home to-day that his father may not chide him.

13. That there may be no suspicion of treachery, guard all the gates.

14. We shall work hard (*diligently*) that we may receive bigger pay.

C

Master and Pupils

[*Some idea of the sane and enlightened view of education which the Romans attained is to be gathered from the following passage based on* QUINTILIAN, *a great Roman writer and teacher, who lived in the latter part of the first century A.D.*]

Habeat igitur ante omnia lūdī magister parentis animum ergā discipulōs suōs et operam det ut intret in eōrum locum ā quibus līberī eī trāditī sunt. Ipse nē habeat vitia, nēve ferat. Plūrimus eī dē rēbus honestīs et bonīs sermō sit. Saepe discipulōs moneat, rārō castīget. Minimē sit īrācundus; sī, tamen, errāverint discipulī, nē neglegat errōrēs. Simplicia sint verba ēius; labor assiduus potius quam immodicus. Sī discipulī interrogant, libenter respondeat; sī tacent, ipse multa dē rēbus eīs quās docuit, roget. Bonōs discipulōs laudet; in laudibus tamen maxima semper cūra sit nē aut malignus aut effūsus videātur. Discipulī enim, sī semper laudās, mox labōribus sunt dēfessī; sī numquam, omnia neglegunt. Ubi ea ēmendat quae discipulī

nōn satis bene aut dīxērunt aut scrīpsērunt, nē sit acerbus nēve
contumēliōsus. Magistrī enim quīdam ā studiīs dīscipulōs
āvertunt cum crūdēliter eōs castīgent. Multa quoque dīcat
cotīdiē magister quae, ubi audīverint, discipulī memoriae
trādent. Librī enim exempla in sē habent plūrima quibus
mōrēs puerōrum cōnfōrmantur, ingenium nūtrītur ; multō
tamen melius docentur vīvā illā vōce magistrī quem dīscipulī,
sī bene ēducantur, amant.

Note :

acerbus, -a, -um, bitter.
assiduus, -a, -um, constant.
cōnfōrmō, -āre, -āvī, -ātum, to
shape.
contumēliōsus, -a, -um, abu-
sive.
cotīdiē, daily.
cūra, -ae, *f.,* care.
effūsus, -a, -um, profuse, lavish.
ēmendō, -āre, -āvī, -ātum, to
correct.
ergā (*prep. gov. acc.*), toward.
error, -ōris, *m.,* mistake.
ferō, ferre, tulī, lātum, to bear.
honestus, -a, -um, honourable.
immodicus, -a, -um, immoderate.

ingenium, -iī, *n.,* ability.
interrogō, -āre, -āvī, -ātum, to
ask questions.
īrācundus, -a, -um, bad-
tempered.
laus, laudis, *f.,* praise.
libenter, gladly, willingly.
malīgnus, -a, -um, grudging.
memoria, -ae, *f.,* memory.
nēve, nor (*used instead of* **neque**
after **nē**)
potius, rather.
rārō, seldom.
simplex, -icis, simple.
trādō, -ere, -didī, -ditum, to
hand over, commit.

WORD STUDY

Can you clear up the derivation and meaning of *ventriloquist,
dormitory, dormant, oral* and *orally, dentist* and *dental, nutriment*
and *nutritious* ? And, by the way, what is the connection
between **plēbs** and *plebiscite* ?

XVI

INDIRECT COMMAND

26. In Latin, verbs meaning *to request, command, advise,* etc., are followed by Final Clauses, e.g. : **Ōrō tē ut veniās,** I beg you to come : **Imperāvī tibi nē manērēs,** I ordered you not to stay.

The two exceptions to this rule are **iubēre,** to order ; **vetāre,** to forbid, to order . . . not, which take the same construction as English, e.g. : **Iūssī tē discēdere,** I ordered you to depart : **Vetuī tē manēre,** I forbade you to stay, I ordered you not to stay.

The following table gives the commonest verbs of this class with their appropriate constructions :

Verb	Person Commanded	Construction
monēre, to advise **rogāre,** to ask **ōrāre,** to beg **obsecrāre,** to beseech **implōrāre,** to implore	Accusative ,, ,, ,, ,,	Final Clause ,, ,, ,, ,,
imperāre, to command **persuādēre,** to persuade	Dative ,,	Final Clause ,,
petere, to seek, ask **pōstulāre,** to demand	**ā, ab** with ablative ,, ,, ,,	Final Clause ,,
iubēre, to command **vetāre,** to forbid, to order . . . not	Accusative ,,	Present Infinitive ,,

Notes.—(1) NEVER write **iubeō . . . nōn.** I order . . . not, must be expressed by **vetāre,** or **imperāre . . . nē.**

(2) When the verb " to tell " means " to order," translate by **iubēre,** or **imperāre,** e.g. :

I told him to stay, **Iūssī eum manēre,** or, **Imperāvī eī ut manēret.**

EXERCISE 16

A

1. (*a*) Translate the following ; then rewrite each, using
      imperāre with a Final Clause :
      (1) Vōs vetō hodiē lūdere. (2) Mē iūssit quam
      celerrimē venīre. (3) Eum vetābō equum ver-
      berāre. (4) Eōs iūssimus portās claudere.
      (5) Puerōs vetuī senēs adiuvāre.
   (*b*) Translate the following : then rewrite each, using
      iubēre or **vetāre** with infinitive :
      (1) Puerō imperāvī ut quam dīligentissimē labōr-
         āret.
      (2) Puellīs imperāveram nē portam aperīrent.
      (3) Servō imperābō ut cibum paret.
      (4) Cīvibus imperēmus ut in hostēs saxa dēiciant.
      (5) Imperā puerīs nē in viā lūdant.
2. Cum dīves sit, eum obsecrābimus ut pauperēs adiuvet.
3. Prīncipī persuādeāmus ut revocet ex exsiliō amīcum
      nostrum.
4. Tē vetō illum tam turpem librum legere.
5. Mī pater, quandō persuādēbō tibi ut mēcum ad fundum
      contendās ?
6. Avus enim nōs rogat ut hodiē ad cēnam veniāmus.
7. Ita vērō ; et benignē tē accipiet avus tuus. Sed tē
      moneō nē in agrīs lūdās nē ā bōbus terreāris.
8. Imperātor mīlitibus imperāvit ut post paucōs diēs
      iterum convenīrent.
9. Senātōrēs cōnsulī imperāvērunt ut dictātōrem dīceret.
10. Quam stultus sum ! Uxor mē rogāvit ut pānem hodiē
      ab urbe domum portārem. Ēheu ! mandāta ēius
      neglēxī.

B

1. I shall not ask you (*pl.*) again to be silent.
2. What persuaded you (*s.*) to frighten the girls ?
3. Master, I beg you to give me back my ball.
4. Why do you (*pl.*) demand that I should resign the consulship ?
5. I told the children not to take the dog with them.
6. No one will persuade me to travel to the city in the dark.
7. My mother has ordered bread to be sent from the shop.
8. Since you (*pl.*) have been lazy, I shall forbid you to play to-day.
9. I have asked the master to recall the boys from the farm.
10. The orator besought the citizens not to send his friend into exile.
11. We were told to walk on the rocks that we might leave no tracks.
12. The women implored the general not to lay waste his fatherland.
13. Hurry, Syrus! Tell Marcus not to enter the wood.
14. Marcus, your mother begs you not to play in that wood. There are many wild beasts in it, and the danger is great.
15. Tell mother not to be frightened. Sextus will be with me. He and I will persuade the wild beasts not to attack us.
16. We are now in the middle of the wood, Sextus. How brave we are !
17. Look, Marcus, a huge bear is coming toward us! Let us flee !
18. Alas! Sextus has fled, and left me alone. How often I implored him to stay with me! Whom shall I now ask to help me ? Who will take (*i.e.* lead) me home ?

C

A crossword puzzle.

CLUES ACROSS

1. Consists of soldiers arranged for battle.
5. The sky (*abl.*).
8. Neuter of 34 across.
9. Our word *general* comes from this.
11. Indicates the state you should be in for attempting cross-words.
14. A colour.
15. Your.
17. Plural of 8 across.
18. By a storm.
19. Don't forget to use this in negative final clauses.
21. Occurs in motto of Scotland.
23. Genitive of 34 across.
26. Hostile (*Gen. pl.*).
29. Applied to last Roman king.
32. A relation (*acc.*).
34. Masculine of 8 across and nominative of 23 across.
35. Arts.
38. Same as 19 across.
39. One more than nom. of 33 down.
40. Distinguished.
41. Often used in prohibitions.
43. Mind (*abl.*).
45. Use this after most verbs of commanding and asking.
47. A burden.
48. When these and 43 across are fixed on anything, it is absorbing your attention.
49. An imperative.
50. Let me remove.

CLUES DOWN

1. Soldiers again, but not arranged as in 1 across.
2. An important event in the Roman day.
3. Only needs an ending to make it a beginning.
4. When you get this one, you'll say " Well done ! "
5. A body.
6. This adjective describes the good pupil.
7. Bones.
8. " Just " in the accusative.
10. Tells when you should be 6 down in school.
12. Right.
13. Hope.
16. *Which* eye ? *which* consul ?
20. Gen. of 8 across and 34 across.

22. Accusative plural of 34 across.
24. A young man.
25. Name of a continent.
27. A short imperative.
28. You may love.
30. A little.
31. A familiar adverb.
32. I increase.
33. Twice the nom. of this makes 39 across.
36. Fear (*noun*).
37. Let it be.
39. Things that are given.
41. " We " or " us."
42. Same as 34 across.
44. Used to introduce some direct questions.
46. Added to 31 down would mean " so well."

REVISION EXERCISES

A

1. Give Gen. sing., Gen. pl., gender and meaning of **bōs, deus, domus, māter, urbs, onus, genū, diēs, virgō, exercitus.**
2. Express in Latin : for goddesses, in the sea, at home, from Rome, by many things, of poor citizens, greater gifts (*acc.*), by arrows, by soldiers, of wounds.
3. Give, with cases which they govern, Latin prepositions for : to, into, without, inside, about.
4. Distinguish : **ipse vīdit, sē vīdit ; nostrum, nostrī ; eīdem senēs, eīdem senī ; amātur, amētur ; amāverō, amāverim ; bene est, bonum est ; alius, alter ; quot ? quantus ?**
5. Compare : **crūdēlis, similis, niger, miser, bonus, male, saepe, celeriter, fortiter, magnopere.**

6. Give Latin for : He stayed many days ; he came on that day ; he will lead us with him ; the camp is large ; since he has been brave ; let us not be cowards ; I told him not to come ; my house is much smaller than yours ; he is like his father ; in order that no one may see us ; either Marcus or Sextus ; Did you (s.) come or not ? ; I neither heard nor saw ; don't come, Cornelius.

B

1. Since he has not recalled ; let them throw away ; may you (s.) not be killed ; since it has been laid down ; do not hire (pl.) ; let us rouse ; since he had not opened ; since she has not been invited ; let it be added : may they not depart.
2. Since the gates had been opened, we left the city.
3. Our friend did not remain even four days in the city.
4. I shall work more diligently that I may learn more.
5. Since it is not late, let us remain for a short time in the city.
6. Since we were at leisure, we invited Quintus and his father.
7. Let us work diligently that no one may blame us.
8. Send the slaves to the shop, Marcus, to procure bread.
9. The boys used to travel to Milan to study.
10. We have come to hear your reply.

C

1. In the following translate only the words in italics :
   (a) We were told *not to throw away* our books.
   (b) Come nearer *that we may hear more easily*.
   (c) We travelled by day *that nothing might frighten us*.
   (d) Post guards *that the camp may not be surrounded*.
   (e) Mother told you (s.) *to hurry*.
2. Since the chief had been killed, the barbarians fled.
3. Since we had marched for many hours, we were tired.

4. The citizens not only blamed the orator but also expelled him from the city.
5. Who asked you to carry so heavy a burden ?
6. The chief advised our men to surround the camp with a rampart.
7. Why is your joy so great, citizens ?
8. Much food has been sent from Sicily that there may not be famine in the city.
9. The consuls ordered the lictors to remove the crowd from the forum.
10. We stayed at home to avoid the storm.

D

1. Give the Latin for :

an alliance	distinguished	how long ?
to be strong	sweat	a limb
a grandson	an altar	the belly
thick	cruel	safety
a cloud	dangerous	a grandfather

2. Give with meanings the Latin words from which are derived : *tacit, colleague, general, audacity, mercenary, sane, deposit, oral, fundamental, timorous.*
3. Surely father did not forbid you to go to the games ?
4. We have hired teachers that our sons may be taught at home.
5. No one has asked us to remain for a short time.
6. By order of the consul we shall cease from this task.
7. Which consul was warned by the old man to be prudent ?
8. Not even his colleague persuaded the consul not to fight.
9. Since this was so, he ordered his men to prepare themselves for battle.
10. Since no reply had been received, we sent a messenger to my friend's country-house.

XVII

INFINITIVE ACTIVE

27. Present, Perfect and Future Infinitives Active of the four regular conjugations and of **esse**, to be, are as follows:

Conj.	Pres. Inf. Act.	Perf. Inf. Active	Future Inf. Active
1st	**amāre,** to love	**amāvisse,** to have loved	**amātūrus esse,** to be about to love
2nd	**monēre,** to advise	**monuisse,** to have advised	**monitūrus esse,** to be about to advise
3rd	**regere,** to rule	**rēxisse,** to have ruled	**rēctūrus esse,** to be about to rule
4th	**audīre,** to hear	**audīvisse,** to have heard	**audītūrus esse,** to be about to hear
esse	**esse,** to be	**fuisse,** to have been	**futūrus esse,** to be about to be

Notes.—(1) The Perfect Infinitive Active of any Latin verb may be formed by adding **-isse** to the perfect stem.

(2) The Future Infinitive Active of any Latin verb is formed of the future participle and **esse.** The participle is declined like **bonus, -a, -um**; and agrees with its subject in Gender, Number and Case, e.g.:

Discipulī scrīptūrī esse dīcuntur, The pupils are said to be about to write.

(3) The future infinitive of the verb **esse** has very commonly the form **fore.**

EXERCISE 17

Note.—The infinitive is used :

(*a*) As subject or object of a verb, e.g. : **Difficile est labōrāre,** To work is difficult, *or*, Working is difficult, *or*, It is difficult to work. **Labōrāre discō,** I learn to work.

(*b*) To complete the sense of many verbs of *wishing, deciding, being able, beginning*, etc., and of passive verbs of *saying, thinking*, etc., e.g. : **Cōnstituit pugnāre,** He resolved to fight ; **Scrīptūra esse dīcitur,** She is said to be about to write ; **Scrīpsisse vidētur,** He seems to have written. This is known as the *Prolative Infinitive.*

A

THE GAULS AT ROME

[*After massacring the old men the Gauls sacked the city and attacked the Capitol. Beaten off, they besieged it until the garrison was ready to buy peace with gold. At the critical moment the great general* CAMILLUS, *who had been living in exile, arrived with an army to take vengeance on the invaders.*]

Gallī, ubi paucōs diēs in urbe mānsērunt ut praedam ē templīs domibusque quam plūrimam comparārent, in arcem impetum facere cōnstituērunt. Prīmā lūce convēnērunt omnēs in forum ; deinde magnō clāmōre ad collem contendērunt. Rōmānī tamen, cum fortiter pugnārent, magnā clāde eōs dēpulērunt. Itaque cum spēs victōriae eō diē nūlla esset, Gallī obsidiōnem parāvērunt. Mox in perīculō ingentī arx erat. Gallī enim, cum aut vestīgium hominis vīdissent aut ipsī viam invēnissent, collem nocte ascendere cōnstituērunt. Cum aliī aliōs per saxa traherent, magnō silentiō ad summum pervēnērunt. Nihil audīvērunt custōdēs Rōmānī ; nē canēs quidem excitātī sunt. Sed erant forte in Capitōliō ānserēs quīdam, quibus, cum Iūnōnī

GALLI PRAECIPITES DEIECTI SUNT

sacrī essent, Rōmānī in tantā cibī inopiā abstinuerant.
Quae rēs tum Rōmānōs servāvit. Clangōre enim ānserum
ālārumque strepitū cum excitātus esset Marcus Manlius, vir
bellō īnsignis, arma cēpit, cēterōs vocāvit, ipse ad locum
contendit et Gallum, quī iam in summō stābat, scūtō
dēturbāvit. Illīus cāsū cum cēterī strātī essent, mox omnēs
Gallī praecipitēs dēiectī sunt.

Cum obsidiōnem Gallī nōn relinquerent, Rōmānī
Camillum ab exsiliō revocāre cōnstituērunt, eumque
dictātōrem dīxērunt. Intereā, nē propter famem, quae
gravissima iam erat, pācem petere vidērentur, in castra
hostium pānem saepe dēiēcērunt. Quā rē Gallī pretiō
Rōmam relinquere cōnstituērunt. Magnum pondus aurī
pretium factum est. Rēs per sē turpissima iniūriā Gallōrum
turpior facta est. Brennus enim, dux Gallōrum inīqua
pondera comparāvit. Īrātī sunt Rōmānī; sed Brennus,

"Vae victīs!" inquit, et ponderī gladium suum addidit.
Ecce tamen, eō ipsō tempore pervēnit cum exercitū Camillus.
Is magnā vōce cīvēs iūssit aurum removēre. "Ferrō enim,"
inquit, "nōn aurō patriam servēmus." Tum Gallīs imperāvit
ut sē ad proelium parārent. Mox Gallī nōn modo superātī
sed omnēs ad ūnum interfectī sunt. Nē nūntius quidem
clādis relictus est.

B

1. To have left ; to have removed ; to be about to call ; we
   have decided to depart ; he is said to be coming ; she
   is said to be about to reply ; he is said to have heard ;
   he has decided to learn.
2. (a) Mī pater, cum hodiē ōtiōsus esse videāris, multa tē
   rogāre cōnstituī.
   (b) Ō mē miserum! Cōnstituistīne mihi molestus esse?
   Nōnne ad vīllam avī tuī hodiē discessūrus esse
   dīcēbāris?
   (c) Ita vērō, sed cum pater meus ōtiōsus futūrus esse
   dīcerētur—
   (d) Satis est, mī Sexte ; parātus sum respondēre. Interrogā.
   (e) Benīgnē respōnsūrus esse, mī pater, vidēris. Hōc igitur
   prīmum rogābō ; nōnne mē hodiē ad spectāculum
   quoddam ductūrus esse dīcēbāris?
   (f) Quam blandum (wheedling) fīlium habeō! Quam
   mātris similem! Cum tamen hoc ōlim dīxisse videar,
   ad spectāculum festīnēmus.
   (g) Grātiās tibi agō, mī pater! Post spectāculum aliīs dē
   rēbus tē interrogāre cōnstituī!
3. Marcus's father is said to have built a new house.
4. How long have you decided to remain in the city?
5. I have told the slave to bring my horse to-morrow morning.
6. You seem to be about to leave the city soon.
7. The Gauls are said to have found a man's tracks on the hill.
8. The sacred geese were said to have saved the citadel.

9. Since we have no bread, we have decided to depart at once.
10. Have I not told you often not to throw away your ball ?
11. It will not be easy to find the horses.
12. The Gauls seemed to be about to depart.
13. It is often easier to blame than to praise.
14. The barbarians were said to be about to attack our camp.
15. It will not be very easy to carry so heavy a burden.

WORD STUDY

What is a *companion* ? A friend ? Yes ; but notice what a flood of light is thrown on the word by your Latin, which shows you that it really means *one with whom you share your bread*. **Pānis** has given us some other interesting words. The *pantry* derives its name from the fact that it was once the place where the bread of the household was stored. Perhaps you have come across the word *pannier*, one of a pair of baskets slung across the back of a horse or donkey and used to convey articles to market, etc. The *pannier* is so called because it was once used mainly for carrying bread.

Look again at **praeceps**. The part **prae-** means " in front " ; in **ceps** we have the root which appears in **caput**, the head. Hence **praeceps** means literally *head in front, head first*. It has given us the English word *precipitate*, which, when a verb, means to throw headlong, hence to throw hastily and violently ; and, when an adjective, means rash, hasty, headlong. **Praeceps** in Latin is often applied to places. What do you think a **praeceps locus** is ? A steep place ? Certainly ; and hence our words *precipice* and *precipitous*.

Lastly, let us *investigate* the *diction* of the following : He was *ponderous* in speech, *precipitate* in *action*. *Obsessed* with the *clamour* of the *multitude*, he had no ear for the *sapient admonitions* of the *prudent minority*. He was *excited* by *temporary success*, *dejected* by *insignificant reverses* of *fortune*. To one so *inconstant*, the *custody* of the *constitution* could never be *committed*.

THE CARTHAGINIAN WARS

The year 270 B.C. marks a turning-point in the history of Rome. By that time she had gained control of all Italy south of the great plain of the Po ; she had met and defeated her first enemy from overseas, Pyrrhus, king of the Greek state of Epirus, whom Tarentum had called in to help in the struggle against Rome. In a few years Rome was to embark upon a series of great wars which were to leave her without a rival in the Mediterranean. For Rome's first movement of expansion after 270 B.C. was towards Sicily with its rich wheat-lands. Here, however, Rome found herself faced by the great African power, Carthage. Carthage was at the moment the wealthiest state in the western Mediterranean. It owned Sardinia and Corsica ; it had many settlements in Sicily. It had trading stations as far afield as Spain ; at sea it was without a challenge to its supremacy. Carthage itself was a Phoenician city, an offshoot of Tyre, about which you may have read in the Old Testament.

The clash of interests between Rome and Carthage led to the outbreak of war in 264 B.C. This First Carthaginian War lasted till 241 B.C. In the first period of the war fighting was confined to Sicily, and the Romans were on the whole victorious. But it was seen that victory meant little as long as Carthage retained command of the sea. In the second phase of the war, therefore, we find the Romans building a fleet, winning some important naval successes, and actually sending an expedition under Regulus to Africa. The expedition ended in disaster, and the war entered its third stage, a long, weary struggle in Sicily which was ended by another bid for naval supremacy by Rome. The victory of the Aegates Insulae ended the war. Carthage withdrew from Sicily and agreed to pay a huge indemnity. Sicily became the first Roman province.

Soon afterwards, the Carthaginian general Hamilcar sailed off to found a Carthaginian empire in Spain to compensate for the loss of Sicily. His command eventually fell to his son Hannibal, the dream of whose life was a war of revenge upon Rome. By 219 B.C. his preparations were complete. He provoked a conflict by wantonly attacking Saguntum, an ally of Rome. Thus began the Second Carthaginian War.

In this war also we may trace three distinct phases. In the first Hannibal crossed the Pyrenees and led his army through Gaul over the Rhône to the Alps. He crossed the Alps with incredible hardships, and then proceeded to inflict defeat after defeat upon the Romans. Yet Rome stood firm. For the most part her allies in Italy were faithful, and she actually sent an army to Spain which did magnificent work in hindering reinforcements from coming to Hannibal. The second part of the war shows the advantage slowly but surely passing to Rome. She secures Sicily, completes the conquest of Spain, and forces Hannibal more and more into the south. In the third and final phase of the war Hannibal's ultimate failure is made certain by the defeat and death of his brother Hasdrubal who had come to reinforce him. Scipio transfers the war to Africa and threatens Carthage which is forced to recall Hannibal for its own defence. In 202 B.C. the grim struggle ended with Scipio's victory at Zama. Spain, Africa, part of Gaul, were among the prizes of victory. More soon followed. Fresh campaigns brought Greece and large parts of Asia Minor under Rome. And finally—for the Romans never ceased to fear that Carthage might revive—an excuse was found for a Third Carthaginian War. The city was besieged, and, after a terrible struggle, taken and utterly destroyed in 146 B.C.

A FAMOUS SAYING

Dēlenda est Carthāgō, Carthage must be destroyed.

With these words, repeated for years in his every speech in the Senate, Cato urged the Romans to undertake the Third Carthaginian War.

XVIII

INFINITIVE PASSIVE

28. The Present, Perfect and Future Infinitives Passive of the four regular conjugations are as follows :

CONJ.	PRES. INF. PASS.	PERF. INFIN. PASS.	FUTURE INFIN. PASS.
1	**amārī**, to be loved	**amātus esse**, to have been loved	**amātum īrī**, to be about to be loved
2	**monērī**, to be advised	**monitus esse**, to have been advised	**monitum īrī**, to be about to be advised
3	**regī**, to be ruled	**rēctus esse**, to have been ruled	**rēctum īrī**, to be about to be ruled
4	**audīrī**, to be heard	**audītus esse**, to have been heard	**audītum īrī**, to be about to be heard

Notes.—

(1) The Perfect Infin. Passive of any Latin verb is formed of the Perfect Participle with **esse**. The participle agrees with its subject in Number, Gender and Case, e.g. : **Amāta esse dīcitur,** She is said to have been loved.

(2) The Future Infin. Passive of any Latin verb is formed of the supine with **īrī**. The supine does not change in form.

(3) The Pres. Infin. Passive of **capiō** is **capī**.
The Perfect and Future Infinitives Passive are formed regularly.

EXERCISE 18

Note.—The nouns *top, bottom, middle, edge, whole, rest,* are expressed in Latin by adjectives, e.g. : **summus collis,** the top of the hill ; **medius ager,** the middle of the field ; **extrēma silva,** the edge of the wood ; **īmum mare,** the bottom of the sea ; **tōtus exercitus,** the whole of the army ; **reliquus exercitus,** the rest of the army.

A

A Band of Heroes

[*By* 265 *B.C. Rome controlled all Italy south of the Rubicon. In* 264 *B.C. war broke out with the great African power, Carthage. Sicily was the main theatre of operations, which dragged on till* 241 *B.C. Here is one episode in the Sicilian campaigns.*]

Atīlius Cālātīnus, cōnsul Rōmānus, magnam Carthāginiēnsium classem superāvisse dīcitur. Posteā tamen in Siciliā, cum exercitum in vallem quamdam dūxisset, ab hostibus est circumventus. Magnā virtūte Calpurniī, tribūnī mīlitum, Rōmānī tum servātī esse dīcuntur. Is enim cōnsulī, " Cūr nōn iubēs," inquit, " mīlitēs quadringentōs ad collem illum altum per mediōs hostēs contendere eumque occupāre ut in eōs hostēs sē convertant, tū intereā reliquum exercitum ā locō īnfēstō dūcās ? Alia enim, nisi haec, salūtis nūlla via est." Cuī cōnsul, " Optimum tū quidem," inquit, " dās cōnsilium ; sed quis quadringentōs illōs sīc ad certam mortem dūcet ? " Et Calpurnius, " Sī alius," inquit, " nēmo hōc factūrus esse vidētur, cūr nōn mihi imperās ut ipse dūcam ? Ego hanc tibi et reī pūblicae vītam dō."

Cōnsul Calpurniō grātiās ēgit, et quadringentōs mīlitēs dedit. Quibus ubi Calpurnius persuāsit ut prō patriā vītam darent, " Agite, mīlitēs," inquit, " morte nostrā līberēmus ex obsidiōne legiōnēs." Tum omnēs nūllā spē salūtis sed ingentī laudis amōre in hostēs contendērunt. Prīmō Carthāginiēnsēs, propter audāciam eōrum attonitī, stābant immōtī ; deinde, ubi iter ā Rōmānīs susceptum esse vidē-batur ut collem occupārent, statim in eōs tōtus Poenōrum exercitus sē convertit. Est proelium diū ācerrimum. Tan-dem superat multitūdō. Quadringentī omnēs ad ūnum interficiuntur. Cōnsul intereā reliquum exercitum in loca tuta dūcit.

Sed dī immortālēs Calpurniō fortūnam virtūtī pārem dedērunt. Multīs ille quidem locīs vulnerātus esse dīcitur, vulnus tamen in capite nūllum accēpisse. Quae cum ita essent, tandem inter mortuōs multīs cōnfectus vulneribus sed vīvus adhuc est inventus. Mox convaluit, et praemium virtūtis accēpit corōnam obsidiōnālem quae nōn nisi eī data est quī tōtum exercitum ex obsidiōne līberāvisse vidēbatur.

B

1. (*a*) Cum equōs tuōs, mī pater, prīmā lūce dūcī iūsseris, longum iter susceptūrus esse vidēris.

   (*b*) Ita vērō, mī fīlī. Cōnstituī enim Brundisium iter facere ut in Graeciam nāvigem.

   (*c*) Mehercule, pater, id iter longissimum esse dīcitur. Num ūnō diē id ā tē cōnficiētur ?

   (*d*) Minimē vērō, mī fīlī ; multōs diēs in itinere futūrus esse videor ; ab eīs quī celeriter contendunt iter decem diēbus cōnficī dīcitur ; facile erit nōbīs quīndecim diēbus Brundisium venīre.

   (*e*) Quam longum iter, mī pater, ā tē susceptum esse vidētur ! Ōlim ego quoque iter faciam ut urbēs Ītaliae et Graeciae praeclārās videam.

2. Our city is said to have been saved by the sacred geese.
3. The brave soldier is said to have been found alive.
4. Marcus seems to be about to leave the city.

5. This great work is said to have been completed in a year.
6. It will not be easy to find your friend in so great a multitude.
7. He is said to have received a reward equal to his courage.
8. No one is said to have been taken alive in that city.
9. Many houses seem to have been built in the city.
10. We shall persuade the enemy to turn (i.e. to turn *themselves*) against us.
11. Four hundred oxen are said to have been sent to our farm.
12. The orator is said to be about to leave Rome of his own accord.

DŌNA MĪLITĀRIA

Various gifts or, as we should say, decorations, were open to the Roman soldier who distinguished himself in war. The commonest was perhaps the **hasta pūra,** a pointless lance, which was awarded for wounding an enemy. For other degrees of distinguished conduct we hear of the award of an **armilla,** bracelet, or of a **torques,** a twisted necklet of gold. These were minor decorations. Much more coveted were the various crowns or **corōnae** which were bestowed for certain exploits. The man who, like Calpurnius in our story, freed a beleaguered army, was given the **corōna obsidiōnālis,** a wreath made of grass. For saving the life of a comrade in battle the appropriate reward was the **corōna cīvica,** which was made of oak-leaves. The leader of a storming party might receive the **corōna mūrālis,** a crown made in the form of a city wall. The first man to break his way into the enemy's camp was eligible for the **corōna vallāris,** a crown made to represent a rampart. For generally distinguished conduct in a campaign the decoration was the **corōna aurea,** a plain crown of gold. In naval warfare the man who first boarded an enemy ship was eligible for the **corōna nāvālis,** a wreath adorned with miniature prows of ships. The supreme distinction of all was however the **corōna triumphālis,** the wreath of bay leaves worn in his triumphal procession by the victorious general to whom the Senate gave the privilege of holding a triumph.

XIX

INDIRECT STATEMENT

29. An indirect statement is a subordinate noun clause depend-
ing on a verb of *saying, thinking, knowing, showing,* etc., e.g.
    We say that he is fighting, **Dīcimus eum pugnāre.**
Notice that in the Latin—
    (*a*) there is no word corresponding to the English " that,"
    (*b*) the subject of the subord. noun clause is in the
        accusative,
    (*c*) the verb of the subord. noun clause is in the infinitive.
Hence this construction is often called the Accusative and
Infinitive Construction. This construction is not unknown in
English, e.g. :
    I believe this to be true.

30. To determine the tense of the infinitive to be used in Latin,
think back to the original direct statement, i.e. the
speaker's actual words, the thinker's actual thought.
    If the direct had the present tense, use present infin. in the
indirect statement ; if the direct had the future tense,
use the future infin. If the direct employed any past
tense whatever, use the perfect infin. in the indirect
statement.

Examples :

1. He said the camp would be taken, **Dīxit castra captum
   īrī.**
   (*Direct was* " will be taken " ; *hence fut. infin. pass.*)

2. He said that the boy was coming, **Dīxit puerum venīre.**
   (*Direct was* " is coming " ; *hence pres. infin. act.*)

3. He thought that the boy had come, **Putāvit puerum
   vēnisse.**
   (*Direct was* " has come " ; *hence perf. infin. act.*)

EXERCISE 19

A

1. Audiō prandium parātum esse. Festīnēmus.
2. Quid novī est, Marce ? Audiō enim tē nūper ē prōvinciā vēnisse.
3. Lēgātiōnem Carthāginem missam esse affirmant.
4. Putō comitēs nostrōs ad portam urbis nōs iam exspectāre.
5. Putāsne ōrātōrem mox ab exsiliō revocātum īrī ?
6. Videō patrem Sextī iam convaluisse.
7. Dīcunt magistrum vestrum hominem esse mītissimum.
8. Videō portās templī iam clausās esse.
9. Audīvī in Britanniā frīgora maxima esse.
10. Putō magistrōs optimīs discipulīs dōna datūrōs esse.

B

1. They say that the wealth of the Roman people has been increased by you (s.).
2. Where is Sextus hurrying to ? I think that he is hurrying to school.
3. I see that the consul is about to sacrifice.
4. Have you (s.) heard that your companion has come ?
5. He declares that he will travel slowly.
6. Sextus says that his father has a boat.
7. They say that the general sleeps on the ground among the soldiers.
8. We heard that the soldiers had been killed to a man.
9. I think that the little boy will be sent to school to-morrow.
10. Have you (s.) heard that the citizens have no bread ?
11. I hear that you (s.) have undertaken a very difficult task.
12. They said that Caesar had held the command for five years.
13. He told me that you (pl.) would come quickly.
14. I told you (s.) to come quickly.
15. We think that those men have been sent to certain death.

C

A Journey to Brundisium—I

LOLLIUS : Salvē, Horātī ! Quid agis, dulcissime rērum ? Sed unde tū vēnistī ? Affirmābant enim omnēs tē ex urbe discessisse. Ubi tam diū fuistī ?

HORĀTIUS : Salvē tū quoque, Lollī. Sed quid est quod dīcis ? Nōnne audīvistī mē longum iter fēcisse ?

LOLLIUS : Minimē vērō. Quō iter fuit ?

HORĀTIUS : Brundisium.

LOLLIUS : Quam longum iter nārrās ! Age, mēcum sedē paulisper ; omnia dē itinere nārrā. Audīre enim cupiō.

HORĀTIUS : Ab initiō omnia, mī Lollī, audiēs. Rōmā cum Hēliodōrō discessī quī doctissimus Graecōrum esse dīcitur. Viā Appiā iter fēcimus. Dīcunt plūrimōs prīmō diē Forum Appiī pervenīre ; sed nōs—

LOLLIUS : Satis est, mī Horātī. Sciō vōs īgnāvōs esse !

HORĀTIUS : Prīmō diē Arīciam, postrīdiē Forum Appiī vēnimus. Affirmant enim omnēs Viam Appiam rēgīnam esse viārum ; iīs tamen quī tardē iter faciunt, multō minus gravis est.

LOLLIUS : Quid dē Forō Appiī nārrās ? Dīcunt enim plūrimī sordidum oppidum esse.

HORĀTIUS : Ita vērō, mī Lollī. Quam malignī ibi caupōnēs sunt ! Quam ingēns errat semper per viās nautārum multitūdō ! Cum aqua dēterrima esset, ego nōn cēnāvī ; comitēs quibus grāta cēna fuit, nōn placidē exspectābam. Tandem, ubi iam nox erat, ad lintrem contendimus. In rīpā ingentem clāmōrem audīmus. Aliī enim aliīs, " Festīnāte, virī," inquiunt, " lintrem iam discessūram esse nūntiant." Nē in rīpā relinquerēmur, omnēs quam celerrimē lintrem intrāmus. Tum aes petitur ; mūla ligātur. Tōta hōra est. Intereā malī culicēs rānaeque somnōs āvertunt. Et nauta quīdam, " Audīte virī," inquit, " dē puellā meā cantāre cupiō, puellārum pulcherrimā." Sed viātor quīdam, " Tacē," inquit, " homō īgnāvissime. Est et mihi puella multō tuā pulchrior. Dē illā ego cantābō." Diū cantant ; tandem dēfessī dormiunt. Paucās hōrās omnēs dormīmus. Tandem quīdam, " Iam diēs est," inquit, " stat tamen linter immōta. Fcce. vidēmus nautam in rīpā placidē dormīre. Īrātus ex lintre contendit ūnus viātōrum ; fūstem capit, et nautae, " Festīnā," inquit, " mūlam ligā." Et caput hominis mūlaeque verberat. Cum magnō omnium rīsū nauta festīnat. Quid multa ? Quārtā hōrā ad Fānum Ferōniae venīmus.

Note :

aes, aeris, *n.*, bronze, money, fare.
cantō, -āre, -āvī, -ātum, to sing.
caupō, -ōnis, *m.*, shopkeeper.
cēnō, -āre, -āvī, -ātum, to dine.
culex, -icis, *m.*, gnat.
cupiō, -ere, -īvī, -ītum, to desire.
dēterrimus, -a -um, very bad.
dulcis, -is, -e, sweet.
ligō, -āre, -āvī, -ātum, to tether.

fūstis, -is, *m.*, cudgel.
malígnus, -a, -um, niggardly.
mūla, -ae, *f.*, mule.
placidē, calmly.
rāna, -ae, *f.*, frog.
viātor, -ōris, *m.*, traveller.
sciō, -īre, -īvī, -ītum, to know.
somnus, -ī, *m.*, sleep.

Horātius, -iī, *m.* (*Q. Horatius Flaccus*), Horace, a great Roman poet, 65 B.C.–8 B.C.
Hēliodōrus, -ī, *m.*, Heliodorus, a Greek teacher of Rhetoric, companion of Horace on the journey to Brundisium.
Lollius, -iī, *m.*, Lollius, a friend of Horace.

XX

INDIRECT STATEMENT—*continued*

31. In an indirect statement, *he, she, it, they*, referring to the subject of the main verb, are translated by **sē**; otherwise by the appropriate part of **is, ea, id**, e.g. :

He says that he is brave, **Dīcit sē fortem esse.**
I say that he is brave, **Dīcō eum fortem esse.**

32. Instead of **dīcō** followed by a negative, Latin employs **negō**, I deny, I say that . . . not. Hence—

for *I say that . . . not* we must use **negō**, *I deny*, etc.
  ,, *I* ,, ,, *no one*   ,,   ,, **negō quemquam** (*I deny that anyone*)
  ,, *I* ,, ,, *no*   ,,   ,, **negō ūllum** (*I deny that any*)
  ,, *I* ,, ,, *never*   ,,   ,, **negō umquam** (*I deny that ever*)
  ,, *I* ,, ,, *nowhere*   ,,   ,, **negō ūsquam** (*I deny that anywhere*)

Notes.—

(1) The above rule applies only to **dīcō** with a negative following. Other verbs of saying are followed by a negative, e.g. :

Affirmō eum numquam vēnisse, I declare that he has never come.

(2) When the negative precedes **dīcō**, it is expressed in the usual way, e.g. :

Numquam dīxī eum vēnisse, I never said that he had come.

(This, of course, *means* something quite different from **negāvī eum umquam vēnisse**.)

EXERCISE 20

A

PRELUDE TO WAR

[*The peace which followed the first Carthaginian war did not
last. With his son* HANNIBAL *the Carthaginian general*
HAMILCAR *set out to build a Carthaginian empire in
Spain and prepare for a war of vengeance on Rome.
He died before preparations were complete. In due
course* HANNIBAL *inherited his task. By attacking
Saguntum, a city allied to Rome, he provoked war in*
219 *B.C.*]

Quae cum ita essent, dīxit Hamilcar in Hispāniam sē
cum exercitū nāvigātūrum esse quō celerius opēs Carthāginiēnsium augēret et novum bellum parāret. Eō diē quō
Carthāgine discessit, ubi dīs sacrificābat, Hannibalem fīlium
suum ad āram vocāvit eīque imperāvit ut iūrāret sē numquam amīcum fore populī Rōmānī. Quod ubi puer fēcit,
patrī persuāsit ut sē cum exercitū in Hispāniam dūceret.

Post Hamilcaris mortem, Hasdrubal gener ēius, medius
inter patrem et fīlium, octo annōs imperium in Hispāniā
obtinēbat. Ubi is interfectus est, Hannibal, maximō
omnium cōnsēnsū, imperātor creātus est. Mīlitibus enim
ab initiō grātissimus fuisse vidētur. Vidēbant enim eum in
perīculīs audācissimum esse, in cōnsiliīs prūdentissimum.
Nūllō labōre aut corpus aut animus ēius superātus est.
Calōris et frīgoris pār erat patientia ; cibī quod satis erat
modo sūmēbat. Quiētem neque cubīlī neque silentiō
petēbat ; saepe humī inter statiōnēs mīlitum dormiēbat.
Prīmus semper in proelium contendēbat ; ultimus discēdēbat.
Vitia tamen ingentia hās tantās virtūtēs aequābant, in-

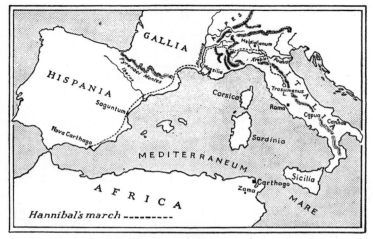

THE WESTERN MEDITERRANEAN, SHOWING HANNIBAL'S ROUTE

hūmāna crūdēlitās, perfidia plūs quam Pūnica, nūllus neque hominum neque deōrum metus.

Ubi sē parātum esse putābat, Saguntīnōs, sociōs populī Rōmānī, oppūgnāvit. Mox audīvērunt Rōmānī urbem obsidērī ; lēgātōs statim mīsērunt ut Hannibal ab obsidiōne dēsisteret. Quibus Hannibal, ubi negāvit sē lēgātiōnēs iam audītūrum esse, imperāvit ut Carthāginem festīnārent. Lēgātī, ubi id fēcērunt, in senātum ductī sunt. Tum Fabius (is prīnceps fuit lēgātiōnis) negāvit sē quidquam nisi hōc rogātūrum esse, " Vestrōne cōnsiliō Hannibal Saguntum oppūgnāvit ? " Deinde sinum ex togā fēcit, et, " Cūr nōn respondētis ? " inquit, " Hīc enim vōbīs bellum et pācem portāmus. Utrum placet, sūmite." Māgnō omnium cōnsēnsū clāmant Carthāginiēnsēs sē bellum sūmere. Tum Fabius, ubi sinum excussit, bellum sē dare dīxit. Et Carthāginiēnsēs, " Accipimus," inquiunt, " et quō animō accēpimus, eōdem gerēmus."

B

1. Translate the infinitives only in the following :
   (*a*) I think that he was hurrying.
   (*b*) We thought that you (*pl.*) would come.
   (*c*) We heard that she had been wounded.
   (*d*) I shall say that you (*s.*) were tired.
   (*e*) He thought that we were afraid.
2. (*a*) Paene cōnstituī tē, Mārce, verberāre. Videō enim īgnāvum tē esse.
   (*b*) Ō magister, nōlī mē verberāre ! Quandō mē īgnāvum esse vīdistī ? Putō enim puerum mē dīligentiōrem in lūdō tuō nōn esse, nōn fuisse, numquam futūrum esse.
   (*c*) Vae tibi, sceleste puer ! Quid dīcis ? Nōnne herī imperāvī omnibus ut hodiē librōs ad lūdum portārētis ? Nōnne iam audiō tē eōs domī relīquisse ?
   (*d*) Nōn negō, magister, mē adhūc mandātōrum tuōrum saepe immemorem fuisse ; negō tamen mē umquam posthāc (*hereafter*) īgnāvum fore.
   (*e*) Satis est, Mārce. Videō tē satis monitum esse ; iam omnēs moneō mē nōn semper mītem fore, īgnāvōs tandem īgnāviae poenās datūrōs esse.

3. He says that he has not taken food to-day.
4. We heard that you (*pl.*) had been frightened by the storm.
5. The old man said he would never come to the island.
6. The children said that there was no bread in the house.
7. The consul said that no one would be taken alive.
8. Where have you (*pl.*) been ? Syrus says that he has not seen you anywhere.
9. I told them to hasten ; but they told me that they would travel slowly.
10. My grandfather says that he is not recovering.
11. Why did you (*s.*) not ask my companions to come to the house ?
12. For I told them that I would be at home to-day.

XXI

INDIRECT STATEMENT—*continued*

33. In English, verbs of *hoping, promising, threatening*, are often followed by the infinitive instead of a " that "-clause containing a future verb.

In Latin, the full accusative and future infinitive construction must be used, e.g. :

I hope to come, **Spērō mē ventūrum esse.**

I promised to come, **Prōmīsī mē ventūrum esse.**

34. In English an indirect statement is often introduced by the impersonal *it is said, it seems*. Latin adopts a personal construction, e.g. :

It seemed that the soldier had departed, **Mīles discessisse vidēbātur.**

(*literally*, The soldier seemed to have departed)

It is said that he is brave, **Dīcitur fortis esse.**
(*literally*, He is said to be brave)

Notes.—(1) In English " that " before an indirect statement is often omitted, e.g. :

I think he will come, **Putō eum ventūrum esse.**

(2) In Latin **esse** of the future infin. active and of the perf. infin. passive are frequently omitted, e.g. :

Prōmīsērunt sē ventūrōs, They promised to come.

Puellās laudātās dīxit, He said that the girls had been praised.

EXERCISE 21

Note.—**Mīlle,** thousand, is an indeclinable adjective, e.g. : **mīlle hominēs,** a thousand men ; **mīlle hominum,** of a thousand men, etc.

In the plural we use the noun **mīlia,** thousands (declined like plural of **cubīle**). Hence, two thousand men becomes " two thousands of men," **duo mīlia hominum** ; with two thousand men, **cum duōbus mīlibus hominum,** etc.

A

ON THE ALPINE SLOPES

[*In* 218 *B.C.* HANNIBAL *crossed the Pyrenees, marched across Gaul and over the Alps into Italy. Difficult as was the ascent of the Alps, the descent was even harder and caused greater losses.*]

Nōnō diē ad iugum Alpium Hannibal pervēnit. Castra posuit ; dēfessīs itinere mīlitibus brevis quiēs data est. Ubi nivis cāsū mīlitēs perterritī sunt, Hannibal, nē spem tōtam abicerent, Ītaliam campōsque Circumpadānōs ostendit ; affirmāvit suōs moenia iam superāvisse nōn Ītaliae modo sed etiam Rōmae. Prōmīsit cētera loca plāna et prōclīvia fore, eōsque ūnō aut alterō proeliō arcem et caput Ītaliae in potestāte habitūrōs. Tertiō diē ex castrīs discessērunt. Iter tamen multō quam in ascēnsū iam difficilius erat. Omnis enim via praeceps, angusta, lūbrica esse vidēbātur. Itaque mīlitēs āmissī esse plūrimī dīcuntur, cum aliī in aliōs caderent neque quidquam eōs in locō prōclīvī servāret. Vēnērunt tandem ad locum ubi tōta via lāpsū terrae dēlēta est. Prīmō alia via petitur ; deinde, cum propter nivem nūlla esse vidērētur, Hannibal castra posuit et novam per rūpēs praecipitēs viam facere cōnstituit. Quae paucīs diēbus parāta est ; in saxīs enim fēcērunt īgnem ingentem Carthāginiēnsēs ; deinde, quō celerius saxa frangerentur, in ea, ubi iam ārdēbant, acētum (*vinegar*) mīlitēs īnfūdērunt.

AN ALPINE PASS.

Quīntō decimō diē in campōs Hannibal pervēnit. Ex copiīs restābant vīgintī mīlia peditum, sex mīlia equitum. In tōtō itinere Hannibal, praeter ingentem equōrum multitūdinem, tria et trīgintā mīlia mīlitum āmīsisse dīcitur.

B

1. No one will come ; he says that no one will come ; I have done nothing ; I say that I have done nothing ; I had hoped that you would come ; I hope to come ; we promise to be diligent ; it will be found ; I hoped that it would be found ; I have promised to hurry.

2. (a) Pater, nōnne dīcitur Hannibal imperātor maximus fuisse ?
   (b) Ita vērō, mī fīlī, omnēs putant paucōs imperātōrēs eō māiōrēs fuisse.
   (c) Ego tamen negō eum imperātōrem maximum fuisse. Nōnne spērāvit urbem Rōmam ā sē et captum et incēnsum īrī ? Num legimus eam captam et incēnsam esse ?
   (d) Minimē vērō, mī fīlī. Legimus tamen eam saepe in perīculō fuisse ingentī, exercitūsque Rōmānōrum multōs et magnōs ab eō superātōs esse.
   (e) Cūr tamen ipse ab Ītaliā revocātus est, et in Āfricā ā Scīpiōne superātus esse dīcitur ?
   (f) Nōnne audīvistī Hannibalem cum parvō exercitū hostēs saepe superāvisse ? Spērāvit enim Rōmānōs ā sociīs relictum īrī. Cum illī in fidē et societāte Rōmānōrum mānsisse dīcerentur, sine eōrum auxiliō per multōs annōs Rōmānōs terrēbat. Hunc ego imperātōrem maximum appellō.

3. It is said that you desire to procure bread.
4. The boys have promised to come home to-morrow.
5. They say that they have found nothing.
6. It seems that snow has fallen on the hills.
7. It is said that many horses were lost on account of the snow.

8. It is said that the farmer has two thousand oxen.
9. The general hoped to reach the city with five thousand soldiers.
10. The girls say they do not like the snow.
11. Did you (*s.*) not promise to show me your crown?
12. It seems that we are being blamed by the farmer.
13. We hoped that gifts would be given to us.
14. But Marcus says that nothing has been given to him.
15. We think we shall leave for Sicily to-morrow.

WORD STUDY

Once again your Latin makes contact with your Science, where by this time you have heard of *calories* and *calorimeters*. From which Latin word that you have met of late are these names derived?

What is a *convalescent*, a *refrigerator*, the *frigid* zone? What does a financier mean by saying that certain shares are at *par*? What sort of plan might be called a *perfidious* design? What is *Perfidious Albion*? To circumvent was originally *to surround*; what does the word mean nowadays?

BATTLE ELEPHANTS

Animals such as these added to Hannibal's difficulties in crossing the Rhône and the Alps.

XXII

PARTICIPLES ACTIVE

35. A Latin verb normally possesses two participles of the active voice :

      (*a*) a Present Participle Active,

      (*b*) a Future Participle Active.

Observe most carefully that it does not possess a perfect (or past) participle active.

The active participles of the four regular conjugations are :

Conj.	Present Participle Active	Future Participle Active
1	**amāns, amantis,** loving	**amātūrus, -a, -um,** about to love
2	**monēns, monentis,** advising	**monitūrus, -a, -um,** about to advise
3	**regēns, regentis,** ruling	**rēctūrus, -a, -um,** about to rule
4	**audiēns, audientis,** hearing	**audītūrus, -a, -um,** about to hear

Notes.—

    (1) Participles are declined like adjectives, agreeing in number and gender with the noun or pronoun which they qualify ; and can themselves govern the same case as the verb to which they belong, e.g. :

Eum epistolam scrībentem vīdimus, We saw him writing a letter.

Eum mīlitibus persuādentem audīmus, We hear him persuading the soldiers.

    (2) The ablative singular, all genders, of the present participle ends in **-e**, not **-ī**.

(3) The future participle active of any Latin verb may be formed by changing **-um** of the supine into **-ūrus**.

(4) The present participle active of **capiō** is **capiēns**.

(5) The verb **esse** has only one participle—the future participle **futūrus**, about to be.

(6) The present participle active may also be translated " *while -ing, when -ing,*" and the future participle active " *going to——, on the point of -ing.*"

EXERCISE 22

A

1. Give, with meanings, present and future participles active of the following verbs : **aequāre, suscipere, cōnficere, mūnīre, convertere, persuādēre.**
2. Audīvī vōs mē culpantēs.
3. Nōnne vīdī Mārcum domum festīnantem ?
4. Gallī arcem captūrī ā Mānliō dēpulsī sunt.
5. Montem ascēnsūrī ā viātōribus monitī sumus viam nōn tūtam esse.
6. Ab Hasdrubale imperium obtinente potestās Carthāginiēnsium aucta est.
7. In lūbricā nive multī equī āmissī sunt.
8. Captīvīs effugientibus nēmō obstābat.
9. Nōnne tē vīdī pilam in sinū togae celantem ?
10. Per saltum venientibus nōbīs obstitērunt barbarī.

B

1. How do you do, Sextus ? I heard that you had left the city yesterday.
2. No, Marcus. Being about to depart I was warned to remain.
3. For Syrus saw the robbers preparing an ambush in the pass.
4. Playing in the wood we did not realise that it was late.
5. The Senate sent messengers to Cincinnatus while (he was) working in the fields.
6. The master saw the boys when (they were) about to break the window.

7. The shepherd saved the boy when he was about to fall from the crag.

8. I gave the letter to Marcus when (he was) leaving.

9. When (I was) leaving I received a letter from Sextus.

10. When about to take food we were ordered to march.

11. Hannibal was called to the altar by his father while (he was) sacrificing.

12. While pouring water into the ditch I myself fell into the water.

WORD STUDY

What of the word *case*? We have used this word throughout our Latin lessons; yet it is by no means clear at first sight why we call the Nominative, Vocative, etc., *cases*.

The story of the word takes us to ancient Greece, where learned men, investigating their own language, hit upon the idea of representing the various forms of a noun by means of a diagram. The Nominative was indicated by an upright line; the other forms by lines *falling* away from it. Hence someone thought of calling those forms which were shown by falling lines "*ptoseis*," which is a Greek word meaning "falls" or "fallings." The name stuck, and before long the Nominative was called the upright *ptosis* and the others were called slant or oblique *ptoseis*. When the Romans learned their Grammar from the Greeks, they translated *ptosis* by **cāsus**, which gave us our word *case*, and, like the Greeks, they frequently called the Nominative the upright case (**cāsus rēctus**), and the others they called slant or oblique cases (**cāsūs oblīquī**). Even to-day we quite often call the Vocative, Accusative, Genitive, Dative, and Ablative collectively the *oblique cases* of a noun.

Now, in conclusion, what is *ostentation*; why is *plane* Geometry so called; what does a *lubricant* really do; what is a *fracture*; what kind of supporter of a cause would you call *ardent*; what is really meant by *infusing* the tea?

XXIII

PARTICIPLES PASSIVE

36. The Latin verb possesses only one participle of the Passive voice, the Perfect Participle Passive.

The perfect participles passive of the four regular conjugations are:

Conj.	Perfect Participle Passive	Meaning
1	**amātus, -a, -um**	loved, having been loved
2	**monitus, -a, -um**	advised, having been advised
3	**rēctus, -a, -um**	ruled, having been ruled
4	**audītus, -a, -um**	heard, having been heard

Notes.—

(1) Observe most carefully that the Latin verb has no present or future participle passive.

(2) The perfect participle passive of any Latin verb may be formed by changing **-um** of the supine into **-us**.

(3) Before translating an English participle into Latin, examine its tense carefully. What at first sight may seem a present participle in English is often really perfect, e.g:

Being seen by the enemy, I fled, **Vīsus ab hostibus fūgī.**

EXERCISE 23

A

NEWS OF BATTLE

[HANNIBAL *entered Italy in October* 218 *B.C. Before the end of the year he defeated* SCIPIO *at the river Ticinus and* SEMPRONIUS *in a great battle on the river Trebia. In spring* 217 *B.C. he crossed the Apennines and at Lake Trasimene destroyed a Roman army under the consul* FLAMINIUS.]

Hannibal, quō magis īram cōnsulis excitāret, agrōs Cortōnēnsium, populī Rōmānī sociōrum, vāstāvit; deinde ad Trasumēnum lacum contendit. Locus īnsidiīs idōneus esse vidēbātur. Via enim est angusta inter montēs et lacum; deinde campus minimus; inde collēs īnsurgunt altī et praecipitēs. In aditū saltūs Hannibal equitēs cēlātōs relīquit; levem armātūram per iuga montium circumductam in īnsidiīs collocāvit; ipse cum reliquō exercitū in mediō campō castra posuit.

Postrīdiē Flāminius, īnsidiārum immemor, saltum intrāvit. Hannibal, ubi hostēs inclūsōs habuit, exspectantibus suīs signum dedit. Cum in campō dēnsa nebula esset, Rōmānī Poenōs dē montibus contendentēs nōn vīdērunt. Tandem clāmōribus hostium excitātī, sē circumventōs esse sēnsērunt. Perturbātīs suīs Flāminius imperāvit ut fortiter stārent et pugnārent; negāvit ūllam inde viam esse nisi vī et virtūte. Trēs hōrās pugnābant, et ubīque ferociter. Circā cōnsulem ipsum ācerrima pugna fuit, quem et hostēs magnā vī petēbant et Rōmānī servābant. Tandem Gallus

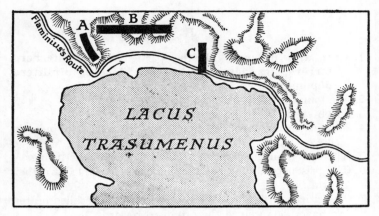

PLAN OF BATTLE OF LAKE TRASIMENE

While Flaminius marched along the road by the lakeside to meet Hannibal's infantry (C), he was attacked on the flank and in the rear by cavalry
and light-armed troops (A) and (B) lying in ambush.

quīdam cōnsulem ostendēns, " Ecce, hīc est," inquit, " quī
legiōnēs nostrās dēlēvit agrōsque et oppida vāstāvit. Iam
ego hanc victimam Mānibus necātōrum crūdēliter cīvium
dabō." Quae ubi dīxit, in Flāminium impetum fēcit,
hastāque interfēcit. Tum vērō Rōmānī in fugam sē con-
vertunt. Fugientibus neque lacus neque montēs obstant.
Quī per montēs iter petunt, aliī super aliōs praecipitantur ;
quōs in lacum terror agit, aut in aquīs dēlentur aut, sī ad
terram redeunt (*they return*), ab hostibus interficiuntur.
Quīndecim mīlia Rōmānōrum illō diē necātī sunt ; vix
decem mīlia ex aciē effugiunt.

Rōmae, ubi clādēs nūntiāta est, ingēns terror fuit.
Mātrōnae per viās errantēs exercitum superātum dēflēbant.
Tandem solis occasū M. Pompōnius praetor multitūdinī
magistrātūs vocantī respondit : " Pūgnā māgnā victī
sumus."

B

1. Give with meanings all the participles of: **sternere, terrēre, frangere, interficere, abicere, dīmittere, dēpōnere, revocāre.**
2. We found the boy sitting outside the closed door.
3. Frightened by the storm we stayed at home.
4. Manlius thrust down the Gauls (as they were) climbing the crags.
5. The consul on the point of sailing to Africa is sacrificing.
6. The prisoners having been sent away safe, laid down their arms.
7. The citizens will give back the house to the recalled orator.
8. We have not received the promised rewards.
9. We have finished the task undertaken by you.
10. This story was told by my grandfather while living in our country-house.
11. The old men were killed sitting at the doors of their houses.
12. The defeat was announced to the citizens as they were hurrying through the streets.
13. Led into an ambush the cavalry were killed to a man.
14. Let us give bread to the boys left in school.

C

A JOURNEY TO BRUNDISIUM—II

LOLLIUS: Ad Fānum Ferōniae tē pervēnisse dīcis. Inde Tarracīnam iter fuisse putō.

HORĀTIUS: Ita vērō. Ōra enim manūsque lāvimus; intereā prandium parātum est. Post prandium tria mīlia passuum ad urbem Tarracīnam in summō monte positam ascendimus. Hūc ventūrus erat Maecēnās vir optimus et Coccēius, missī magnīs dē rēbus lēgātī. Quōs, ubi pervēnērunt, magnō gaudiō salūtāvimus.

LOLLIUS : Nec mīrum, cum poētās Maecēnās semper amet et maximō honōre trāctet.

HORĀTIUS : Postrīdiē Fundōs vēnimus, et libenter, mī Lollī, relīquimus, togam praetextam Aufidiī Luscī praetōris et īnsignia rīdentēs. Paulō ante noctem Formiās pervēnimus ubi iam itinere dēfessī in vīllā Murēnae, Maecenātis amīcī, mānsimus. Postrīdiē Sinuessam iter fēcimus. Eō vēnērunt ad nōs Vergilius et Plōtius et Vārus. Quam libenter eōs vīdīmus ! Quantum gaudium fuit ! Mehercule, mī Lollī, nihil in vītā melius est iūcundō amīcō ! Inde Capuam iter fēcimus ; ibi pilā sē exercēbant amīcī ; ego tamen et Vergilius dormiēbāmus.

Alinari

LOLLIUS : Quō inde contendistis ?

HORĀTIUS : Caudium, ubi vīlla Coccēiī nōs accēpit ; deinde Beneventum pervēnimus ubi magnō in perīculō fuimus.

THE COLUMN AT BRINDISI MARKING THE END OF THE VIA APPIA

LOLLIUS : Quid audiō ? Magnō vōs in perīculō fuisse dīcis ? Quam ob rem ?

HORĀTIUS : Quod domus, dum (*while*) cēna parātur, paene incēnsa est. Edepol, perturbātī sumus omnēs ; satis

HORACE'S JOURNEY TO BRUNDISIUM

magnum enim perīculum fuit, et tumultus ingēns factus est. Omnēs tamen servātī sumus, et nostrō servōrumque auxiliō magna pars cēnae servāta est. Deinde posterō diē Trivīcum vēnimus ; inde ad oppidulum (*little town*) ubi aqua dēterrima, pulcherrimus pānis esse vidēbātur. Decimō diē Canusium nōs accēpit ; deinde Barium ; inde Egnātia. Tandem quīntō decimō diē Brundisium pervēnimus. Ecce, Lollī, omnia audīvisti. Brundisium enim longae viae fābulaeque longae fīnis est.

Note :

os, ōris, *n.,* face.
lavō, -āre, lāvī, lautum, to wash.
prandium, -iī, *n.,* lunch.
hūc, hither, to this place.

nec mīrum, and no wonder.
libenter, gladly.
tumultus, -ūs, *m.,* tumult.
dēterrimus, -a, -um, very bad.

A ROMAN PROVERB

Quī sibi sēmitam nōn sapiunt, alterī mōnstrant viam.
Those who do not know their own path, show the way to another. *i.e.* The blind are leading the blind.

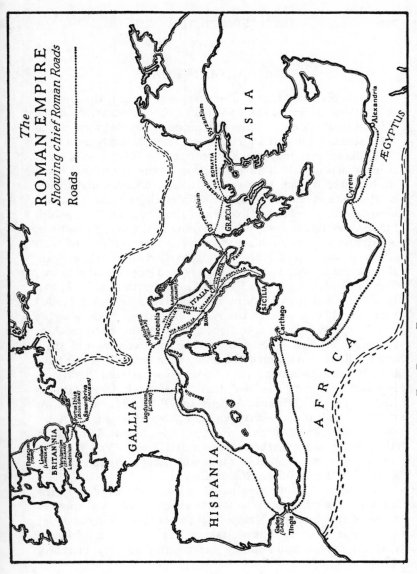

THE ROMAN EMPIRE, SHOWING MAIN ROADS

ABOUT ROMAN ROADS

It has been said that road-making was perhaps the greatest of the Roman arts. Once we realise the vast extent of the Roman road system and the excellence of the highways which the Romans built that statement will seem no exaggeration.

Look at your map and try to trace the lines of the great roads which ran in all directions from Rome as centre. First, we have the Appian Way running south to Capua and thence to Brundisium on the Adriatic. From there a short voyage brought the traveller to Greece and the Egnatian Way, which ran to Constantinople or, to give it its ancient name, Byzantium. South also ran the Poplilian Way to the Strait of Messina from where it was not a long crossing to Carthage. Here again Roman roads ran west to Tangiers and east to Alexandria. The Flaminian Way was Rome's Great North Road. It ran to Rimini, and from there by the Aemilian Way one travelled north to Milan and over the Alps. The coast route was the Aurelian Way. Trace it to Genoa, then by the Maritime Alps to the Riviera and so across the Rhône and Pyrenees into Spain and finally to its terminus at Cadiz. Then notice how you have branch lines radiating from these great arterial highways. For instance, note the road that led through Lyons up the Rhône valley to Rheims, Amiens and Boulogne, the port for Britain. And observe that, crossing from Boulogne to Kent, the traveller found again a great road leading to London, St Albans and away north to Lincoln and York. You begin to see now the vast system of roads which made communication so quick and easy in the Roman Empire.

Those great roads were made in the first instance by the legions. Their first purpose was to enable troops and supplies to move fast from point to point. Hence the roads ran as far as possible in straight lines, taking heights in their stride so that the troops could survey the country as they marched.

A ROMAN ROAD IN ENGLAND

Watling Street at Stony Stratford

Rivers were crossed by magnificent bridges, marshes and valleys by viaducts. If masses of rock were encountered they were tunnelled.

The method of construction was this : a foundation was made by levelling the earth and ramming it hard. On this foundation was laid a layer of small stones, on top of it a layer of rubble, next cement, and finally a close-set pavement of dressed stones. This top pavement was made somewhat convex to allow of quick drainage. For drainage also, culverts were frequently provided. The road had regularly raised side-walks. Such were the roads that ran for mile after mile across hill and dale, hardly varying an inch in breadth throughout their course. On all the main roads stood milestones giving the distance from the centre at Rome. The roads were wide enough to allow two quite big vehicles to pass.

It is worth while to try to imagine the kind of life that flowed along these great highways of empire and civilisation. Try to think of it—bodies of troops on the move, now and then government couriers galloping along with important letters, news and dispatches to or from Rome, messengers between town and town, business men going from market to market, private travellers on foot or in carriages, rich men in their luxurious litters in which they could recline at full length, carried by six or eight slaves, or in carriages ; and in any case with a great retinue and all kinds of equipment. For on his travels a great man either stayed at the house of a friend, or, if that were impossible, made his own encampment. Inns were dirty, smoky places used only by rough characters and poor travellers. And in addition to all this there was a perpetual stream of commerce, manufactured goods and raw materials being conveyed in carts, wagons, by pack-horses and by mules. Think of all that activity going on year after year over thousands of miles and you will begin to realise what the Roman roads meant for civilisation.

XXIV

DEPONENT VERBS

37. A deponent verb is one which is Passive in form but Active in meaning. Deponent verbs occur in all four conjugations, e.g. :

Conj.	Verb	Meaning	Inflection
1st	cōnor, cōnārī, cōnātus sum hortor, hortārī, hortātus sum	to try ,, exhort	like **amārī** ,, ,,
2nd	vereor, verērī, veritus sum	,, fear	,, **monērī**
3rd	sequor, sequī, secūtus sum loquor, loquī, locūtus sum proficīscor, proficīscī, profec- tus sum adipīscor, adipīscī, adeptus sum patior, patī, passus sum morior, morī, mortuus sum prōgredior, prōgredī, prō- gressus sum	,, follow ,, speak ,, set out ,, obtain ,, suffer, allow ,, die ,, advance	,, **regī** ,, ,, ,, ,, ,, ,, ,, **capī** ,, ,, ,, ,,
4th	experior, experīrī, expertus sum coorior, coorīrī, coortus sum	,, try, test ,, arise	,, **audīrī** ,, ,,

In addition to its passive forms a deponent verb has a present and a future participle, also a future infinitive formed as though from an active verb, e.g. :

cōnāns, trying ; **cōnātūrus,** about to try ; **cōnātūrus esse,** to be about to try.

Thus, deponent verbs have three participles, all with active meaning, e.g. :

sequēns, following ; **secūtūrus,** about to follow ; **secūtus,** having followed.

Note.—The future participle of **morior** is formed irregularly— **moritūrus,** about to die.

EXERCISE 24

A

1. Sequāmur ; profectus ; prōgrediēns ; cōnētur ; nē
   vereantur ; morientur ; nē loquātur ; nē verērē-
   minī ; adipīscitur ; cooritur.
2. Aenēās terrā marīque multa passus, tandem ad Ītaliam
   pervēnit.
3. Cūr loqueris, Sexte ? Nōnne mē audīvistī puerōs
   monentem nē loquerentur ?
4. Pater moriēns fīliōs monuit nē umquam occāsiōnem
   beneficiī āmitterent.
5. Haec locūtus mortuus est.
6. Illō diē sex mīlia passuum prōgressī, ad urbem ante
   noctem pervenīre cōnātī sumus.
7. Dēnsa nebula coorta omnem campum cēlāvit.
8. Puerōs hortēmur nē vēra loquī vereantur.
9. Cum equum adeptus sit, bovēs facile sequētur.
10. Vim maris tempestātumque expertus quam laetus
    domum veniō !

B

1. About to advance ; to have followed ; having spoken ;
   since they had experienced ; about to suffer ; we shall
   set out ; he is dying ; it will arise ; since she has tried ;
   they had obtained.
2. We (who are) about to die salute thee, Caesar !
3. Shall we allow such brave men to die ?
4. I hope we shall soon obtain a boat.
5. We are afraid to set out ; for a storm is arising.

6. While trying to follow the dogs Marcus fell into the water.
7. Do not speak, boys! I do not allow pupils to speak in school.
8. Since I have already experienced the master's anger, I am afraid to speak.
9. They say that the consul is dead.
10. Set out at once, friends; I hope to follow in a few days.
11. Obtaining a suitable place the consul joined battle.
12. Having advanced for many miles we tried to pitch our camp.
13. The soldiers encouraged the general to entrust the matter to fortune.
14. The old man encouraged the children to follow him to the river.

WORD STUDY

Iugum is a particularly interesting word. If you were to look it up in a good Latin dictionary, you would probably find *yoke* given as the first meaning; further on, you would find the meaning *ridge, mountain ridge*. How does this one word bear two meanings which seem so different? The reason becomes clear when we consider the shape of an ancient yoke:

Is the outline of the yoke not very reminiscent of the contour of a lofty ridge uniting two mountain peaks?

Insurgō, I rise up, gives us the word for one who *rises up in revolt* against his government. Can you think of it? **Nebula,** again, gives us our word *nebulous*, which is an excellent word to describe promises, statements or explanations which are vague, cloudy and lacking in conviction.

XXV

DEPONENT VERBS—*continued*

38. The following common deponent verbs govern the Ablative case :

ūtor	**ūtī**	**ūsus sum**	to use
abūtor	**abūtī**	**abūsus sum**	to use up, exhaust
fungor	**fungī**	**fūnctus sum**	to perform, fulfil
fruor	**fruī**	**frūctus (fruitus) sum**	to enjoy
potior	**potīrī**	**potītus sum**	to gain possession of
vescor	**vescī**	———	to feed on, live on

e.g. :

Mīles gladiō ūtitur, The soldier uses a sword.

Castrīs potītus est, He gained possession of the camp.

Carne et lacte vescuntur, They live on flesh and milk.

Patientiā meā abūsus est, He has exhausted my patience.

Notes.—(1) **Ūtor** has a wide range of meanings—to enjoy, to experience, to avail one's self of, to turn to advantage, e.g. :

> **Optimā valētūdine ūtēbātur,** He enjoyed (experienced) excellent health.
> **Ventō ūsus est,** He availed himself of the wind.

(2) *To abuse, to misuse,* is regularly **male ūtī,** not **abūtī.**

EXERCISE 25

A

CANNAE

[*After Trasimene*, Q. FABIUS MAXIMUS *as dictator employed a policy of caution, discontent with which led the consuls* TERENTIUS VARRO *and* AEMILIUS PAULUS *to join battle with* HANNIBAL *in* 216 *B.C. at Cannae in Apulia. The result was a Roman defeat and the loss of* 70,000 *men.*]

Contrā Hannibalem profectus Q. Fabius dictātor novā bellī ratiōne ūtēbātur. Doctus enim priōrum ducum clādibus, nusquam sē fortūnae committēbat, sed per alta loca exercitum dūcēns iter Hannibalis impediēbat et agmen ēius secūtus pālantēs (*stragglers*) excipiēbat. Ita Fabius, cunctātiōne ūsus, impetum Hannibalis frēgit ; Rōmae tamen plūrimī, quod novum cōnsilium non probābant, īrātī, " Quō ūsque tandem," inquiunt, " dictātor patientiā nostrā abūtētur ? Quamdiū īgnāviam eius patiēmur ? Imperium dēpōnat ; novī cōnsulēs creāti contrā Hannibalem prōgrediantur bellīque fortūnam experiantur quō celerius Hannibal victus ex Ītaliā discēdat."

Cōnsulēs creātī sunt Aemilius Paulus et Terentius Varrō. Paulus cunctātiōnem Fabiī probābat ; Varrō tamen, vir ferōx et temerārius, ācriōra cōnsilia sequēbātur. Contrā Hannibalem profectī ad Cannās cōnsulēs castra posuērunt. Ibi Varrō in levibus proeliīs quibusdam optimā fortūnā ūsus est. Aciem tandem īnstrūxit et signum pugnae dedit. Omnia Rōmānīs adversa fuērunt ; locus enim inīquus erat, ventusque coortus multum pulverem in oculōs mīlitum volvēbat. Victus igitur caesusque exercitus Rōmānus est, neque gravius umquam vulnus accēpit rēs pūblica. Aemilius Paulus graviter vulnerātus, ā comitibus est relictus ; quem ubi Cn. Cornēlius Lentulus tribūnus mīlitum sedentem in saxō vīdit sanguine maculātum, " L. Aemilī," inquit, " quī ūnus extrā culpam huius clādis es, cape hunc equum. Occāsiōnem fugae adeptus, nōlī hunc diem morte cōnsulis nefāstum (*unlucky*) facere. Etiam sine tuā morte satis lacrimārum et dolōris est." Sed cōnsul, " Frustrā mē, Cn. Cornēlī," inquit, " servāre cōnāris. Discēde ; patribus imperā ut urbem mūniant. Mē in hāc strāge mīlitum meōrum patere morī." Sīc locūtus ab hostibus prōgredientibus Paulus interfectus est ; vix ipse Lentulus fugā sē servāvit.

B

1. (*a*) Quid agis, Quīnte ? Quā fortūnā hodiē ūsus es ?
   (*b*) Fortūnā ūsus sum pessimā, mī amīce ; tōtam enim per urbem frātrem meum secūtus sum sed nusquam invēnī.
   (*c*) Quid est, Quīnte ? Ālīsne ūtitur Marcus frāter tuus ?
   (*d*) Fortāsse ! Hōc quidem sciō, eum patientiā meā abūsum esse.
2. (*a*) Senēs iuvenēs hortantur ut arcem dēfendant.
   (*b*) Hostēs igitur urbe potītī arcem capere frustrā cōnātī sunt.
   (*c*) In arce mīlitēs frūmentō vescuntur. Etiam in castra hostium pānem coniciunt.
   (*d*) Nōn diū hostēs bonā fortūnā ūtēbantur. Mox enim omnēs ad ūnum ā Camillō caesī sunt.

3. How long shall we live on this bread ?
4. Fabius tried to hinder Hannibal's march.

5. Since you (s.) have exhausted the master's patience, you will be punished.
6. Since the general has drawn up his line, we shall follow the standards.
7. Since he has not spoken, he shows that he is afraid.
8. Setting out in the morning we reached the top of the mountain in a few hours.
9. Did not the Roman soldiers live on corn ?
10. We hope soon to gain possession of the town.
11. Having already experienced the violence of the storm I shall stay at home to-day.
12. I hope to use my new book to-morrow.
13. Do not abuse the books which I gave you.
14. Since one consul is dead, the citizens will be disturbed.
15. Since no one has spoken, all will be blamed.

C

MAHARBAL'S ADVICE

Post pugnam Cannēnsem, ubi Hannibal tam bonā fortūnā ūsus ā cēterīs laudābātur, plūrimī monēbant ut quiētem et ipse sūmeret et mīlitibus dēfessīs daret. Maharbalis tamen, praefectī equitum, longē alia sententia fuit. Hortātus enim Hannibalem ut statim Rōmam peteret, " Diē quīntō," inquit, " victor in Capitōliō epulāberis." Ubi Hannibal respondit sententiam sē Maharbalis laudāre sed dē rē diūtius dēlīberātūrum, tum Maharbal, " Mehercule," inquit, " nōn omnia eīdem virō dī dedērunt ; vincere scīs, Hannibal, sed victōriā ūtī nescīs."

Note :

Cannēnsis, -is, -e, of, belonging to, Cannae.
Maharbal, -alis, m., Maharbal.
praefectus, -ī, m., commander.
sententia, -ae, f., view, opinion.

victor, -ōris, m., victor.
epulor, -ārī, -ātus sum, to sup.
dēlīberō, -āre, -āvī, -ātum, to deliberate.
longē, far, by far.

FABIAN TACTICS

When the brief impatience of 217 B.C. had run its course and the disaster of Cannae had taught the Romans the price that had to be paid for rash counsels, men realised the wisdom that had inspired the Fabian policy. After Cannae, Fabius exercised a virtual leadership in the Senate ; on several occasions he commanded armies in the field ; his policy was declared to have been the salvation of the state. Notice very carefully what that policy was : to avoid a major conflict ; to harass the enemy at every turn, hinder his communications, wear down his strength while gradually building up that of Rome and improving the morale and discipline of her officers and men. To this day we often apply the term " Fabian tactics " to a policy of wise and vigilant caution. Fabius was surnamed **Cunctātor**, *Delayer*, and later Roman poets and historians are loud in his praise. Here is a tribute paid to him by the first great Latin poet, Q. Ennius, who was himself a young man of twenty-two in the year when Fabius was dictator :

Ūnus homō nōbīs cunctāndō restituit rem ;
Nōn enim rūmōrēs pōnēbat ante salūtem.
Ergō postque magisque virī nunc glōria clāret.

One man by delaying restored our fortunes ; for he did not set rumours before safety. Therefore afterwards and in greater degree the glory of the hero now shines bright.

A FAMOUS SAYING

Rōmānus populus victus vī et superātus proeliīs Saepe est multīs, bellō vērō numquam.

The Roman people has often been beaten by force and overcome in many battles, but never in a long campaign.

XXVI

SEMI-DEPONENT VERBS

39. Latin possesses the following semi-deponent verbs, so called because some of their tenses are Active in form, some Passive :

audeō, audēre, ausus sum, to dare (*takes prolative infin.*).
gaudeō, gaudēre, gāvīsus sum, to rejoice (*takes* **quod** *with indic. or Acc. and Infin.*).
soleō, solēre, solitus sum, to be accustomed (*prolative Infin.*).
fīdō, fīdere, fīsus sum, to trust (*governs dative case*).
cōnfīdō, -ere, cōnfīsus sum, to trust (,, ,,).
diffīdō, -ere, diffīsus sum, to distrust (,, ,,).

The above verbs have passive forms with active meanings in the Perfect, Future Perfect and Pluperfect Indicative ; Perfect and Pluperfect Subjunctive ; Perfect Infinitive ; Perfect Participle.

EXERCISE 26

A

THE LAST PHASE

[*After Cannae Rome gradually won the initiative in the war. For twelve years* HANNIBAL *stood at bay. By 205 B.C. young* SCIPIO *cleared the Carthaginians from Spain.* HASDRUBAL, *brother of* HANNIBAL, *managed to reach Italy with an army, only to be defeated and killed at the River Metaurus. In 204* SCIPIO *attacked Carthage itself, and next year* HANNIBAL *was recalled for its defence.*]

Cum iam in tantō essent perīculō, Carthāginiēnsēs Hannibalem ex Ītaliā revocāre cōnstituērunt. Missī sunt

igitur lēgātī quōrum verba maximō cum dolōre Hannibal
audīvisse dīcitur. Ubi data sunt mandāta, " Iam palam,"
inquit, " eī mē revocant, quī, cum novās cōpiās et pecūniam
mittī vetārent, iam diū mē retrahēbant. Vīcit igitur
Hannibalem nōn populus Rōmānus totiēns caesus fugātusque, sed senātus Carthāginiēnsis. Neque magis hāc
dēfōrmitāte reditūs meī P. Scīpiō gaudēbit quam Hannō,
quī, cum nūllā aliā ratiōne id factūrus esse vidērētur, ruīnā
Carthāginis domum nostram oppressit." Iam hōc ipsum
exspectāns Hannibal nāvēs comparāverat. Inūtilem
suōrum multitūdinem in oppida quaedam Ītaliae dīmīsit ;
praesidia fore simulābat. Quod rōbur mīlitum fuit, cum
eō in Āfricam nāvigāvit. Negant quemquam ex patriā
tam trīstem in exsilium profectum esse quam Hannibalem
ex hostium terrā discēdentem. Saepe enim oculōs in lītora
Ītaliae dēfīxit, deōs hominēsque accūsāns et sē ipsum
culpāns quod nōn cruentōs ab Cannēnsī victōriā mīlitēs
Rōmam dūxit. " Ausus est Scīpiō," inquit, " Carthāginem
prōgredī, quī cōnsul hostem Pūnicum in Ītaliā nōn vīdit ;
ego ubi centum mīlia Rōmānōrum ad Trasumēnum et ad
Cannās caesī sunt, diffīsus fortūnae circā Cūmās et Nōlam
sedēns cōnsenuī." Sīc sē accūsāns ex Ītaliā est dētractus.

Proximō annō ad Zamam, quae urbs quīnque diērum
iter ā Carthāgine abest (*is distant*), proelium commissum
est ; victusque Hannibal cum quattuor equitibus Carthāginem fūgit. Cum iam cīvibus invīsus esset, ad Antiochum,
Syriae rēgem, sē recēpit. Ibi post paucōs annōs nē in
potestātem Rōmānōrum venīret sē venēnō necāvit.

B

1. Let him dare ; since you (*s.*) have rejoiced ; we had been accustomed ; I had trusted ; having distrusted ; about to dare ; we rejoiced ; we shall dare ; we are accustomed ; let us rejoice.

2. (*a*) Cum ausus sīs eum montem ascendere, temerārius, nōn fortis, vidēberis.
   (*b*) Age, Mārce, nōnne gaudēs quod cōnsilium nostrum ā patre probātur ?
   (*c*) Quā ratiōne bellī Fabius ūtēbātur ?   Dīc mihi, Sexte.
   (*d*) Cum sibi copiīsque diffīderet, cunctātiōne ūsus proelium nūllum committēbat.
   (*e*) Iam palam cīvēs gaudent quod temerārius homō cōnsul creātus est.

3. Having dared to join battle the consul was defeated.
4. Since we trust Syrus, we have left him at home.
5. The general had been accustomed to leave garrisons in the towns.
6. Why do you (*s.*) dare to exhaust the master's patience ?
7. We have tried in vain to remove the huge rock.
8. Why do you pretend that you will trust us ?
9. Since he employs violence, we are accustomed to distrust him.
10. While trying to reach the shore I was hindered by the wind.
11. Since father was angry, I did not dare to speak.
12. When shall we set out for the shore ?
13. Having advanced for a few miles we were accustomed to pitch our camp.
14. Father warned us not to employ violence.
15. They say that no one will dare to set out to-day.

C

A crossword puzzle.

CLUES ACROSS

1. A useful thing to find when you lose your way.
10. Deponent verb governing ablative (*inf.*).
13. 2 down rides on one of these.
14. A conjunction.
15. The shore.
16. He withstands.
17. So.
20. Personal pronoun (*acc.*).
21. To neuter of this prefix 14 across and you get etc.
22. The same.
23. Not " she " nor " it."
24. There.
26. I remove.
30. Not many things.
33. An infinitive ending.

34. Same as 10 across.
35. Let me die.
37. Either " where " or " when."
39. Your state " post negotium."
42. Adorn.
43. Former.
45. You need this verb to say " I thank."
46. Some wishful thinking about this one.
48. Same as 32 down.
50. I carry on an action or engagement. (It went on all night in Ex. 14 A.)
52. Just " dare ! "
53. The Trojan one lasted ten years.
54. A participle of 10 across.

CLUES DOWN

1. Once over the threshold this is where you find yourself (*abl. case*).
2. Rides on one of 13 across.
3. They undertake.
4. O Titus !
5. Would have been more appropriate as No. 1.
6. A relation by marriage.
7. A " moving " word.
8. Last (*fem. sing.*).
9. Gentle (*dat. sing.*).
10. In order that.
11. Then.
12. Same as 23 across.
18. When Fortune is like this she is not kind.
19. By love.
25. One of them cost an old Roman magistrate his life.

27. This with 46 down and a pronoun makes a prayer.
28. You (*s.*) will escape.
29. This is the word you would use for " which ? " with " hand " or " foot " or " ear " or " eye."
31. To arise.
32. Art (*dative*).
36. A form of Nom. Pl. of 12 down.
38. Self.
40. Perf. Part. of verb of which 31 down is a compound.
41. A semi-deponent verb.
44. Same as 27 down.
46. See 27 down.
47. Perf. Indic. of 45 across.
49. Neuter of 23 across.
51. What does this abbreviation mean ?

REVISION EXERCISES

A

1. Give with meanings all the Infinitives of the following verbs : *committō, sequor, impediō, caedō, cadō, instruō, frangō, cōnor, retrahō.*

2. Give with meanings all the Participles of the following verbs : *ūtor, audeō, augeō, cadō, patior, volvō, soleō, suscipiō, sternō, proficīscor.*

3. Give ablative singular, genitive plural, meaning and gender of : *rūpes, eques, linter, ānser, frīgus, cāsus, saltus, lītus, clādēs, pedes.*

4. Give nominative, genitive singular and gender of the Latin nouns meaning : *heat, cold, praise, blame, cruelty, a kindness, wealth, want, faith, treachery.*

5. A Roman poet describes the hero of his poem as **pietāte īnsignis.** What kind of man would you expect that hero to be ?

B

1. He says he did not break the window.
2. Since you (*s.*) desire to escape, I shall open the gate.
3. Let us set out soon ; for it is dangerous to remain.
4. Do you (*pl.*) dare to accuse me of cruelty ?
5. We are glad that father has hired a chariot.
6. The boys say that they saw nothing.
7. The citizens said that they would never trust the enemy.
8. (While) deliberating about a new plan we heard a great noise.
9. Marcus says that no one spoke.
10. The poor men say that they have no money.
11. Since we have neither money nor food, we are very wretched.
12. Since there were robbers everywhere, we decided to stay at home.

C

1. The old man begged his sons not to neglect the worship of the gods.
2. (When) about to sail we were hindered by the storm.
3. The geese having been terrified roused the guards.
4. (While) trying to save the dog I fell into the water myself.
5. Tell (*s.*) the soldiers to desist from the slaughter.
6. Frightened by the arrival of Caesar the Gauls fled.
7. The general is said to have slept on the ground.
8. Whether are infantry or cavalry more useful to us ?
9. How long shall I wait for you, Lucia ?
10. I think I have exhausted your patience, Marcus.
11. Having advanced a few miles we pitched camp.
12. It is most disgraceful to accuse a good man of treachery.

D

1. Since there is no suspicion of treachery, let us receive the general kindly.

2. Order (*pl.*) the lictors to come here. Let them prepare the axes.
3. Why do you (*s.*) pretend to be wise ?
4. Everyone knows that you (*s.*) are very foolish.
5. Do you (*pl.*) think that we shall escape ?
6. I have heard that the city has been surrounded with a rampart and a ditch.
7. Having tried in vain to remove the rock we desisted from the task.
8. Having been advised to leave the city I shall set out to-morrow morning.
9. Father says that no one will dare to advance through the pass.
10. The master declares that these boys will be expelled from the school.
11. The citizens encouraged the young men to fight.
12. We hope to come home at midnight.

E

Write down in ten minutes the Latin for as many of the following words as you can :

old woman	slaughter	slippery
friendship	considerably	glad
dear	to resign	to swear
scarcity	true	lake
to roll	last	to call together
reward	neither	to come together
to be silent	siege	forces
to grow old	to overwhelm	track
distinguished	slowly	payment
to stain	on the next day	reply (*noun*)
example	far	pride
beard	thick	to strew, lay low
sweat	limb	to equal
to arise	to waken	easily.

XXVII

ABLATIVE ABSOLUTE

40. Consider the following sentences :

    (a) *The boy having been found* was led home.
    (b) *The boy having been found,* we led him home.
    (c) *The boy having been found,* we gave him food.
    (d) *The boy having been found,* we gave the soldier a reward.

In (a), *boy* is subject of the main verb *was led* ; therefore it stands in the nominative case, with the participle *having been found* in agreement—

Puer inventus domum ductus est.

In (b), *boy* is identical with the direct object *him.* The sentence might be expressed, " We led home the found boy " and *MUST* have this form in Latin—

Puerum inventum domum dūximus.

In (c), *boy* is identical with the indirect object *him.* The sentence might be expressed, " We gave food to the found boy " and *MUST* have this form in Latin—

Puerō inventō cibum dedimus.

In (d), *boy* neither is, nor is identical with, subject, object or indirect object of the sentence. The noun *boy* with the participle *having been found* forms an independent phrase within the sentence. Such a phrase is called an Absolute Phrase. In Latin the noun and participle which form an Absolute Phrase agree with each other in the ablative case—

Puerō inventō, mīlitī praemium dedimus.

This construction is known as the Ablative Absolute.

Note.—Ablative Absolute phrases are most naturally rendered into English by a subordinate adverbial clause of time, cause, etc., or by an adverbial phrase, e.g. :

Puerō inventō, mīlitī praemium dedimus, might be rendered—

When the boy had been found,
After the boy had been found,
Since the boy had been found, we gave the soldier a reward.
As the boy had been found,
On the discovery of the boy,

Conversely, an English subordinate adverbial clause is often most neatly expressed in Latin by an Ablative Absolute phrase.

EXERCISE 27

A

[In the following sentences translate any Ablative Absolute phrases into natural English.]

1. Clāmōre audītō, ad forum festīnāvimus.
2. Clāmōrēs hostium in urbe audītī cīvēs terruērunt.
3. Hannibal patriā expulsus ad rēgem Antiochum fūgit.
4. Hannibale expulsō, cum Rōmānīs pāx erat.
5. Manū porrēctā, cōnsul rēgem salūtāvit.
6. Cum nēmō in cōnspectū esset, mūrum ascendimus.
7. Agricolā vīsō, fūgimus.
8. Domum ambulāns plēnum orbem lūnae vīdī.
9. Plēnus orbis lūnae in caelō vīsus canem terrēbat.
10. Aciē īnstrūctā, cōnsul mīlitēs hortātus est.
11. Cēnam parātam scelestus servus incendit.
12. Cēnā parātā, Sextum nē exspectēmus.
13. Lūnā obscūrātā, iter per silvam nōn faciēmus.
14. Cīvibus convocātīs cōnsul victōriam nūntiāvit.

6

B

1. In the following sentences translate phrases in italics by means of the Ablative Absolute Construction :

   (a) *War having been declared*, the citizens left their homes.
   (b) *Prodigies having been seen*, the citizens were afraid.
   (c) *The ball having been found*, we played in the street.
   (d) *The wild beast having been seen*, all fled.
   (e) *The work having been finished*, let us leave for home.

2. In the following translate the subordinate adverbial clause by an Ablative Absolute phrase :

   (a) Since the leader has been killed, the robbers will flee.
   (b) When we saw the moon we were glad.
   (c) As no reply had been given, the master was angry.
   (d) After the door had been shut, my father called me.
   (e) Since the state had been saved, the consul was praised.

3. In translating the following, first decide whether or not the Ablative Absolute Construction can be used :

   (a) The letter having been sent to Rome was given to my father.
   (b) Since he pretends that he is tired, let him depart.
   (c) Hannibal having been recalled was angry.
   (d) The old man having called his sons gave them instructions.
   (e) Hannibal having been recalled, the Romans feared nothing.
   (f) The horses having been found, we led them home.
   (g) The horses having been found were led home.
   (h) The horses having been found, we hurried home.
   (i) The work having been undertaken was hindered by storms.
   (j) The work having been undertaken, we were hindered by storms.

XXVIII

ABLATIVE ABSOLUTE—*continued*

41. Since the only Latin verbs that possess Perfect Participles Active are deponents and semi-deponents, many English participial phrases containing a Perfect Participle Active cannot be translated literally into Latin. Methods of dealing with such phrases are as follows :

(*a*) When the English participial phrase contains the Perfect Participle Active of a Transitive verb, e.g. :

Having heard this the soldiers rejoiced,

change the participial phrase into passive form and use the Ablative Absolute Construction—

This having been heard, the soldiers rejoiced.
Hōc audītō, mīlitēs gāvīsī sunt.

Note, however, that when a deponent verb is available, this type of sentence can be translated literally, e.g. :

Having encouraged the soldiers Caesar went away.
Mīlitēs hortātus Caesar discessit.

(*b*) When the English participial phrase contains the Perfect Participle of an Intransitive verb, then—
If a deponent verb is available, translate literally, e.g. :

Caesar having advanced reached the river.
Caesar prōgressus ad flūmen pervēnit.

If no deponent verb is available, such phrases MUST be rendered in Latin by a clause with **ubi** and the Perfect Indicative, or **cum** (*when, since*) and the Pluperfect Subjunctive, e.g. :

Caesar, having come, built a bridge.
Caesar, ubi vēnit, pontem aedificāvit, *or*—
Caesar, cum vēnisset, pontem aedificāvit.

EXERCISE 28

A

ROMA VICTRIX

[*After Zama, Rome embarked upon a career of conquest which in less than a century made her supreme in the Mediterranean world. In the following lesson we see her crush the pride of Macedonia, in* 168 *B.C.*]

Cōnsul creātus Aemilius Paulus, eius quī ad Cannās ceciderat fīlius, in Macedoniam missus est. Ibi enim, armīs captīs, Perseus rēx bellum Rōmānīs indīxerat. Cum duae aciēs iam in cōnspectū essent, Sulpicius Gallus, tribūnus mīlitum, exercitum Rōmānum gravī metū līberāvit. Is enim, cum lūnae dēfectiōnem proximā nocte futūram esse scīret, mīlitibus convocātīs, " Nocte proximā," inquit, "ab hōrā secundā ad quārtam lūna dēfectūra est. Nē cui prōdigium id esse videātur ! Sīcut nēmō verētur quod lūna nunc orbe plēnō, nunc parvō cornū fulget, ita minimē est mīrābile eam umbrā terrae obscūrārī." Quibus dictīs, Rōmānī immōtī sunt illā dēfectiōne ; Macedonēs tamen perterrēbantur, cum trīste prōdigium vidērētur. Proeliō igitur commissō, Macedonum exercitus caesus fugātusque est. Victus Perseus in templum quoddam fūgit, ubi paulisper sē cēlāvit ; captus tandem ad cōnsulem dūcitur.

Perseus sordidīs vestīmentīs indūtus in castra intrāvit. Plūrimīs ex mīlitibus ad eum quasi ad mīrābile quoddam spectāculum prōgressīs, vix ipsī līctōrēs iter eī ad praetōrium fēcērunt. Paulus, ubi audīvit Perseum pervēnisse, prōgressus paulum, intrantī rēgī manum porrēxit ; eum ad genua prōcumbere vetuit ; tandem in praetōrium ductum

AEMILIUS PAULUS AND KING PERSEUS

rēgem sedēre iussit. Deinde, " Quā iniūriā excitātus,"
inquit, " bellum contrā populum Rōmānum tam īnfestō
animō suscēpistī? " Perseus tamen, nūllō datō respōnsō,
oculīsque in terram dēfīxīs, diū flēbat. Tum cōnsul,
" Bonum," inquit, " animum habē : populī Rōmānī
clēmentia nōn modo spem tibi sed prope certam fīdūciam
salūtis praebet."

Deinde Paulus, sermōne iam ad ipsōs Rōmānōs conversō,
" Vidētis," inquit, " exemplum īnsigne mūtātiōnis rērum
hūmānārum. Itaque vōs moneō, iuvenēs, nēminem debēre
in quemquam superbē agere neque semper crēdere fortūnae." Quibus dictīs, cōnsul Perseum ad cēnam eō diē
vocāvit et posteā omnī honōre tractāvit.

B

1. In translating the following sentences render the Ablative Absolute phrases in natural English :
   (a) Locō idōneō inventō, castra posuimus.
   (b) Strepitū audītō, ferās in silvā esse putāvī.
   (c) Caesīs hostibus et fugātīs, praedā potītī sumus.
   (d) Cane domī relictō, quā ratiōne mē dēfendam ?

2. Translate the following sentences and explain carefully why they cannot use the Ablative Absolute Construction :
   (a) Puerīs convocātīs persuādēbō ut taceant.
   (b) Tria mīlia passuum prōgressī castra posuimus.
   (c) Equōs bovēsque inventōs domum agam.
   (d) Canis nōs secūtus tandem invēnit.

3. Translate the following sentences using an Ablative Absolute phrase for the words in italics :
   (a) *Since the ball had been lost,* the little girl was weeping.
   (b) *Hearing a shout* I opened the door.
   (c) *When the task was finished,* we hurried home.
   (d) *Having hired horses* we reached the city before sunset.
   (e) *Having seen a wolf* the boys fled.

4. In the following sentences you must first of all decide whether or not the Ablative Absolute Construction can be used:
   (a) Having advanced slowly we reached the river at sunset.
   (b) Having found the money the old woman was glad.
   (c) Having read the book I gave it back to the master.
   (d) Having read the book I walked in the Campus.
   (e) When the rocks had been removed, the soldiers advanced.
   (f) Having taken the city the Greeks burned it.
   (g) Having spoken these words the old man departed.
   (h) Since footprints have been seen, we are posting guards.
   (i) Hindered by their heavy burdens the slaves did not advance quickly.
   (j) Having found the gold the slaves said nothing.

XXIX

ABLATIVE ABSOLUTE—*continued*

42. In the Ablative Absolute Construction the Perfect Participle
Passive is most commonly used, but Ablative Absolute
phrases occur

(*a*) With a Present Participle, e.g. :

Magistrō loquente, omnēs tacēbant.
While (As, Since, When) the master was speaking,
all were silent.

N.B. ending
in -e (not i)
for Abl,
Abs,

(*b*) With a noun or adjective, e.g. :

Caesare duce, Caesar being leader ; Under the
leadership of Caesar.
Rōmulō rēge, Romulus being king ; In the reign of
Romulus.
Amīcō meō vīvō, My friend being alive ; In the
lifetime of my friend.

EXERCISE 29

A

1. Hāc rē cognitā, equum nōn vēndidī.
2. Tē duce, Caesar, nihil timēmus.
3. Imperātōre hortante, mīlitēs per noctem labōrābant.
4. Mihi interrogantī puer nihil respondit.
5. Mē dē fēriīs interrogante, magister intrāvit.
6. Numā rēge, cīvēs fēlīcēs erant.
7. Hortō fossō, cum tempestās ad labōrem nōn idōnea
esset, fēriās agēbāmus.
8. Occāsiōne datā, ex urbe effūgimus.
9. Patre monente, pecūniam mēcum nōn portāvī.
10. Nōbīs discentibus, magister dormīvit.

B

1. Having ascertained these things I decided to sell the farm.
2. While you (*s.*) were speaking, Marcus laughed.
3. Under Caesar's leadership we conquered many nations.
4. Having seen the moon in the sky the wolves were afraid.
5. On the foundation of the city Romulus was the first king.
6. Two cohorts having been surrounded, Caesar roused the soldiers.
7. After the window had been opened, the cold was severe.
8. Since father is sleeping, all the children are silent.
9. Since thick clouds had been seen, we did not travel to town.
10. Having procured bread I carried it home.
11. Since father has been roused by the noise, all the children have fled.
12. With your help (i.e. you helping), my friend, I shall do everything.

C

A Roman Betrothal

[*A Roman betrothal was very much a family ceremony. The following account of one is given in the form of an imaginary letter from* VERANIUS *to his friend the poet* CATULLUS. *Note the formula with which the letter opens*—**s.p.d.** *is for* **salūtem plūrimam dīcit,** " *gives heartiest greeting to.*"]

Verānius Catullō suō s.p.d.

Petis, mī Catulle, ut, rēbus relictīs, ad tē contendam. Grātiās agō ; et mē ad vīllam tuam mox ventūrum esse spērō. Intereā tamen, multa mē Rōmae dētinent. Cotīdiē enim aut ad officium togae virīlis vocor aut ad spōnsālia quaedam aut ad nūptiās. Ēheu ! quot in hīs officiīs hōrae cōnsūmuntur ! Herī tamen, maximō cum gaudiō spōnsālibus Aurunculeiae,

Cottae nostrī fīliae, interfuī. Est enim Aurunculeia puella amābilis ; et Cottam, patrem eius, magnopere amāmus. Laetus igitur domum Cottae festīnāvī. Eō cum pervēnissem, in ātrium ductus, multōs amīcōs invēnī quī iam convēnerant. Cum fēstus ille diēs esset, ātrium est rosīs aliīsque flōribus tōtum ōrnātum. Dum (*while*) inter nōs loquimur, intrat Cotta cum uxōre et fīliā ; intrat eōdem tempore cum patre et mātre Mānlius Torquātus quī Aurunculeiam uxōrem petit. Quam nōbilis iuvenis est ! quam Aurunculeiā dignus ! Hinc Aurunculeia cōnstitit ; ā dextrā pater, ā sinistrā māter fuit : illinc et Mānlius stetit inter parentēs. Tum silentiō factō, magnā vōce pater Mānliī, " Quod bonum et fēlīx sit," inquit " mihi tibique et nostrīs līberīs, fīliam tuam fīliō meō uxōrem petō. Spondēsne ? " Et Cotta, " Dī bene vertant," inquit, " Spondeō." Tum Mānlius paulum prōgressus, " Hunc ānulum," inquit, " Aurunculeia ā mē accipiat, pignus spōnsālium nostrōrum." Tum sinistrā manū eius captā, ānulum quārtō digitō imposuit. Quō factō, Aurunculeia dōna quaedam Mānliō dedit. Tum nōs exclāmāmus, " Fēlīciter ! " et Mānliō Aurunculeiaeque grātulāmur. Deinde agunt paulisper parentēs dē dōte Aurunculeiae; nōs intereā in triclīnium dūcimur ubi cēna iam parāta erat. Valē.

amābilis, -is, -e, amiable, lovable.
ātrium, -iī, *n.*, hall.
cōnsistō, -ere, -stitī, to halt, stop, stand still.
cōnsūmō, -ere, -sūmpsī, -sūmptum, spend, consume, use up.
cotīdiē, daily.
dextra, -ae, *f.,* right hand ; **ā dextrā,** on the right.
dētineō, -ēre, -tinuī, -tentum, detain.
dī bene vertant, may the gods bless it.
digitus, -ī, *m.,* finger.
dignus, -a, -um, worthy.
dōs, dōtis, *f.,* dowry.
eō, thither, there, to that place.
fēstus, -a, -um, festal.
flōs, flōris, *m.,* flower.

grātulor -ārī, -ātus sum, congratulate (*object in dative*).
hinc . . . illinc, on this side . . . on that side.
intersum, -esse, -fuī, to be present at, take part in, attend.
officium, -iī *n.,* duty, function, ceremony.
pignus, -oris, *n.,* pledge, token.
sinistra, -ae, *f.,* left hand ; **ā sinistrā,** on the left.
s(alūtem) p(lūrimam) d(īcit), gives heartiest greetings to.
spondeō, -ēre, spopondī, spōnsum, to promise, pledge, guarantee, betroth.
spōnsālia, -ium, *n.pl.,* betrothal.
toga virīlis, *f.,* the toga virilis.
triclīnium, -iī, *n.,* dining-room.

XXX

THE VERB POSSUM

43. The conjugation of **Possum,** I can, I am able, is as follows :

TENSE	INDICATIVE		SUBJUNCTIVE	
PRES.	pos-sum	pos-sumus	pos-sim	pos-sīmus
	pot-es	pot-estis	pos-sīs	pos-sītis
	pot-est	pos-sunt	pos-sit	pos-sint
FUT.	pot-erō	pot-erimus		
	pot-eris	pot-eritis		
	pot-erit	pot-erunt		
IMP.	pot-eram	pot-erāmus	pos-sem	pos-sēmus
	pot-erās	pot-erātis	pos-sēs	pos-sētis
	pot-erat	pot-erant	pos-set	pos-sent
PERF.	potuī, potuistī, etc.		potuerim, potuerīs, etc.	
FUT. PERF.	potuerō, potueris, etc.			
PLUP.	potueram, potuerās, etc.		potuissem, potuissēs, etc.	

INFINITIVE

Present, **posse,** to be able. *Perfect,* **potuisse,** to have been able

Notes.—(1) **Possum** has no imperatives, no future infinitive and no participle. The form **potēns, -entis** is found, but it is used only as an adjective meaning *powerful.*

(2) It is important to realise that **possum** is a compound of **sum, esse, fuī,** to be. It is made up of **pot** (from adjective **potis,** able) and **sum.** The **t** of **pot** becomes **s** before **s** ; in the perfect forms **f** is lost. Thus—

pot+sumus gives **possumus.**
pot+fuī   „   **potuī.**

EXERCISE 30

A

LETTER ON FARMING

[*The acquisition of a great empire brought with it grave problems. The old simplicity of Roman life tended to disappear. Italy, once a land of small farms owned and worked by a sturdy peasantry, became largely a land of great estates owned by wealthy men and worked, as our lesson shows, by slave labour.*]

Valerius Fundānō suō s.p.d.

Quō melius fundum tuum colās, petis ut pauca dē agricultūrā ad tē scrībam. Magnō cum gaudiō id faciō. Ipse enim agricultūram diū amāvī, et gaudeō quod iam tū fundum tantum et tam bonum comparāvistī.

Ante omnia, igitur, operam dā ut ipse quam saepissimē ad vīllam contendās. Sīc enim fundum meliōrem habēbis ; servī minus peccāre poterunt ; frūctūs plūs capiēs. Ubi ad vīllam vēneris, eōdem diē, sī poteris, circum fundum iter faciēs ut servōs, agrōs, bovēs videās et ipse ea īnspiciās quae iam facta erunt. Quibus vīsīs, vīlicum ad tē vocātum sīc interrogābis : " Satisne tempore omnia facta sunt ? Poterisne reliqua cōnficere ? Quantum vīnī, frūmentī aliārumque rērum omnium hōc annō facere potuistī ? " Quibus cognitīs, sī satis factum esse nōn vidēbitur et vīlicus affirmābit sē melius facere nōn potuisse cum neque servī valuerint neque tempestāte idōneā ūsī sint, cum fēriae plūrimae fuerint et servī multī aufūgerint, tum tū, " Quid ? " inquiēs, " Nōnne multa et ūtilia facere potestis ubi pluvia tempestās est ? Quandō melius vīlla pūrgātur aut frūmentum ex aliō in aliud horreum portātur ? Quid ? Nōnne tum possunt servī vestīmenta sibi facere ? Per fēriās tamen, sī bene exercentur, veterēs fossās reficere possunt, viam pūblicam mūnīre, hortum fodere. Dīcis servōs aegrōtāvisse. Cūr, igitur, tantum eīs cibī dedistī ? Audīsne ? sī quis aegrōtābit, multō minus cibī accipiat quam is quī et valet et dīligenter labōrat."

Quibus rēbus cōnstitūtīs, vīlicō imperā ut reliqua opera dīligenter et celeriter cōnficiat. Deinde ratiōnēs rērum omnium petēs et maximā cum cūrā īnspiciēs. Sī quid deerit, imperā ut statim comparētur ; sī quae supererunt, imperā ut vīlicus ea vēndat. Dominus enim, sī prūdēns est, operam dat semper ut bovēs veterēs, senēs servōs, omnia dēnique quae vetera et inūtilia sunt, sī pretium habent, quam celerrimē vēndat. Valē.

B

1. We can ; they will be able ; he could not ; you (s.) had been able ; since I have not been able ; in order that we may be able ; you (pl.) will be able ; we could.
2. Ut possent ; cum potuerint ; nē possint ; potuerātis ; potestis ; potuērunt ; potuerint ; potuisse.
3. I shall soon help you (s.) if I can.
4. When the rocks had been removed (abl. abs.), we were able to advance.
5. I shall send the bailiff with you (s.) that you may be able to ascertain everything.
6. Since I cannot dig, by what means shall I obtain food ?
7. Since wine is lacking, I cannot prepare a good dinner.
8. Since we have procured a new horse (abl. abs.), we shall be able to sell the old (one).
9. Since the slaves were ill, they could not work.
10. Since we do not enjoy suitable weather, we cannot work in the fields.
11. Since I often inspect the farm, the slaves cannot do wrong.
12. Since we had not been able to come more quickly, father was angry.

13. Since I cannot trust that man, I shall not take him with me.
14. Since the work is now finished (*abl. abs.*), we shall be able to play in the garden.
15. Under your leadership we can do everything.
16. Since you are king (*abl. abs.*), we dare to speak the truth.

WORD STUDY

Valēre has given us a great number of interesting words. To begin with, there is *valour*, which at first meant " strength," and nowadays means rather " bravery " than mere strength. *Valour* reminds us of *valorous* and *valiant*. A little further thought brings us to *prevail*, *prevalent* and *prevalence*. Make sure of the meaning of all these. Less obvious derivatives of **valēre** are *value* and *valuable*. What did these words originally mean in English ?

From **ūtor** and **abūtor** we have, of course, *use* and *abuse* ; *utility* and *useful*. To *utilise* a thing is to turn it to use. What do *utilitarian* and *utilitarianism* mean ? A *utensil* is really something designed for use. In history and elsewhere we often come across the words *usurp*, *usurpation* and *usurper*. To *usurp* power is literally to seize for one's self the use of it.

What is a *unit* ? How does it get its name ? What is a *unicorn*, and from what two Latin words that you know does it derive its name ? What is an *impeccable* person ? Why is an *inspector* so called ? What is a *prodigy*, and what do we mean by a *prodigious* feat ? What kind of eclipse is called *lunar* ?

You recently met the verb **flēre**. From that word came a Latin adjective **flēbilis**, which means " able to be wept over," and so " lamentable." The interesting thing is that from **flēbilis** has come the English word " feeble."

Have you ever heard of an *exorbitant* demand? It is one that goes too far, one that is excessive. As one might say in slang, it goes " beyond the limit." Your Latin shows you that it is one that goes right " outside the circle."

XXXI

THE VERB VOLO

44. The conjugation of **Volō, velle, voluī,** to wish, to be willing, is as follows :

Tense	Indicative		Subjunctive	
Pres.	volō vīs vult	volumus vultis volunt	velim velīs velit	velīmus velītis velint
Fut.	volam volēs volet	volēmus volētis volent		
Imp.	volēbam, volēbas, etc.		vellem, vellēs, etc.	
Perf.	voluī, voluistī, etc.		voluerim, voluerīs, etc.	
Fut. Perf.	voluerō, volueris, etc.			
Plup.	volueram, voluerās, etc.		voluissem, voluissēs, etc.	

INFINITIVE
Present, **velle,** to wish, to be willing. *Perfect*, **voluisse,** to have wished, to have been willing

PARTICIPLE
Present, **volēns, -entis,** willing

Notes.—(1) **volō** has no imperative, no future infinitive and no future participle.

(2) The present subjunctive is like **sim, sīs, sit,** etc.

EXERCISE 31

A

1. We are willing ; you (*s.*) cannot ; let us wish ; since she was willing ; to have wished ; in order that they might not be able ; we shall have wished ; in order that they may be willing.
2. Volumus rogāre ; vīsne respondēre ? ; cum vidēre vellem ; nē aufugere vellet ; vēndere voluerat ; manēre voluī ; cum stāre voluisset ; nē mē culpāre vellētis.
3. Cum manēre nōn audeat, statim proficīscī vult.
4. Comitibus diffīsus sōlus iter facere volēbam.
5. Domum vīsam comparāre voluī.

B

1. Marcus wishes to be distinguished for learning.
2. I am willing to remain all summer in this pleasant country house.
3. But in winter do you (*s.*) wish to live in the city ?
4. Since you (*pl.*) wish to dine at a poor man's house, bring food and wine with you.
5. Since the general is desirous of money, he wishes to lay down his command.
6. Since you are at leisure, I wish to question you, my friend.
7. Since I wish to learn from you (*s.*) tell me this.
8. Where do swallows fly away to in winter ?
9. We cannot sell corn, since none is left over.
10. Marcus is glad that you (*s.*) wish to live for a few days at his house.

XXXII

THE VERB NOLO

45. The conjugation of **Nōlō, nōlle, nōluī,** to be unwilling, to refuse, is as follows :

TENSE	INDICATIVE		SUBJUNCTIVE	
PRES.	nōlō	nōlumus	nōlim	nōlīmus
	nōn vīs	nōn vultis	nōlīs	nōlītis
	nōn vult	nōlunt	nōlit	nōlint
FUT.	nōlam	nōlēmus		
	nōlēs	nōlētis		
	nōlet	nōlent		
IMP.	nōlēbam, nōlēbās, etc.		nōllem, nōllēs, etc.	
PERF.	nōluī, nōluistī, etc.		nōluerim, nōlueris, etc.	
FUT. PERF.	nōluerō, nōlueris, etc.			
PLUP.	nōlueram, nōluerās, etc.		nōluissem, nōluissēs, etc.	

IMPERATIVE

Sing. **nōlī,** be thou unwilling. *Plur.* **nōlīte,** be ye unwilling

INFINITIVE

Present, **nōlle,** to be unwilling. *Perfect,* **nōluisse,** to have been unwilling

PARTICIPLE

Present, **nōlēns, -entis,** unwilling

Notes.—(1) **nōlō** has no future infinitive and no future participle.
(2) The present subjunctive is like **sim, sīs, sit,** etc.

EXERCISE 32

A

PORTRAIT OF A RICH MAN

[*Displaced by slave labour, thousands of free workers flocked to Rome to form a large semi-pauper population. The Senate became selfish and inefficient. Wealth poured into Rome, but it was in the hands of a few and was largely lavished upon personal show and selfish ends. The ancient simplicity of life was disappearing.*]

Lūcius Lūcullus ingeniō, doctrīnā, virtūte īnsīgnis erat. Quaestor enim in Asiam profectus, illī prōvinciae māgnā cum laude praefuit. Posteā contrā Mithridātem, rēgem Pontī, missus, multīs proeliīs eum superāvit, bellumque cōnficere magis nōluit quam nōn potuit. Vitia tamen ingentia virtūtēs eius aequābant. Cupidus enim erat pecūniae quam habēre volēbat ut luxuriae indulgēret. Itaque cum Mithridātem superāvisset, ōtiō et luxuriae sē dēdidit ; glōriam mīlitārem diūtius petere nōlēbat. Vīllās igitur omnibus rēbus ōrnātās in multīs Ītaliae partibus ingentī sūmptū aedificāvit. Mōlēs ingentēs in locīs quibusdam ipsī marī iniēcit ut in eīs vīllās suās pōneret. In aliīs locīs, marī in terram ductō, lacūs pulcherrimōs fēcit. Quae cum ita essent, amīcus quīdam Xerxem togātum eum vocāvit. Xerxēs enim, rēx ille Persārum, cum pontem in Hellēspontō factum tempestās et fluctūs dēlēvissent, nōn sōlum imperāvit ut mare verberārētur sed et vincula eī inicī iūssit.

Pompeius ōlim cum ad vīllam Lūcullī vēnisset, pulcherrimam eam esse affirmāvit, sed, " Quid hoc est," inquit, " Lūculle ? Cūr tū vīllam aedificāre voluistī quae aestāte quidem satis amoena est, sed hiemī minimē idōnea vidētur ?"

LUCULLUS APUD LUCULLUM

Cui Lūcullus, "Putāsne," inquit, "mē stultiōrem esse quam hirundinēs quae ineunte hieme (*at the approach of winter*) ex aliā in aliam sēdem āvolant?" Et vīllārum magnificentiae respondēbat cēnārum sūmptus. Saepissimē enim, ut ipsī sōlī cēna parārētur, sex talenta expendēbantur. Cum in cēnīs ipse sibi imperāre Lūcullus neque vellet neque posset, ē servīs cuidam mandāta dedit ut, cum satis cibī cēpisse vidērētur, fercula ē manibus suīs tolleret. Neque hōc officium servus ausus est neglegere nē tum quidem cum Lūcullus in Capitōliō cum prīncipibus cīvitātis cēnābat. Parva cēna ōlim parāta est Lūcullō cum sōlus esset; quā vīsā, culpābat servum, eīque negantī sē debuisse magnam cēnam parāre cum nēmō vocātus esset, īrātus Lūcullus, "Quid dīcis?" inquit, "Nesciēbāsne Lūcullum hodiē cēnātūrum esse apud Lūcullum?"

B

1. We shall refuse   to have wished ; let us refuse ; do not speak (*pl.*) ; since you (*s.*) were unwilling ; we have refused ; let them be willing ; since I had refused ; to be unwilling ; you (*pl.*) are unwilling.
2. Since the bridge has been destroyed (*abl. abs.*), we refuse to set out.
3. Since I am in command of the legion, I wish to encourage the soldiers.
4. Why do you (*s.*) refuse to spend a talent ?   Are you not very rich ?
5. Since you have neglected your duty, soldiers, I refuse to help you.
6. The farmers are unwilling to construct a road.
7. Do you (*s.*) wish to procure a house at small expense ?
8. I hear that you (*s.*) have refused to dig the garden.
9. The bailiff will tell us to clean the granary.
10. But we shall refuse to work on holidays.
11. The master declares that he is unwilling to sell the old slave.
12. The general says that he is not desirous of ease.
13. Having cleaned the granary I refuse to do more.
14. Having seen the slave I am willing to procure him.
15. Marcus having neglected his duty will be punished.

WORD STUDY

You are now able to state exactly what is meant by an *ingenious* device. It is worth while to recall that **ingenium** came to acquire a kind of concrete sense—a clever notion—and that hence comes the English word *engine*.

You see now that the *Doctrines* of Christianity are not merely what Christianity believes but what it actively *teaches*.

You will remember **insignis** better if you realise that from it comes *ensign*, a flag ; and that the word **insignia** which we know as meaning emblems, distinctions, distinctive marks, is just its neuter plural used as a noun.

Possum, as you might expect, has given us a host of important English words, e.g. *possible, possibility, potent.* Can you think of any more ? You see now why the *indulgent* parent is so called ; and you can at once say what is really meant by *sumptuous* fare. Look carefully at **mōlēs** ; it has given us our word *mole,* meaning a breakwater—perhaps you have read or heard of the Mole at Zeebrugge and the heroic attack made on it in the Great War. Curiously, the word **mōlēs** had in Latin what we call a diminutive, i.e. there was a form **mōlēcula** meaning a small mass, and that has given us a word for an exceedingly tiny particle of matter. Can you find or guess it ?

THE END OF THE REPUBLIC

Our recent reading lessons have shown us great changes at work in the Roman state after the Carthaginian Wars. For example, we have seen something of changes in the land system resulting in the rise of a large unemployed and discontented class at Rome. We have seen also how the wealth which was won from Rome's conquests tended to be spent in foolish and selfish ways. There were other troubles as well. The system of administering the provinces was thoroughly bad ; the Senate became strangely inefficient ; the Italians at large were debarred from the Roman citizenship which, by their services to Rome, they had richly deserved.

The first attempts to deal with those problems were made in 133 and 123 B.C. by two brothers, Tiberius Gracchus and Gaius Gracchus. Their proposals were good, but unfortunately in their methods they provoked much hostility and broke the constitution of the state. Each perished amid disorder, and the ills which the Gracchi had nobly tried to cure continued to grow and menace the republic.

About thirty years later a great soldier, Gaius Marius, rose to singular power. He had saved Italy by crushing vast hordes of Germans who threatened to pour into it from the north. Year after year he was made consul. However, he was no statesman and failed to grapple with any of the problems that confronted Rome. When already an old man he quarrelled with a younger general, Lucius Sulla, about the command in a war in Asia Minor against a king called Mithridates. The result was a civil war which left Sulla supreme in the state. Sulla tried to set matters right by restoring the power of the Senate. The attempt proved fruitless, simply because it did not touch and remove the real causes of the trouble, the grievances of the poor, the wrongs of the provinces, the claims of the Italians, the inefficiency of the Senate. Within a few years of Sulla's death civil war broke out again.

The cause was this : a general called Pompey had won a series of brilliant successes in the east. The Senate very foolishly disputed many of Pompey's arrangements in Asia Minor and the east, and refused to reward his soldiers as he had wished. This led to a coalition in which Pompey made common cause with Julius Caesar who was well known in politics as an opponent of the Senate. As a result of this coalition Pompey had his wishes gratified and Caesar, with Pompey's help, attained the consulship. This meant that next year he was sent to govern a province as proconsul. He was given the province of Gaul, which was in a very unsettled condition, fighting being rife among the Gallic tribes, and German tribes constantly threatening invasion from the east. This state of affairs gave Caesar his chance. He rapidly restored peace in the province of Gaul, and then proceeded to the conquest of the far greater part of Gaul which as yet lay outside Roman sway. There followed nine years of brilliant work, ending in the conquest of all Gaul. But, strangely, Caesar's success aroused the enmity of a large part of the Senate. It was feared that he would return from Gaul with his victorious army to make himself master of the state. Pompey was induced to share this opinion. The result was a quarrel between Caesar and the Senate which developed into civil war. Pompey and the Senate were defeated ; Caesar was left master of the state, but in a few months was murdered by conspirators, chief among whom were Brutus and Cassius.

Caesar's murder was a tragic mistake. It did not bring peace or restore Roman liberty. On the contrary it left two rival parties at Rome, that of the Senate under Brutus and Cassius, and an anti-senatorial party under Mark Antony, the friend of Caesar, and Octavius, Caesar's nephew and adopted son. Antony and Octavius gained control of Italy, drove Brutus and Cassius to Greece, then crossed over and defeated them at Philippi. Antony and Octavius next divided the rule of the Roman world between them. Antony took over the East ; Octavius the West. Antony, however, soon gave the Romans cause for grave fear. He fell in love with Cleopatra, queen of Egypt, and seemed to be aiming at making himself something like an eastern despot. The consequence was a quarrel between him and Octavius. War flared up. The fleets of the rivals met at Actium, off the west of Greece. Octavius proved victor ; Antony and Cleopatra fled to Egypt where both committed suicide.

Octavius was left sole ruler of Rome. He was named Augustus by the Senate. Taking great care not to offend Roman sentiment, he did not call himself emperor or king, nor did he abolish the Senate or any of the old time-honoured republican magistracies. Instead, he either himself held, or had conferred upon himself, the powers of the most important offices, so that while the old form of government was retained, power was now centred in one man. The republic, in all but form, was ended; the Roman Empire was inaugurated.

A MEMORABLE LINE

Tantae mōlis erat Rōmānam condere gentem.
So great a task it was to found the Roman race.

XXXIII

THE VERB MALO

46. The conjugation of **Mālō, mālle, māluī,** to prefer, is as
follows :

Tense	Indicative		Subjunctive	
Pres.	mālō māvīs māvult	mālumus māvultis mālunt	mālim mālīs mālit	mālīmus mālītis mālint
Fut.	mālam mālēs mālet	mālēmus mālētis mālent		
Imp.	mālēbam, mālēbās, etc.		māllem, māllēs, etc.	
Perf.	māluī, māluistī, etc.		māluerim, māluerīs, etc.	
Fut. Perf.	māluerō, mālueris, etc.			
Plup.	mālueram, māluerās, etc.		māluissem, māluissēs, etc	

INFINITIVE

Present, **mālle,** to prefer.   *Perfect,* **māluisse,** to have preferred

Notes.—(1) **mālō** has no imperatives, no future infinitive, no participles.
(2) The present subjunctive is like **sim, sīs, sit,** etc.

EXERCISE 33

A

THE GRACCHI

[*Much-needed reforms were attempted by two brothers* TIBERIUS *and* GAIUS GRACCHUS *of whom the former was tribune of the plebs in* 133 B.C., *the latter in* 123 B.C. *Both proposed good laws, but to carry them through, broke the constitution and perished in the ensuing disorders.*]

Tiberius Gracchus et Gaius frāter eius minor, Scīpiōnis eius quī Hannibalem ad Zamam superāvit nepōtēs erant. Quī cum puerī optimae speī essent, ā Cornēliā mātre bene ēducātī, mox ingeniō, doctrīnā, virtūte īnsignēs erant. Cornēlia enim ipsa cūrābat studia līberōrum et mōrēs eōrum suīs verbīs et exemplō cōnfōrmāvit. Nōn modo virtūtem sed etiam sermōnis ēlegantiam eōs docuisse dīcitur. Itaque cum mātrōna quaedam apud Cornēliam ōrnāmenta sua, fībulās, ānulōs, gemmās pretiōsissimās ostendisset, Cornēlia līberōs vocāvit, et eōs, ubi vēnērunt, mātrōnae ostendēns, " Ecce, haec," inquit, " mea sunt ōrnāmenta."

Tiberius tribūnus plēbis creātus nova dē rē pūblicā cōnsilia cēpit. Mālēbat enim adiuvāre pauperēs quam senātuī indulgēre. Itaque cum plūrimās Ītaliae partēs incultās esse pauperēsque ex agrīs ā dīvitibus expulsōs esse vidēret, lēgem rogāvit ut ager pūblicus plēbī dīviderētur. Nōbilēs tamen (dīvitiās enim suās augēre quam omnium salūtem cūrāre māluērunt), magnōs tumultūs excitāvērunt, neque sine magnā difficultāte lēx illa lāta est. Posterō annō, ubi Tiberius iterum tribūnus esse voluit, lēgēs ab eō violātās esse rēgnumque petī nōbilēs exclāmābant. Deinde,

cum ingēns tumultus esset, Scīpiō Nāsīca, impetū in Tiber-
ium factō, suā manū eum interfēcit.

Decem post annīs Gaius tribūnus creātus nōn modo,
sīcut frāter, agrum pūblicum plēbī dīvidere volēbat,
sed lēgem tulit ut frūmentum pauperibus vīlī darētur.
Operam dedit ut ipse senātus iūstīs cōnsiliīs ūterētur.
Deinde lēgēs rogāvit quō melius prōvinciae regerentur.
Tandem monēbat ut omnēs Ītalicī iam cīvēs essent Rōmānī.
Tum vērō senātus, sīcut maximīs in perīculīs facere solitus
est, dēcrēvit ut vidērent cōnsulēs nē quid dētrīmentī rēs
pūblica caperet. Quō factō, cōnsul Opimius Montem Aven-
tīnum in quō Gracchus erat, obsēdit. Mox Gracchus, ā
superiōre locō dēpulsus, salūte iam dēspērātā, cervīcēs
servō praebuit quī dominum et super dominī corpus sē ipsum
necāvit.

B

1. We shall prefer; I shall refuse; let me wish; since you (s.)
preferred; since I have preferred; to have preferred;
we were preferring; he had preferred; we shall have
preferred; they will prefer.
2. We prefer to be silent. Do not divide (s.). You (pl.) refuse
to speak. Did they not prefer to sell? Let us be willing to
be warned. We are willing to help. Let them not refuse
to advance. Did you (s.) refuse to answer? Do you (s.)
prefer to remain? I did not prefer to sit.
3. Having finished his task Valerius is desirous of ease.
4. Perhaps you (s.) prefer to say nothing about the defeat.
5. Syrus says that he is not accustomed to be idle.
6. Cornelia preferred to teach her sons herself.
7. Why did the citizens refuse to pass that law?
8. Having examined the farm I sold it cheap.
9. I preferred to dig the garden (rather) than be idle.
10. Why did the citizens refuse to give the citizenship (cīvitās)
to the allies?

11. Having made a long journey yesterday we wish to be at leisure to-day.
12. Since you (*s.*) have always preferred to play (rather) than to work, you are poor.
13. I say that I never preferred to play (rather) than to work.
14. Having roused a great tumult the orator was in great danger.
15. Weary of war the soldiers wished to hasten home.
16. Surely you (*pl.*) do not wish to neglect your duty ?

C

A ROMAN MARRIAGE

Catullus Verāniō suō s.p.d.

Laetus hīc diēs fuit ; immō laetissimus, nisi quod tū mēcum nōn fuistī. Vocātus enim ad nūptiās Aurunculeiae hodiē māne cum plūrimīs amīcīs domum Cottae, patris eius, contendī. Ō quantum gaudium in itinere fuit ! Quam fēlīcem Mānlium appellāmus, quam fēlīcem Aurunculeiam ! Tandem in ātrium Cottae ductus multa statim dē Aurunculeiā rogō. " Quid ? " inquam, " Satisne hodiē valet ? Fēlīxne esse vidētur ? Estne iam ad nūptiās parāta ? " Affirmat quīdam eam optimē valēre et laetissimam hodiē pulcherrimamque vidērī ; dīcit eam herī togam praetextam et bullam et crepundia Lāribus dedisse. Tum, " Audiō eam," inquit, " hodiē māne ad nūptiās ā mātre esse ōrnātam." Dum (*while*) haec et similia dīcimus, ecce, veniunt auspicēs. Ōmina fēlīcia esse nūntiant. Gaudēmus omnēs. Tum, patre et mātre sequentibus, dūcitur ā prōnubā in ātrium Aurunculeia. Quam pulchra nōbīs esse vidētur ! Mehercule, affirmant plūrimī deae eam esse simillimam. Est et antīquō mōre Rōmānō ōrnāta. Tunica alba est ; capillī antīquō mōre dīviduntur ; flammeō ōrnātur ; est in capite corōna pulcherrima.

Eōdem tempore intrat cum parentibus Mānlius togātus corōnāque īnsignis. Is et Aurunculeia statim in medium ātrium

A ROMAN MARRIAGE

prōgrediuntur ; decem testēs sequuntur. Tum prōnuba manūs iungit Mānliī et Aurunculeiae. Quō factō, Aurunculeia, " Ubi tū Gaius," inquit, " ego Gaia." Deinde sacerdōtēs ad āram prōgrediuntur. Farreum lībum in ignem impōnitur ; Iovem Iūnōnemque, deōs deāsque omnēs ōrant ut hae nūptiae semper fēlīces sint. Quibus factīs, nōs exclāmāmus, " Fēlīciter ! Vīvat Mānlius, vīvat Aurunculeia ! ". Ecce, vōx audītur Cottae nōs ad cēnam vocantis. Quid multa ? Optima cēna est ; mustāceum dīviditur ; sermō inter nōs exoritur grātissimus ; laetissimī diem agimus.

Tandem, ubi iam nox est, Aurunculeiam domum Mānliī dūcimus. Ō mī Verānī, quantō nōs gaudiō prōgredimur ! Quantus rīsus, quantus clāmor est, dum magnā vōce omnēs exclāmāmus, " Talassiō, Talassiō ! " et nucēs spargit Mānlius ! Edepol, paene dēfessī sumus ubi domum Mānliī pervēnimus. Ibi prīmum ōrnat postēs Aurunculeia, deinde aquam et ignem eī praebet Mānlius. Quibus acceptīs, Aurunculeia cum magnō omnium clāmōre ab ipsō Mānliō in ātrium portātur.

Ecce, mī Verānī, omnia habēs ; immō habēbis, ubi carmen quod dē nūptiīs Aurunculeiae scrībere cōnstituī, accēperis. Spērō mē paucīs diēbus id ad tē missūrum. Valē.

Note :

albus, -a, -um, white.
ātrium, -iī, *n.,* hall.
auspex, -icis, *m.,* soothsayer.
capillus, -ī, *m.,* a hair.
crepundia, -iōrum, *n.pl.,* toys.
exorior, -īrī, -ortus sum, to arise.
farreum lībum, *n.,* spelt-cake, cake made of spelt (a coarse cereal).
flammeum, -ī, *n.,* bridal veil (so called from its flame-colour).
immō, nay rather.
iungō, -ere, iūnxī, iūnctum, to join.

Iūnō, -ōnis, *f.,* Juno.
Larēs, -um (-ium), *m.pl.,* The Lares, household gods.
mustāceum, -ī, *n.,* wedding cake.
nūptiae-ārum, *f.pl.,* wedding.
nūx, nūcis, *f.,* nut.
ōmen, -inis, *n.,* omen.
postis, -is, *m.,* doorpost.
prōnuba, -ae, *f.,* bride's attendant.
spargō, -ere, sparsī, sparsum, to scatter.
Talassiō, Talassio ! (cry used in escorting Roman bride to new home).
testis, -is, *m.,* witness.
vīvō, -ere, vīxī, vīctum, to live.

BIRTH, MARRIAGE AND DEATH

It sounds rather startling, but is nevertheless true, that the Roman father was not absolutely compelled to rear a child that was born to him. Willingness to rear the newly-born infant was signified by a piece of ceremony in which the baby was laid on the ground before the father, and the father solemnly took it up in his arms. On the ninth day after birth the Roman baby figured in another ceremony, when it was solemnly purified and received its name. At the same ceremony, also, there was suspended from its neck the **bulla**, a kind of locket, made of gold if the parents were sufficiently wealthy, of bronze or even of leather if they were poorer. Boys wore the bulla as a protection against evil influences until, at the age of seventeen or eighteen, they laid aside the purple-bordered **toga praetexta** which was the garb of free-born boys and assumed the plain white toga of manhood, the **toga virīlis.** Girls, on the other hand, wore the bulla and the toga praetexta till marriage.

Marriage, as a rule, came early. Generally the bridegroom would be in his early twenties, the bride still in her teens. A Roman marriage was normally a matter of family arrangement as marriages still are in many Continental countries. The first piece of ceremony was the betrothal, **spōnsālia**, when, in the presence of parents and friends at his fiancée's home, the man gave her a betrothal ring. Some time later came the actual wedding. Once again, parents and friends were assembled at the bride's home. The auspices were taken, and the wedding contract was signed and witnessed. The bride was dressed in a special form of dress, the **tunica rēcta**, over which she wore the **flammeum**, an orange-coloured veil. She was attended by the **prōnuba**, an attendant who had to be a married lady. In the presence of the assembled guests the pronuba joined the hands of bride and bridegroom, and the bride signified her assent in the formula **Ubi tū Gaius, ego Gaia**—Where you are Gaius, I am Gaia, i.e. Where you are husband, I am wife. Prayer and sacrifice followed. Then came good wishes and congratulations from the guests, and a banquet at which a special wedding cake, the **mustāceum**, was shared. In the evening the bride was escorted to her new home in a procession with torch-bearers and flute-players. On arrival at the bridegroom's house the bride garlanded the doorposts, received the symbolic gifts of fire and water from her husband, and to prevent the unlucky omen of a stumble, was lifted over the threshold into her new home.

A Roman funeral was another occasion for ceremony. When a Roman died, the body was arranged for the funeral by professional undertakers. The dead man was laid upon a couch in the **ātrium** or hall of the house, and in front of the house was set a branch of cypress or pine. A distinguished man was usually given a public funeral. A crier went through the streets calling citizens to attend. A long procession was formed in which were musicians, hired mourners, often a professional mummer who imitated the walk and gestures of the dead man, and a whole retinue of men who wore the portrait masks of all ancestors of the dead man who had held high office in the state. The corpse itself was borne on a bier. When the procession reached the forum, the bier was set down and a **laudātiō** or speech of praise about the deceased was delivered. When this was over, the procession formed again and went to the burying ground of the family. This was outside the city, generally close to one of the great roads. Here the body was burned on a pyre, the ashes were collected, placed in a funeral urn and deposited in the tomb. When the last farewell, **valē**, was given, the mourners returned, to observe a period of nine days' mourning, at the end of which offerings were made at the tomb.

A FAMOUS SAYING

Hōrae pereunt et nōbīs imputantur, The hours perish, and are charged to our account.

TOMBS ON THE APPIAN WAY

XXXIV

INDIRECT QUESTIONS

47. An indirect (i.e. reported) question is a subordinate noun clause introduced by an interrogative word, e.g. :

Tell me *why he came,* **Dīc mihi *cūr vēnerit.***

In Latin the verb in an indirect question is in the subjunctive mood. The tense of the subjunctive is determined (*a*) by the sense required, (*b*) by the Rule of Sequence of Tenses, i.e. the rule that a primary subjunctive is employed in a clause depending on a primary main verb, a historic subjunctive in one depending on a historic main verb. In translating an indirect question into Latin :

(*a*) Any past tense whatever is represented by a perfect subjunctive if the verb in the main clause is primary.

(*b*) In all other cases the tense of the subjunctive in the Latin indirect question corresponds with the tense used in the English.

(*c*) " Will " and " would " in indirect questions are signs of the future subjunctive which is formed of the future participle and **sim, sīs, sit,** etc., in primary sequence ; of the future participle and **essem, essēs, esset,** etc., in historic sequence. Consider the following tables :

PRIMARY SEQUENCE

I ask (**Rogō**)			he is doing (**faciat**)
I shall ask (**Rogābō**)			he was doing (**fēcerit**)
I have asked (**Rogāvī**)	what		he has done (**fēcerit**)
I shall have asked (**Rogāverō**)	(**quid**)		he did (**fēcerit**)
Ask (**Rogā, Rogāte**)			he will do (**factūrus sit**)

HISTORIC SEQUENCE

I was asking (**Rogābam**)		he was doing (**faceret**)
I asked (**Rogāvī**)	what (**quid**)	he did (**fēcisset**)
I had asked (**Rogāveram**)		he had done (**fēcisset**)
		he would do (**factūrus esset**)

Notes :

(1) The verb on which an indirect question depends need not be one of asking.

(2) The interrogative words used in indirect questions are in general the same as those used in direct questions. Remember that **quandō** must be used in questions for " when ? ", and **quis** for " who ? "

EXERCISE 34

A

1. Change the following direct into *indirect* questions (*a*) after **Rogō**, (*b*) after **Rogābam** :

   (*a*) Quandō domum veniēs ?

   (*b*) Quid in hortō facitis ?

   (*c*) Cūr anum nōn adiūvistis ?

   (*d*) Quotiēns tē monueram ?

   (*e*) Quantus est canis vester ?

2. Nesciō cūr puellae fleant.

3. Dīc mihi, nauta, quandō lintrem refectūrus sīs.

4. Nōn audīveram quō Mārcus profectūrus esset.

5. Dīc nōbīs cūr fundum tam vīlī vēndere velīs.

6. Mātrem rogābō quandō mē ad urbem ductūra sit.

7. Nescīmus cūr iūcundum vōbīs videātur rūrī habitāre.

8. Quis mihi dīcet quot mīlia passuum prōgressī sīmus ?

9. Puerōs rogābō cūr labōrāre quam ōtiōsī esse māluerint.

10. Nesciēbam cūr opus celerius cōnficere servī nōn possent.

7

B

1. Tell me, citizens, why you have broken the laws.
2. I asked Valerius how many talents he had spent.
3. I do not know how long I shall remain here.
4. Ask Marcus to come home with me.
5. Ask Marcus when he will come home.
6. I have ascertained who wrote the letter.
7. Tell me by what means I shall procure food.
8. Valerius told me that he had sold his farm.
9. Valerius told me why he had sold his farm.
10. Valerius told me not to sell my farm.
11. I do not know why we have not been able to finish the work.
12. I asked my father why he wished to pursue the horseman.
13. Ask the general why he refuses to lead the army through the pass.
14. Have you (*pl.*) ascertained why Sulla has resigned his dictatorship?
15. Tell me why you (*s.*) prefer to live in the city (rather) than in the country.

C

ANOTHER LIMERICK IN LATIN

Aufidium morbus temptāvit.
Mortem sē timēre clāmāvit.
    Medicum arcessīvit;
    Venīre nequīvit.
Aufidius mortem vītāvit!

Note:

Aufidius, -iī, *m.,* Aufidius.
morbus, -ī, *m.,* illness.
temptō, -āre, -āvī, -ātum, to attack.

medicus, -ī, *m.,* doctor.
arcessō, -ere, -īvī, -ītum, to summon.
nequeō, nequīre, nequīvī, to be unable.

XXXV

INDIRECT QUESTIONS—*continued*

48. The English *if, whether*, introducing a single indirect question is translated by **num**, e.g. :

Ask if (whether) he has come, **Rogā num vēnerit.**

Observe that **num** introducing an *indirect* question does not convey any suggestion as to answer expected.

Alternative indirect questions are introduced by **utrum . . . an** as in direct questions, but *or . . . not* in an indirect question must be rendered by **necne** instead of **an nōn,** e.g. :

Rogā utrum discesserit an mānserit, Ask whether he went away or stayed.

Rogā utrum discesserit necne, Ask whether he went away or not.

EXERCISE 35

A

CIVIL WAR AND DICTATORSHIP

[*In less than forty years after the death of* C. GRACCHUS, *civil war broke out between the rival generals* MARIUS *and* SULLA. *The result was* SULLA'S *victory and dictatorship with its notorious proscriptions.*]

Cum Sulla cōnsul creātus contrā Mithridātem, rēgem Pontī, profectūrus esset, Marius illud imperium sibi petiit. Quam ob rem īrātus Sulla Rōmam contendit. Urbe occupātā Mariōque expulsō, cum tranquilla omnia vidērentur, Sulla ad bellum discessit. Marius tamen, ubi Sullam ex Ītaliā nāvigāvisse audīvit, Rōmam festīnāvit. Vī et armīs urbem occupāvit ; inimīcōs plūrimōs necāvit. Mox tamen,

SULLA—DICTATOR NO LONGER

labōribus cōnfectus ē vītā discessit.   Intereā Sulla, Mithri-
dāte superātō, cum victōre exercitū ad Ītaliam nāvigāvit.
Brevī tempore Rōmam cēpit ;   quī Marium adiūverant,
superāvit omnēs ;   tandem dictātor est creātus.

    Nihil umquam fuit eā victōriā crūdēlius.   Tabulae enim
prōpositae sunt in quibus nōmina eōrum scrīpta sunt quōs
Sulla capitis damnāverat.   Posteā   plūra nōmina saepe
addidit.   Captīvī etiam quibus Sulla vītam lībertātemque
prōmīserat, interfectī sunt.   Quōrum clāmōribus audītīs,
Sulla senātuī causam rogantī, " Cīvēs quīdam," inquit,
" paulō turbulentiōrēs iūssū meō castīgantur."   Tandem
in senātū ausus est C. Metellus Sullam rogāre quandō fīnem
caedis factūrus esset.   Cui Sulla respondit sē nescīre quot
hominēs interfectūrus esset, sed dē rē dēlīberātūrum.   Postrīdiē, tabulīs prōpositīs in quibus nōmina erant quīngentum

hominum, cīvēs in forum convocāvit et, " Ecce," inquit,
" omnēs iam prōscrīpsī quōrum nōmina meminī (*I re-*
member) ; sī quōrum oblītus sum (*if I have forgotten any*),
posteā prōscrībentur." Cum ingēns praemium darētur sī
servus caput dominī prōscrīptī tulerat, avāritia causam
caedibus praebēbat et multī innocentēs propter dīvitiās
interfectī sunt. Cīvis quīdam innocēns quī magnum in agrō
Albānō fundum habēbat, nōmen suum inter prōscrīptōs
vīdisse dīcitur. " Ō mē miserum ! " inquit, " Mē fundus
Albānus persequitur ! "

Post paucōs annōs Sulla dictātūrā sē abdicāvit, līctōri-
busque dīmissīs, inter cīvēs in forō ambulāvit. Attonitus
est populus eum prīvātum vidēns cuius tanta fuerat potestās. Diū tacēbant omnēs ; tandem ūnus adulēscēns
Sullam culpāre ausus eum ad iānuam domūs probrīs per-
secūtus est. Quod Sulla aequō animō tulit ; sed domum
intrāns, " Hīc adulēscēns," inquit, " efficiet nē quis posteā
tantum imperium dēpōnat."

B

1. I do not know if I can help you (*pl.*).
2. We do not think we can help you (*s.*).
3. We do not know whether you (*s.*) are innocent or not.
4. Tell me whether you (*pl.*) prefer to sleep or to play.
5. Having closed the door I asked the young man who he was.
6. Do you (*pl.*) know how many names are on the lists ?
7. I asked my father if we should set out in the morning.
8. But he told me to be silent.
9. Ask your mother, Sextus, if dinner is ready.
10. Tell me when you (*s.*) can speak with me.
11. We did not know whether the general was dead or not.
12. Ask (*s.*) these men whether they are friends or enemies.
13. I do not know whether I have written all the names or not.
14. I shall find out whether the children have come home.
15. Tell me, boy, whether you have seen my brother.

C

Here is a crossword puzzle which will refresh your memory of the proper names you have met in your reading.

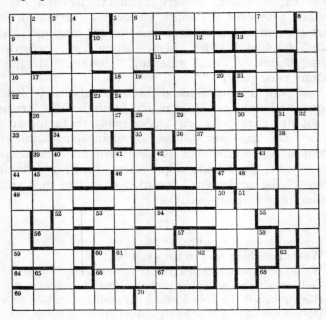

Clues Across

1. Goddess of the hearth.
5. Friend of poets (*abl.*).
9. I.
10. Treachery brought a terrible death to her.
13. A Roman of the old school.
14. Wife of a rustic hero.
15. The East (*dat.*).
16. A common Roman praenomen.
18. You met him at Cannae and in Macedonia (*voc.*).
21. Vocative of 16 across reversed.
22. A familiar abbreviation, *that is* a contraction.
24. A town on the way to Brundisium.
25. With 8 down gives the name of the home of a line of kings.

26. New (*neuter sing. nom.*).
28. With 31 down gives name of one who settled a strike (*abl.*).
33. See 22 across.
34. A short imperative.
36. " An honourable man " (*abl.*).
38. 2 down reversed.
39. A continent.
42. In English a flower, in Latin a goddess.
44. A great dictator.
46. These mountains took a heavy toll of Hannibal's army.
47. This town is near Brundisium (*gen.*).
49. Scene of a Roman disaster (alternative spelling).

51. Personal pronoun (*neuter plural nom.*).
52. Pliny thought it a pity boys should go here to school.
55. This occurs in the formula that begins a Roman letter.
56. Rome's first province overseas.
57. Seaport of Rome.
59. I adorn.
61. Domestic gods.
64. " Ubi tu 16 *across* ego *this*."
66. Among Rome's early enemies.
68. For a long time.
69. I throw away.
70. Rēgīna viārum.

Clues Down

1. Most famous of Roman poets.
2. A common abbreviation.
3. The allies.
4. This word means *one of a group of three men*.
5. A goddess.
6. An altar.
7. Made fatal bargain with 10 across (*voc.*).
8. See 25 across.
11. Great rival of Julius Caesar (*Gen.*).
12. " Others " reversed.
19. Accusative of 21 down.
20. God of the door.
21. Personal pronoun (*fem. sing. nom.*).
23. A woman's name.
27. Accusative of 9 across.
29. Another common abbreviation.
30. Thus.
31. See 28 across.
32. Horace calls him the most learned of the Greeks.

35. I am strong.
37. With a smile.
40. Roman consul who fell at the disaster of 49 across (*gen.*).
41. He delivered Rome in 390 B.C. (*abl.*).
43. To-morrow.
45. The city.
48. Same as 18 across.
49. For Titus.
50. Kingdom of Mithridates (*reversed*).
53. Gods.
54. Singular of 61 across.
58. Preposition gov. acc.
60. I have gone.
62. Small word but often makes a world of difference.
63. My (*voc.*).
65. By *or* from.
67. Same as 62 down.
68. Same as 53 down.

REVISION EXERCISES

A

1. (a) What is a deponent verb ? Give three parts of the
       deponent verb **proficīscor** which do not conform to
       your definition.
   (b) Give the principal parts and meaning of four semi-
       deponent verbs.
   (c) Give meanings of : nōlīte caedere ; mālētis ; nōn vultis ;
       velīmus ; cum māluerim ; cum vellētis ; poterunt ;
       potuerint ; cum effugere nōn potuerit ; aufugere
       nōlēmus.
2. Give four deponent verbs which govern the ablative case.
   What are their principal parts ?
3. Give Ablative singular, genitive plural, gender and meaning
       of : gener ; socius ; genus ; socer ; genū ; diēs ;
       vir ; vīs ; deus ; comes.
4. (a) Give Latin words for eight parts of the body.
   (b) Give Latin for : sun, moon, summer, winter, storm,
       wind, dawn, midnight.
   (c) Give Latin words for : army, infantry, cavalry, reinforce-
       ments, victory, defeat, to retreat, to advance.

B

(Revise Purpose and Indirect Command)

1. (a) Cibum sūmite ut valeātis.
   (b) Cīvēs monēte nē strepitū perturbentur.
   (c) Ipse fundum īnspice nē vīlicus īgnāvus sit.
   (d) Imperā servō ut hortum fodiat.
   (e) Multum cibum comparāte nē quid dēsit.
2. Do not ask (*pl.*) me to trust such a man.
3. That he himself might escape, he accused his brother.
4. That nothing may be lost, often examine (*s.*) the farm.
5. Work hard, my friend, that your granaries may be full.

6. Who told you (s.) to follow us ?
7. The master warned the boys not to exhaust his patience.
8. I shall ask this old man to show us the way.
9. The children were warned not to play on the shore.
10. The swallows have flown away to spend the winter in other lands.

C

(Revise Indirect Statement)

1. The poets say that the worship of the gods is being neglected.
2. You (s.) promised to sell the house cheap.
3. I hope the camp will not be surrounded by the barbarians.
4. The old man said that you (s.) laughed at his beard.
5. Did you (pl.) not say that the horse had been lost ?
6. We said that the horse had not been lost.
7. Marcus says that he cannot suffer the cold.
8. Valerius writes that he is being killed by the heat.
9. The boys say that they heard nothing.
10. The old men say that they will never be safe in the city.

D

(Revise Participles and Ablative Absolute)

1. After trying in vain to save the boat, we swam to the shore.
2. Under your leadership, my friend, we shall easily climb the mountains.
3. Obtaining a horse I hurried to the camp.
4. Hearing the speech we were astounded.
5. Coming home at midnight I found no food prepared.
6. Being accused of cowardice I left the camp.
7. Advancing for three miles we reached the pass.
8. Since help has been promised, we shall defend the walls.
9. When the booty was divided, the soldier thought that he was rich.
10. Since the ball is lost, we cannot play.

XXXVI

THE VERB EO

49. The conjugation of **Eō, īre, īvī, itum,** to go, is as follows :

TENSE	INDICATIVE		SUBJUNCTIVE	
PRES.	eō	īmus	eam	eāmus
	īs	ītis	eās	eātis
	it	eunt	eat	eant
FUT.	ībō	ībimus		
	ībis	ībitis		
	ībit	ībunt		
IMP.	ībam, ībās, ībat, etc.		īrem, īrēs, īret, etc.	
PERF.	īvī, īvistī, īvit, etc.		īverim, īverīs, etc.	
FUT. PERF.	īverō, īveris, etc.			
PLUP.	īveram, īverās, etc.		īvissem, īvissēs, etc.	

IMPERATIVE

Sing., **ī,** go.   *Plur.,* **īte,** go

INFINITIVE

Pres., **īre,** to go.   *Perf.,* **īvisse,** to have gone.   *Fut.,* **itūrus esse,** to be about to go

PARTICIPLE

Pres., **iēns, euntis,** going.   *Fut.,* **itūrus, -a, -um,** about to go

Notes.—(1) In the simple verb the **v** of the perfect stem is occasionally dropped, e.g. : **iī, iistī,** etc. : **ierō, ieris,** etc. : **ieram, ierās,** etc.

(2) In compounds the **v** of the perfect stem is *regularly* dropped, e.g. :

abeō, abīre, abiī, abitum, to go away
redeō, redīre, rediī, reditum, to return
trānseō, trānsīre, trānsiī, trānsitum, to cross
pereō, perīre, periī, peritum, to perish

EXERCISE 36

A

POMPEY THE GREAT—I

[*In Rome, during* SULLA's *dictatorship, were three men, each of whom was to play a great part in history*—POMPEY, CICERO *and* CAESAR. *In this and the next lesson we review the career of* POMPEY *down to* 60 *B.C.*]

Bellō cīvīlī Cn. Pompeius, iuvenis trēs et vīgintī annōs nātus, cum audīvisset quantō in perīculō rēs pūblica esset, Sullam adiuvāre cōnstituit. Exercitū igitur comparātō, optimum sē imperātōrem brevī tempore praebuit. Mīlitibus enim nēmo cārior umquam fuit ; nēmo magis in sē mentēs oculōsque omnium convertit. Erant enim eī virtūtēs imperātōris omnēs, labor in negōtiīs, in perīculīs virtūs, celeritās mīrābilis, maxima prūdentia. Cum cognōvisset ubi Sulla esset,

Brogi

POMPEY

statim ad eum cum suīs contendit, et in itinere trēs hostium exercitūs superāvit. Quem ubi Sulla adīre audīvit, ē sellā surrēxit paulumque prōgressus Pompeium salūtāvit imperātōrem.

Prīmō in Siciliam, deinde in Africam profectus Pompeius hostēs Sullae intrā sexāgintā diēs oppressit. Quō factō, litterās ā Sullā accēpit in quibus scrīptum erat ut, exer-

citū dīmissō, Rōmam quam celerrimē contenderet. Eā rē
magnopere mōtus est Pompēius ; quid Sulla vellet, īgnōrā-
bat. Exercitum tamen dīmīsit ; ipse domum rediit.
Redeuntī eī incrēdibilis multitūdō obviam īvit. Quae cum
ita essent, ipse Sulla māximō cum gaudiō eum accēpit,
Magnumque appellāvit. Deinde Pompeius triumphum,
praemium victōriae, petēbat ; quem honōrem ubi Sulla
dare nōlēbat, Pompeius minimē sollicitus (potestātem enim
suam quam Sullae maiōrem iam esse putābat) ausus est
affirmāre plūrēs ad orientem (*rising*) quam ad occidentem
(*setting*) sōlem sē convertere. Quid Pompeius significāret,
Sulla intellēxit, et cōnstantiā iuvenis attonitus, " Triumphet ! " inquit, " triumphet ! "

B

1. Let us go ; don't go (*s.*) ; about to go ; go ! (*s.*) ; since we
   have gone ; they will go ; we are going ; you (*pl.*) were
   going ; to have gone ; you (*s.*) are going.
2. Nōlīte īre ; ībisne ? ; māvīsne īre ? ; quō ībātis ? ; īverit ;
   hominis domum euntis ; nōbīs ad urbem itūrīs ; īverint ;
   cum īvissent ; quō īverās ?
3. Since you (*s.*) are unwilling to go with me, I shall go alone.
4. When do you (*s.*) hope to return ?
5. The poor men will perish of cold (*abl.*).
6. Yesterday we tried in vain to cross the river.
7. Where has father gone ? I think he has gone to the city.
8. My friend, when sixty years of age, crossed to Africa.
9. I shall tell the slave to meet you (*s.*) at midday.
10. I thought you (*pl.*) had gone away from home.
11. I did not know when you (*pl.*) would return.
12. Ask your brother, Sextus, if he will go to the games with me.
13. I asked my brother to go with you (*s.*).
14. Caesar had gone to the province.
15. No one knew when he would return.
16. My little brother, when ten years old, went to the forum alone.

XXXVII

THE VERB FERO

50. The conjugation of **Ferō, ferre, tulī, lātum,** to bear, is as
follows :

A. ACTIVE VOICE

TENSE	INDICATIVE		SUBJUNCTIVE	
PRES.	ferō	ferimus	feram	ferāmus
	fers	fertis	ferās	ferātis
	fert	ferunt	ferat	ferant
FUT.	feram, ferēs, etc.			
IMP.	ferēbam, ferēbās, etc.		ferrem, ferrēs, etc.	
PERF.	tulī, tulistī, etc.		tulerim, tulerīs, etc.	
FUT. PERF.	tulerō, tuleris, etc.			
PLUP.	tuleram, tulerās, etc.		tulissem, tulissēs, etc.	

IMPERATIVE

Sing., **fer,** bear. *Plur.,* **ferte,** bear

INFINITIVE

Pres., **ferre,** to bear. *Perf.,* **tulisse,** to have borne.
Fut., **lātūrus esse,** to be about to bear

PARTICIPLE

Pres., **ferēns, -entis,** bearing. *Fut.,* **lātūrus, -a, -um,** about
to bear

B. Passive Voice

Tense	Indicative		Subjunctive	
Pres.	feror	ferimur	ferar	ferāmur
	ferris	feriminī	ferāris	ferāminī
	fertur	feruntur	ferātur	ferantur
Fut.	ferar	ferēmur		
	ferēris	ferēminī		
	ferētur	ferentur		
Imp.	ferēbar	ferēbāmur	ferrer	ferrēmur
	ferēbāris	ferēbāminī	ferrēris	ferrēminī
	ferēbātur	ferēbantur	ferretur	ferrentur
Perf.	lātus sum, etc.		lātus sim, etc.	
Fut. Perf.	lātus erō, etc.			
Plup.	lātus eram, etc.		lātus essem, etc.	

Imperative
Sing., **ferre**, be borne. *Plur.*, **feriminī**, be borne

Infinitive
Pres., **ferrī**, to be borne. *Perf.*, **lātus esse,** to have been borne. *Fut.*, **lātum īrī**, to be about to be borne

Participle
Perf., **lātus, -a, -um,** having been borne

EXERCISE 37

A

POMPEY THE GREAT—II

Intereā bellum in Hispāniā prō Sullā gerēbat Metellus quī, fortissimus ōlim et ācerrimus, iam īgnāviae et lūxuriae sē dēdiderat. Ut bellum cōnficeret missus est in Hispāniam Pompēius, ubi variā fortūnā contrā hostēs rem gessit. Saepe enim ingentī in perīculō fuit, cum Sertōrius, dux hostium, per alta loca exercitum dūcēns, agmen Rōmānōrum sequerētur et īnsidiīs levibusque proeliīs multōs dēlēret. Pompēius ōlim, gravī vulnere acceptō, ā suīs relictus in hostium potestāte erat. Cum ad equum, tamen, Pompeiī optimē ōrnātum hostēs sē convertissent, et inter sē dē praedā pugnārent, Pompeius occāsiōne ūsus in salūtem effūgit. Alterō in proeliō Pompeius paene victus nōn nisi auxiliō Metellī servātus est. Quō factō, Sertōrius, " Ēheu ! " inquit, " Cūr illa anus vēnit ubi ego hunc puerum verberibus castīgātum Rōmam dīmissūrus eram ? " Posteā tamen, Sertōriō interfectō, Pompeius tōtam prōvinciam occupāvit.

Brevī tempore Sulla mortuus est ; sed nē tum quidem Pompeius sē quiētī dedit. Nūllam enim prōvinciam tenēbat populus Rōmānus ā praedōnibus līberam per illōs annōs ; aut metū relictae aut ā praedōnibus captae sunt plūrimae urbēs sociōrum. Nōn nisi mediā hieme ausī sunt exercitūs Rōmānī in Graeciam trānsīre ; ipsīus Ītaliae portūs saepe in praedōnum potestāte erant. Quae cum ita essent, missus est Pompeius cum imperiō ut praedōnēs opprimeret. Quid multa ? Ineunte vēre bellum suscēpit ; mediā aestāte cōnfēcit. Praedōnum aliī captī interfectīque sunt ; aliī imperiō et potestātī Pompeiī sē dēdidērunt.

Praedōnibus oppressīs, Pompeius contrā Mithridātem, rēgem Pontī, profectus proelium quam celerrimē committere volēbat, sed, cum rēx in castrīs suōs tenēret, id facere diū nōn poterat. Tandem occāsiōnem pugnae adeptus Pompeius cōpiās rēgis nocte oppugnāvit. In proeliō lūna Rōmānōs magnopere adiuvābat. Ā tergō enim cum eam Rōmānī habērent, umbrae corporum longiōrēs factae paene ad prīmōs ōrdinēs hostium pertinēbant. Quā rē dēceptī hostēs tēla in umbrās omnia, nōn in corpora Rōmānōrum mittēbant. Quō factō, cum impetum Rōmānōrum ferre nōn possent, caesī fugātīque sunt. Rēx ipse ē clāde suōrum effūgit, sed mox, ubi spēs esse salūtis nūlla vidēbatur, venēnō sē necāvit. Bellō tandem cōnfectō rēbusque Asiae compositīs, Pompeius in Ītaliam rediit.

B

1. We shall bear ; since we were bearing ; to be about to bear ; having been borne ; bear ye ! ; to have borne ; we had borne ; it has been borne ; you (*pl.*) may bear ; they may be borne.
2. What parts of **ferō** are the following ? : fertis ; ferte ; ferēs ; ferrēs ; feriminī ; ferāminī ; ferrēminī ; ferēminī ; fers ; fer.
3. Does he wish to bear ? ; let us refuse to bear ; since it has been borne ; we hope to bear ; I think it has been borne ; they say it will not be borne ; do you (*pl.*) prefer to bear ?
4. I do not think the enemy will bear the attack of the Romans.
5. I do not understand why we are being borne towards the shore.
6. Whither has the wind borne the ships ?
7. Sailor, do you know where (i.e. *whither*) my boat has been borne by the storm ?
8. Let us not any longer bear the cruel power of the king.
9. We had been advised to bring (i.e. *bear*) help to our allies.
10. But we could not bear the words of the orator.
11. I saw your father going slowly through the wood.
12. The soldiers say that the smoke is being borne by the wind towards the camp.

XXXVIII

THE VERB FĪŌ

51. The conjugation of **Fīō, fierī, factus sum,** to be made, to be done, to become, is as follows:

TENSE	INDICATIVE		SUBJUNCTIVE	
PRES.	fīō fīs fit	—— —— fīunt	fīam fīās fīat	fīāmus fīātis fīant
FUT.	fīam fīēs fīet	fīēmus fīētis fīent		
IMP.	fīēbam fīēbās fīēbat	fīēbāmus fīēbātis fīēbant	fierem fierēs fieret	fierēmus fierētis fierent
PERF.	factus sum, factus es, etc.		factus sim, factus sīs, etc.	
FUT. PERF.	factus erō, etc.			
PLUP.	factus eram, etc.		factus essem, etc.	

IMPERATIVE
none

INFINITIVE
Pres., **fierī,** to be made. *Perf.*, **factus esse,** to have been made. *Fut.*, **factum īrī,** to be about to be made

PARTICIPLE
Perf., **factus, -a, -um,** made, done, become

Notes.—
(1) **Fīō, fierī, factus sum** is used as passive of **Faciō, facere, fēcī, factum,** to make, to do
(2) In the present indicative no forms are found for 1st and 2nd person plural.
(3) **Factum īrī** means to be about to be made *or* done. To be about to become is **futūrus esse** *or* **fore.**
(4) Compounds of **faciō** formed with a preposition have regular passive forms, e.g.: **reficiō**, *I repair,* **reficior**; **perficiō**, *I complete,* **perficior** ; **interficiō**, *I kill,* **interficior.**
(5) Compounds of **faciō** *not* formed with a preposition have passives like **fīō**, e.g. : **patefaciō**, *I lay open,* **patefīō.**

EXERCISE 38

*Note.—*Like **esse,** and certain passives such as **vocārī, appellārī, creārī,** the verb **fierī** requires a complement, i.e. a noun or adjective which completes the sense. With **fierī** as with **esse** and the passives given above, the complement stands in the nominative case, e.g. :

> **Certiōrem eum faciō,** I inform him.
> But— **Certior fit,** He is informed.

A

MARCUS TULLIUS CICERO

SEXTUS : Pater ! pater ! Num dormīs tū in sellā tuā ? Pater, inquam.

VALERIUS : Quid est, mī Sexte ? Cūr tam subitō tantus clāmor fit ?

SEXTUS : Quis M. Tullius Cicerō fuit ? plūrimae sunt in hōc librō ōrātiōnēs eius, sed dē virō ipsō nihil. Age, pater, fac mē certiōrem quis et quālis fuerit.

VALERIUS : Dē vītā mōribusque eius, mī fīlī, certior fīēs. Cicerō enim ingeniō, doctrīnā, virtūte fuit īnsignis, summus ōrātor, scrīptor praeclārus, vir in omnī sermōne facētus.

SEXTUS : Dīc ubi nātus fuerit.

VALERIUS : Arpīnī ; quod oppidum est Volscōrum. Ā
    prīmīs annīs, cum artēs disceret quibus puerī ēducārī
    solent, cēterī discipulī ingeniō ēius attonitī domum ē
    lūdō eum summō cum honōre dūcēbant. Et parentēs
    eōrum ībant saepe ad lūdum ut Cicerōnem vidērent
    dīcentemque eum audīrent.

SEXTUS : Dī immortālēs !

VALERIUS : Iam adulēscēns Cicerō Rōscium, cīvem
    Ameriae, contrā Chrysogonum, lībertum Sullae, dē-
    fendit. Quā rē glōriam est maximam adeptus ; sed,
    cum dictātōris potestātem timēret, prīmum Athēnās,
    deinde Rhodum nāvigāvit ut ōrātōrēs Graecōs audīret.
    Post mortem Sullae Rōmam rediit. Posteā quaestor in
    Siciliam profectus, frūmentō ex Siciliā missō, cīvēs
    Rōmānōs in maximā frūmentī inopiā adiūvit. Ipsīs
    Siculīs propter iūstitiam dīligentiamque grātissimus
    factus, honōrēs accēpit maiōrēs quam ūllus umquam
    praetor est adeptus. Paucīs annīs post, Verrēs, quī
    praetor Siculōs crūdēlissimē tractāverat, reus factus,
    propter Cicerōnis ēloquentiam damnātus in exsilium
    abiit. Posteā cōnsul factus Cicerō—

SEXTUS : Meminī ; Catilīnam oppressit.

VALERIUS : Ita vērō, mī fīlī : is enim ipsum Cicerōnem
    interficere, senātum necāre, urbem incendere cōn-
    stituerat. Dīligentiā tamen Cicerōnis tōta rēs est
    patefacta. Catilīna, cum ex urbe fūgisset, mox in
    proeliō necātus est. Cicerō, cīvibus ex maximō terrōre
    līberātīs, pater patriae appellātus est.

SEXTUS : Quid ? Nōnne mox in exsilium Cicerō expulsus
    est ?

VALERIUS : Ita vērō. Reus enim factus est ā Clōdiō,
    tribūnō plēbis, quī ā Cicerōne cīvēs Rōmānōs quōsdam
    interfectōs esse affirmāvit. Sed brevī tempore Cicerō in

patriam revocātus est. Redeuntī eī ingēns multitūdō obviam iit. Summō honōre est in urbem ductus ; domus eius pūblicā pecūniā restitūta est. Paucīs annīs post, Cicerō in cīvīlī bellō Pompeium contrā Caesarem secūtus, ā Caesare victōre veniam accēpit. Caesare tamen interfectō, Cicerō nōn sōlum gaudēbat sed summā ēloquentiā senātum hortātus est ut Antōnium opprimeret. Tandem ab Antōniō prōscrīptus crūdēliter est necātus.

SEXTUS : Sed quid dīcis, pater ? Nōnne facētum fuisse Cicerōnem affirmāvistī ? Hāc dē rē plūra audīre cupiō.

VALERIUS : Cēnābat ōlim Cicerō apud hominem quī, cum mediocre vīnum amīcīs praebuisset, " Bibite," inquit, " Falernum (i.e. *Falernian wine—a choice variety*) hoc ; annōrum quadrāgintā est." Sed Cicerō, " Mehercule," inquit, " bene aetātem fert."

SEXTUS : Age, pater, plūra nārrā.

VALERIUS : Mātrōna quaedam dīcere solēbat sē trīgintā annōs modo nātam esse. Cui Cicerō, " Vērum est," inquit, " hoc enim vīgintī iam annōs audiō." Sed sērō est, mī fīlī. Abī.

SEXTUS : Abeō.

B

1. Sapientior fīēs ; cōnsul factus est ; cum mītiōrēs factī sītis ; certiōrēs factī erāmus ; negāmus hoc factum īrī ; cum nihil fieret ; cum cōnsilium patefactum esset ; opus perficiētur ; cōnsilium patefīet ; quid factum erat ?
2. (*a*) Cum difficultās tanta sit, quid fīet ?
   (*b*) Nōn certior factus eram tē praemissum esse.
   (*c*) Opere perfectō, quid iam fīēbat ?
   (*d*) Rogō num hoc iūssū imperātōris factum sit.
   (*e*) Mox certiōrēs fīēmus quandō nāvis perventūra sit.

3. Upon my word, I have been deceived ; I did not know what was being done.
4. I cannot understand why nothing has been done.
5. I have been informed that you wish to cross the river.
6. I informed the sailors that the harbour would be closed.
7. Do you (*s.*) wish this to be done ?
8. Thanks to (i.e. *by*) the diligence of the consul the whole affair will be exposed.
9. When will the work be completed ?
10. We hope it will be completed to-morrow morning.
11. Ask (*pl.*) the sailor when he will repair the boat.
12. What will happen (i.e. *be done*) now ? The ship is being borne by the wind towards the rocks.

WORD STUDY

Why is a *Nonconformist* so called ? What is the secret of *elegance* ? Where does one go to *rusticate* ? What exactly do we mean by *posterity* ? *Vile* is an example of a word that has degenerated in meaning as compared with its Latin parent. Can you give any more examples ? Next, derive and so establish the meaning of *tumult, detriment, persecute, rural* and *rustic*.

You are now able to tell what *avarice* is, what is meant by an *adolescent*, what is the main thing about an *intelligible* statement and what is meant by bearing a misfortune with *equanimity*. Why should something rare and strange be called *extraordinary* ? Where do *fumes* get their name, what is a *fumigant* and what do we do to a thing when we *fumigate it* ? Here are some more words for study—*effective, reverberate, intellect, missile*, and, hardest of all, *meridian*.

XXXIX

CONSECUTIVE CLAUSES

52. A Consecutive Clause is a subordinate clause of result, e.g. :

> He fights so bravely *that we praise him.*
> **Tam fortiter pugnat ut eum laudēmus.**

In Latin a consecutive clause is introduced by **ut,** and its verb is in the subjunctive mood. In general, the tense is as in English, e.g. :

He fought so bravely that
(Tam fortiter pugnāvit ut)
$\left\{\begin{array}{l}\text{we praise him (} \textbf{eum laudēmus} \text{).} \\ \text{we have praised him (} \textbf{eum laudā-} \\ \quad \textbf{verimus} \text{).} \\ \text{we praised him (} \textbf{eum laudārēmus} \text{).}\end{array}\right.$

Notes :

(1) Frequently, when stress is laid on the actual occurrence of a result, a perfect subjunctive is used after a historic main verb with the meaning of a past definite indicative, e.g. :

> **Tanta tempestās fuit ut nāvēs dēlēverit.**

So great was the storm that it (actually) destroyed the ships.

(2) When a consecutive clause follows, the main clause usually contains one of the following : **tantus, -a, -um,** so great ; **tālis, -is, -e,** such, of such a kind ; **tot** (*indecl.*), so many ; **totiēns,** so often ; **tam,** so (*qualifying adjective or adverb*) ; **adeō,** so, to such an extent (*qualifying verb*) ; **ita,** so, in such a way (*qualifying verb*).

(3) Whether positive or negative, a consecutive clause begins with **ut.** " That not," " that never," etc. is **ut nōn, ut numquam,** etc., according to sense.

EXERCISE 39

A

1. Puer tam facētus erat ut attonitus essem.
2. Fluctūs erant tantī ut nūlla nāvis in portum inīre posset.

3. Canis meus tam ferōx erat ut eum vēnderem.
4. Ille discipulus tam molestus mihi est ut eum verberāre cōnstituerim.
5. Tanta fuit aquae altitūdō ut in eā cōnsistere nōn possēmus.
6. Estisne tam īgnāvī, mīlitēs, ut aquilam prōdere velītis ?
7. Adeō hunc ōrātōrem cīvēs laudant ut eum audīre velim.
8. Tam audācēs erant praedōnēs ut nōn nisi hieme nāvēs tūtae essent.
9. Tantus fuit ignis ut fūmus tōtam regiōnem obscūrāret.

B

1. Such was the nature of the island that few ships went there.
2. The barbarians were so numerous (i.e. *so many*) that our men halted.
3. Having spurred on our horses we quickly reached the shore.
4. Are you (*s.*) so foolish that you prefer to do nothing ?
5. The young man was so lazy that he rose from his bed at midday.
6. I had not noticed that the difficulty was so great.
7. Tell (*s.*) me what is being done here.
8. We have travelled so quickly that we shall reach home about midday.
9. So many ships have been sighted that we are afraid.
10. We have hesitated (use *cunctārī*) so long that we do not wish to go.
11. The wind and tide are so favourable that I shall go at once.
12. Read carefully the following pairs of sentences and then translate :
    (*a*) Go away so quickly that no one will see you (*s.*).
    Go away quickly so that no one may see you (*s.*).
    (*b*) You (*s.*) are so good that I can never distrust you.
    He has told me everything so that I may never distrust him.

XL

DEFECTIVE VERBS

53. Defective verbs are those of which only some forms are found, e.g., the following are used mainly in the perfect and in forms derived from the perfect :

> **coepī, coepisse,** I have begun, I began.
> **meminī, meminisse,** I remember.
> **ōdī, ōdisse,** I hate.

Observe carefully that **coepī** has perfect meaning ; but **meminī** and **ōdī** have present meaning. Conjugations are as follows :

A. Coepī

Indicative	*Subjunctive*
Perf. **coepī, coepistī,** etc.	**coeperim, coeperīs,** etc.
Fut. Perf. **coeperō, coeperis,** etc.	
Pluperf. **coeperam, coeperās,** etc.	**coepissem, coepissēs,** etc.

Infinitive, **coepisse**
Fut. Partic., **coeptūrus, -a, -um**

B. Meminī

Indicative	*Subjunctive*
Perf. **meminī, -istī,** etc.	**meminerim, -īs,** etc.
Fut. Perf. **meminerō, -is,** etc.	
Pluperf. **memineram, -ās,** etc.	**meminissem, -issēs,** etc.

Imperative, **mementō, mementōte**
Infinitive, **meminisse**

C. Ōdī

Indicative	*Subjunctive*
Perf. **ōdī, ōdistī,** etc.	**ōderim, -īs,** etc.
Fut. Perf. **ōderō, -is,** etc.	
Pluperf. **ōderam, -ās,** etc.	**ōdissem, -issēs,** etc.

Infinitive, **ōdisse**
Fut. Partic. **ōsūrus, -a, -um**

Notes :

(1) The present, imperfect and future tenses of **coepī** are supplied by **incipiō, -ere, incēpī, inceptum,** to begin.

(2) The passive forms **coeptus sum, coeptus eram, coeptus erō,** etc., are used with passive infinitives, e.g. : **Urbs obsidērī coepta est,** The city began to be besieged. BUT, **Urbem obsidēre coepit,** He began to besiege the city.

(3) **Meminī** governs genitive of a person, accusative or genitive of a thing, accusative of a neuter pronoun or neuter adjective used as a noun, e.g. :

Tuī meminī, I remember you.
Nōmen tuum meminī, ⎫
Nōminis tuī meminī, ⎬ I remember your name.
Hoc meminī, I remember this.
Omnia meminī, I remember everything.

EXERCISE 40

A

Caesar Lands in Britain

[*To prevent the Britons from sending help to the Gauls* Caesar *decided to invade Britain. His first expedition late in 55 B.C. was rather a reconnaissance in force than a serious invasion. His second expedition in 54 B.C. was on a much greater scale. Our lesson deals with* Caesar's *landing somewhere between Walmer and Deal on the 26th of August 55 B.C.*]

Ipse Caesar hōrā circiter diēī quārtā cum prīmīs nāvibus ad Britanniam pervēnit. Ibi in omnibus collibus īnstrūctās hostium cōpiās cōnspexit. Cuius locī haec est nātūra : ita montibus altīs mare continēbātur ut ex locīs superiōribus in lītus tēlum conicī posset. Cum hic locus minimē idōneus esse vidērētur, ad hōram nōnam in ancorīs cēterās nāvēs exspectāvit. Tum et ventum et aestum ūnō tempore nactus secundum, datō signō et sublātīs ancorīs, circiter mīlia

THE LANDING OF THE ROMANS NEAR DEAL

passuum septem ab eō locō prōgressus, in apertō et plānō
lītore nāvēs cōnstituit. Sed barbarī, cōnsiliō Rōmānōrum
cognitō, equitēs praemīsērunt et essedāriōs quibus in bellō
ūtī solent. Cum reliquīs cōpiīs secūtī nostrōs ē nāvibus
ēgredī prohibēbant. Erat multās ob causās summa difficultās : nāvēs enim propter magnitūdinem nisi in altō
cōnstituī nōn poterant ; mīlitēs loca īgnōrābant ; manibus
impedītīs, magnō et gravī onere armōrum oppressī ūnō
tempore dē navibus dēsiliēbant et in fluctibus cōnsistēbant
et cum hostibus pugnābant. Hostēs intereā tēla in nostrōs
coniciēbant et equōs in eōs incitāre coeperant. Quibus
rēbus perterritī nostrī nōn eādem virtūte et studiō quō in
Galliā ūtī solēbant, ūtēbantur. Quod ubi Caesar animadver-
tit, nāvēs longās paulum removērī ab onerāriīs nāvibus et
ad latus apertum hostium cōnstituī, et inde hostēs omnī
genere tēlōrum expellī iūssit. Quae rēs nostrōs magnopere
adiuvābat. Nam novā rē commōtī barbarī cōnstitērunt et

paulum sē recēpērunt. Tum nostrīs mīlitibus cunctantibus, maximē propter altitūdinem maris, is quī decimae legiōnis aquilam ferēbat, " Dēsilīte," inquit, " mīlitēs, nisi vultis aquilam hostibus prōdere : ego certē meum reī pūblicae et imperātōrī officium praestiterō." Hoc cum magnā vōce dīxisset, ē nāve dēsiluit atque in hostēs aquilam ferre coepit. Tum nostrī, inter sē hortātī nē aquila ab hostibus caperētur, omnēs ex nāve dēsiluērunt.

B

1. We shall remember ; they began to fight ; he hates ; we might hate ; since they have begun ; we began to be attacked ; you (s.) will hate ; you (pl.) had begun ; to remember.
2. Valerius says that he hates war.
3. Therefore he prefers to die rather than to fight.
4. We were attacked so suddenly that we could not escape.
5. Such was the depth of the water that we were afraid to swim.
6. Do you (pl.) remember when you caught sight of the island ?
7. The ships began to be wrecked (use *frangere*) by the waves.
8. The boys say that they do not hate the master.
9. The anchor began to be raised about the fourth hour.
10. I did not notice whether the tide was favourable or not.
11. Remember (s.) to warn me when I ought to leave.
12. Leap down, soldiers, lest you betray the eagle.
13. The old man says he does not remember my name.
14. Let us wait for a few days that we may obtain a suitable tide.
15. The ships were so large that the barbarians feared them.
16. Marcus does not remember me ; but I remembered his brother.

XLI

DESCRIPTIVE PHRASES

54. Descriptive phrases consisting of a noun and adjective stand

    (*a*) in the genitive (genitive of description), e.g. :

        Vir magnae virtūtis, a man of great bravery.

    (*b*) in the ablative (ablative of description), e.g. :

        Homō nigrīs capillīs, a man with black hair.

The genitive of description *must* be used—

    1. In expressions denoting class or kind, e.g. : **bellum huius modī,** a war of this kind.

    2. In descriptive expressions containing a numeral, e.g. : **clāssis vīgintī nāvium, a** fleet of twenty ships.

The ablative of description *must* be used—

    1. To express a mere physical or bodily characteristic, e.g. : **statūrā fuit humilī,** he was of low stature.

    2. To express a purely temporary quality, e.g. : **es bonō animō,** be of good cheer, cheer up !

Either genitive or ablative of description may be used to express permanent qualities, e.g. :

        Vir magnae virtūtis ⎱
        Vir magnā virtūte ⎰ A man of great valour.

EXERCISE 41

A

THE DRUIDS

[*In his Gallic campaigns* CAESAR *had a keen eye for the life and culture of the natives. Our lesson to-day is based upon his account of the Druids whom you have heard of in your English history.*]

In omnī Galliā Druidēs cultum deōrum, sacrificia pūblica et prīvāta, rēs dīvīnās omnēs cūrant. Ad eōs ingēns multitūdō adulēscentium disciplīnae causā convenit, magnōque Druidēs sunt apud Gallōs honōre. Nam dē omnibus paene contrōversiīs pūblicīs prīvātīsque Druidēs cōnstituunt et sī iniūria facta est, sī caedēs fuit, sī dē fīnibus contrōversia est, illī iūdicant et praemia poenāsque cōnstituunt. Omnibus tamen Druidibus praeest ūnus, quī summam inter eōs habet auctōritātem. Hōc mortuō, aut is quī ex reliquīs maximā est dignitāte, honōrem eius adipīscitur, aut, sī sunt plūrēs pārēs, suffrāgiō Druidum, saepe etiam armīs, dē prīmō locō contendunt. Hī certō annī tempore in fīnibus Carnutum, quae regiō tōtīus Galliae media esse dīcitur, cōnsīdunt in locō cōnsecrātō. Hunc ad locum omnēs quī contrōversiās habent, conveniunt ut dē iīs Druidēs cōnstituant. Disciplīna in Britanniā exorta esse atque inde in Galliam lāta esse vidētur, et nunc, quō melius eam rem cognōscant, plūrimī in Britanniam proficīscuntur.

Druidēs nōn in bellō pugnant neque tribūta solvunt. Multī igitur et suā sponte in disciplīnam conveniunt et ā parentibus mittuntur. Magnum ibi numerum versuum ēdiscere (*to learn by heart*) dīcuntur. Itaque plūrimī vīgintī annōs in disciplīnā manent. Neque eās rēs litterīs mandant, etiamsī in cēterīs rēbus pūblicīs prīvātīsque Graecīs litterīs ūtuntur. Ante omnia hoc volunt docēre, nōn perīre animās, sed ab aliīs post mortem trānsīre ad aliōs. Hoc enim maximē hominēs ad virtūtem excitārī putant, metū mortis neglēctō. Multa quoque dē sīderibus atque eōrum mōtū, dē mundī terrārumque magnitūdine, dē rērum nātūrā, dē deōrum immortālium vī et potestāte docent.

B

1. A boy of six years ; he is of great height ; a three days' journey ; a man of great wisdom ; a long-haired race.
2. The ships are of such a size that they cannot reach the shore.
3. Hannibal (when) a boy of nine years, crossed into Spain.
4. The man is of such low stature that he cannot see the triumph.
5. Be of good cheer ! The controversy will soon be settled.
6. The stars are so many that they cannot be counted.
7. The Druids are men of such wisdom and dignity that all disputes are brought to them.
8. The man is so poor that he cannot pay tribute.
9. I have learned so many verses that I do not remember them all.
10. Hercules was a man of such great strength that he could perform (*perficere*) wonderful labours.
11. We have advanced so many miles that we cannot return to-day.
12. This will be done without any difficulty.
13. The pirates were men of such boldness that they destroyed our warships.
14. Since nothing is being done here, let us cross the river.
15. While going home I tried to count the stars.
16. I am going to the city to see the triumph.
17. Where does this road lead (*use* **ferre**) ? All roads lead (*use* **ferre**) to Rome.
18. The master said he would not bear the noise.

XLII

SOME DATIVE USAGES

55. The dative of certain nouns is commonly used in Latin to express the purpose aimed at or achieved by the subject. Such datives are known as Predicative Datives, e.g. :

>**Hoc dēdecorī est nōbīs,** This is a disgrace (*lit. " for a disgrace "*) to us.
>
>**Legiō praesidiō est castrīs,** The legion is a garrison (*lit. " for a garrison "*) for the camp.

Common predicative datives are :

auxiliō esse,	to be a help to ;
bonō esse,	to be an advantage to ;
praesidiō esse,	to be a protection *or* garrison to ;
dēdecorīesse,	to be a disgrace to ;
dētrīmentō esse,	to be hurtful to ;
honōrī esse,	to be an honour to ; *or* a distinction to;
exitiō esse,	to be a cause of destruction to ;
salūtī esse,	to be a means of safety to ;
ōdiō esse,	to be hateful to ;
onerī esse,	to be a burden to ;
admīrātiōnī esse,	to be a wonder to.

Notes.—(1) The verb **esse** is used with most predicative datives ; but **auxiliō** and **praesidiō** can be used with other verbs, e.g. **mittere, relinquere.**

(2) A predicative dative is never qualified by any adjective except a simple one of quantity, e.g. **magnus, parvus.**

56. Note the following common verbs which govern the dative case :

imperō, -āre, -āvī, -ātum, to command.

crēdō, -ere, -idī, -itum, to believe, to trust, to trust to.

diffīdō, -ere, diffīsus sum, to distrust.

fīdō, -ere, fīsus sum, to trust.

ignōscō, -ere, ignōvī, ignōtum, to pardon.

invideō, -ēre, -ī, invīsum, to envy.

īrāscor, -ī, īrātus sum, to be angry with.

praesum, praeesse, praefuī, to be in command of.

noceō, -ēre, -uī, to hurt.

nūbō, -ere, nūpsi, nūptum, to marry (*with a woman as subj.*)

pāreō, -ēre, -uī, to obey.

parcō, -ere, pepercī, parsum, to spare.

persuādeō, -ēre, -suāsī, -suāsum, to persuade.

subveniō, -īre, -vēnī, -ventum, to help, to come to the help of.

resistō, -ere, restitī, to resist.

EXERCISE 42

A

SECOND SIGHT

[CAESAR *completed his conquest of Gaul in* 50 *B.C. to find himself in opposition to* POMPEY *and the Senate. Civil war broke out in* 49 *B.C.* POMPEY *was speedily driven from Italy ; Spain was secured for* CAESAR, *who then crossed into Greece and in* 48 *B.C. routed* POMPEY *at Pharsalia.*

Many stories grew up about the battle. Our lesson gives one of the best known.]

Eō ipsō diē quō C. Caesar et Cn. Pompeius proelium in Thessaliā commīsērunt, rem mīrābilem Patāviī in Ítaliā audītam esse dīcunt. Erat enim in illā urbe Cornēlius quīdam sacerdōs, vir nōbilis et omnī virtūte īnsignis. Is subitō, mōtā mente, " Quid videō ? " inquit, " Ecce, pugna fit ācerrima. Duo exercitūs in pugnam īnstrūctōs videō. Peditēs Caesaris iam in hostēs impetum faciunt, sed eīs fortiter Pompeiānī resistunt. Equitēs Pompeiī exitiō sunt equitibus Caesaris quōs caesōs fugātōsque ex aciē expellunt. Iam in cornua peditum Caesaris contendunt. Peditēs tamen nōn fugiunt ; fessīs vulnerātīsque integrī subveniunt. Magna fit caedēs ; superātī tandem in fugam sē vertunt equitēs Pompeiī. Iam in legiōnēs eius ex omnibus partibus prōgrediuntur peditēs Caesaris. Quid hoc est ? Dī immortālēs ! Mīlitibus tertiae aciēī Caesar imperat ut statim in pugnam contendant. Pārent imperātōrī ; tantā vī veniunt ut hostēs eīs diūtius resistere nōn possint, sed ad castra fugiant. Ēheu ! haec rēs exitiō eīs est, nōn salūtī. Festīnant enim ad ipsa castra mīlitēs Caesaris ; nōn fossa, nōn vāllum eīs est impedīmentō ; iam in castra intrant ;

nēminī parcunt ; maxima fit strāgēs Pompeiānōrum.
Fortūnae diffīsus fugit ipse Pompeius."

Quae cum dīxisset, tacēbat paulisper Cornēlius ; deinde
magnā vōce Caesarem vīcisse affírmāvit. Quī audiēbant
tamen, omnēs eī crēdere nōlēbant ; Cornēlium dēlīrāre
dīcēbant. Mox tamen rēs magnae admīrātiōnī fuit, cum
cognitum esset eum nōn modo pugnae diem victōriamque
Caesaris praedīxisse, sed ita dē ipsā pugnā, dē caede, dē
fugā, de gemitū vulneribusque locūtum esse ut facile crēderēs
eum ipsum in mediō proeliō fuisse.

B

1. (*a*) Magnō auxiliō mihi fuistī.
   (*b*) Fuga eīs exitiō erat.
   (*c*) Relinque equitēs praesidiō castrīs.
   (*d*) Victōria honōrī erit ducī.
   (*e*) Clādēs nōbīs dēdecorī fuit.
   (*f*) Rēx ōdiō erat cīvibus.
   (*g*) Haec arma onerī sunt mihi.
   (*h*) Dīvitiae nōn bonō sunt aegrō hominī.
2. (*a*) Honōrī erit tibi ignōvisse inimīcō.
   (*b*) Nōlī dīvitibus invidēre ; dīvitiae saepe exitiō sunt
       hominibus.
   (*c*) Cūr mihi īrāsceris ? Num ego tibi umquam nocuī ?
   (*d*) Num tam scelestō hominī subvēnistī ? Quantō dēdecorī
       id tibi erit !
   (*e*) Hīc ventus nautīs magnō dētrīmentō erit.
3. Why do you (*s.*) beat the horse ? He has often been a help
   to us.
4. Tell (*s.*) me why Catiline was hateful to the citizens.
5. It is a distinction to the boy to have read so many books.
6. Have you (*pl.*) heard that Lucia has married Marcus ?
7. Ye immortal gods ! what a great storm has arisen ! Perhaps
   this house will be a protection to us.

8

8. Having taken the city the general spared the prisoners.
9. It will be a great distinction to the priest to have foretold the victory.
10. I have persuaded Caesar to send soldiers as a protection for the camp.
11. The king was a man of such great cruelty that he was hateful to all.
12. I have often helped your father ; but I do not believe that he remembers me.
13. Caesar often pardons his enemies. This is a wonder to everyone.
14. You (*s.*) have deceived me so often that I distrust you.

XLIII

NUMERALS

57. The Cardinal Numbers from 11 upwards are as follows :

11	ūndecim	XI	70	septuāgintā	LXX
12	duodecim	XII	80	octōgintā	LXXX
13	tredecim	XIII	90	nōnāgintā	XC
14	quattuordecim	XIV	100	centum	C
15	quīndecim	XV	200	ducentī, -ae, -a	CC
16	sēdecim	XVI	300	trecentī, -ae, -a	CCC
17	septendecim	XVII	400	quadringentī,-ae,-a	CCCC
18	duodēvīgintī	XVIII	500	quīngentī, -ae, -a	D
19	ūndēvīgintī	XIX	600	sescentī, -ae, -a	DC
20	vīgintī	XX	700	septingentī, -ae, -a	DCC
30	trīgintā	XXX	800	octingentī, -ae, -a	DCCC
40	quadrāgintā	XL	900	nōngentī, -ae, -a	DCCCC
50	quīnquāgintā	L	1000	mīlle	M
60	sexāgintā	LX	2000	duo mīlia	MM

Notes.—(1) Of the above **ūndecim** to **centum** are indeclinable.
(2) **Ducentī** to **nōngentī** are declined like plural of **bonus, -a, -um,** except that genitive plural ends in **-um.**

(3) Compound numbers between 20 and 100 are expressed
in the form *smaller* **et** *larger*, or *larger smaller*, e.g. for 25
we may say **quīnque et vīgintī** *or* **vīgintī quīnque.**

(4) In compound numbers above 100 the larger comes first,
with or without **et**, e.g. for 205 we can say **ducentī
quīnque** *or* **ducentī et quīnque.**

(5) For use of **mīlle** and **mīlia** see Exercise 21, note.

58. The ordinals from eleventh to twentieth are :

eleventh, **ūndecimus, -a, -um**	seventeenth, **septimus decimus**
twelfth, **duodecimus, -a, -um**	eighteenth,**duodēvīcēsimus, -a, -um**
thirteenth, **tertius decimus**	
fourteenth, **quārtus decimus**	nineteenth, **undēvīcēsīmus, -a, -um**
fifteenth, **quīntus decimus**	
sixteenth, **sextus decimus**	twentieth, **vīcēsimus, -a, -um**

EXERCISE 43

A

THE FINAL YEARS OF THE REPUBLIC

[*In* 45 *B.C.* CAESAR *fought his last battle at Munda in Spain ;
but his long-delayed work of reform was cut short by
his murder in* 44 *B.C. Civil war was renewed.*
ANTONY *and* OCTAVIUS *defeated* BRUTUS *and* CASSIUS
at Philippi in 42 *B.C. Presently strife arose between*
ANTONY *and* OCTAVIUS, *ending with the victory of the
latter at Actium in* 31 *B.C.*]

Caesar, ubi Rōmam rediit, lēgēs quidem cīvitātī ūtilissi-
mās tulit, sed multa contrā lībertātem populī Rōmānī
facere coepit. Itaque in eum coniūrāvērunt sexāgintā
senātōrēs equitēsque Rōmānī inter quōs īnsignēs erant M.
Brūtus ex genere Brūtī eius quī prīmus Rōmae cōnsul fuerat
rēgēsque expulerat, et C. Cassius et Servīlius Casca. Ā
quibus in cūriā Caesar, vīgintī tribus vulneribus acceptīs,
interfectus est.

Morte Caesaris audītā, in Ītaliam contendit Octāvius quem Caesar adoptāverat hērēdemque fēcerat. Is, auxiliō Antōniī, Caesaris amīcī, proelium ad Philippōs cum Brūtō et Cassiō commīsit. Prīmō proeliō Cassius, cum Brūtum superātum esse putāret, salūte dēspērātā, cervīcēs lībertō praebuit et est ab eō interfectus. Paucīs post diēbus, Brūtus in aciē victus sē in fugam vertit. Cum equitēs Antōniī ācerrimē sequerentur, Lūcīlius Lūcīnus, Brūtī amīcus, nē Brūtus caperētur, sē suā sponte equitibus obiēcit ; et exclāmāns sē Brūtum esse, ōrāvit ut sibi parcerent et ad Antōnium sē dūcerent. Antōnius vērō, cum Brūtum captum esse audīvisset, suīs in castra redīre iussīs, ipse captīvō īnsignī obviam īvit. Ubi equitēs tamen satis appropinquāvērunt, captīvum nōn Brūtum sed amīcum eius fidēlem esse cognōvit. Sed Lūcīlius, " Nōlī putāre, Antōnī," inquit, " ab ūllō hoste Mārcum Brūtum vīvum aut captum esse aut umquam captum īrī. Ego mē in potestātem tuam trādidī ut eī salūtī sim : iam morī parātus sum sī dignus tibi morte videor quod virō tam praeclārō ita auxiliō fuī." Quae cum audīvisset, Antōnius cōnstantiam Lūcīliī mīrātus nōn modo eī īgnōvit sed maximō honōre tractāvit. Brūtus intereā sē in collem quemdam recēpit. Ubi patriam, rem pūblicam, senātum, lībertātem, tot et tam fortēs amīcōs interfectōs dēflēvit, tandem comitibus, " Fugiāmus," inquit, " sed manibus nostrīs." Quae cum dīxisset, gladiō sē trānsfīxit.

Nē tum quidem pāx reddita est cīvitātī. Antōnius enim cōnsiliīs excitātus Cleopatrae, rēgīnae Aegyptī, ingēns bellum cīvīle mōvit. Victus tandem ab Octāviō pugnā nāvālī ad Actium factā fūgit in Aegyptum. Tum rēbus dēspērātīs, cum omnēs ad Octāvium trānsīrent, ipse sē suā manū interfēcit ; Cleopatra sibi aspidem admōvit et venēnō eius necāta est.

B

1. On the nineteenth day ; of four hundred soldiers ; three hundred and fourteen ; of the fifth son ; in twenty-three days ; three thousand soldiers ; of eight hundred and twenty pupils ; in the seventeenth year ; with ten thousand soldiers ; with nine hundred and fifty horsemen.
2. Brutus, a man of great courage and dignity, killed Caesar.
3. Do you (s.) remember how many oxen Valerius has ?
4. Upon my word, they are so many that I do not remember.
5. My son hopes to come home within twenty-eight days.
6. It is said that Caesar has crossed the Alps with six thousand men.
7. Writers declare that Hannibal lost twenty thousand men in the passes of the Alps.
8. To-day I saw an old man of ninety-one years.
9. They say that the enemy have a fleet of a hundred and thirty-five ships.
10. He is a man of such pride that he is hateful to the citizens.
11. Tell me why you (s.) hate this man. He has often come to your help.
12. Valerius says that eighteen farms are a burden to him.
13. Two thousand soldiers will be a protection to the province.
14. It is a distinction to Marcus to have completed this task.
15. In nineteen days I shall have made a long journey.
16. I shall stay in my country house for ten days. I wish to fish in the river.

MORE BREVITIES

(a)

Nōn amo tē, Sabidī, nec possum dīcere quārē :
　　hōc tantum possum dīcere, nōn amo tē.

(b)

Difficilis facilis, iūcundus acerbus es īdem :
　　nec tēcum possum vīvere nec sine tē.

XLIV

TIME AND PLACE

59.   *A*. Time

(1) Time *throughout which* an action goes on—Accusative, e.g. :
Vīxit multōs annōs, He lived many years.

(2) Time *at which* something happens—Ablative, e.g. :
Tertiō diē vēnit, He came on the third day.

(3) Time *within which* something takes place—Ablative, e.g. :
Tribus diēbus vēnit, He came within three days.

Notes.—(1) Time " how long ago " is expressed by **abhinc** and accusative, e.g. :
Abhinc annōs decem, Ten years ago.
In this usage **abhinc** must stand first.
(2) Time " before " or " after " can be expressed by an ablative
with the adverbs **ante, post** ; or by the prepositions
ante, post, and the accusative, e.g. :
Multīs post annīs } Many years after.
Post multōs annōs }

B. Place

(1) Place *towards which* there is motion—**ad, in,** and
Accusative, e.g. :
Ad castra contendit, He hastened to the camp.
In castra vēnit, He came into the camp.

(2) Place *from which* there is motion, **ā, ab, ex, ē,** and
ablative, e.g. :
A castrīs contendit, He hastened from the camp.
Ex castrīs vēnit, He came out of the camp.

BUT—With proper names of towns and small islands, with
domus and **rūs,** no prepositions are employed, e.g. :
Rūs profectus est, He set out to the country.
Rōmam rediit, He returned to Rome.
Domō vēnit, He came from home.

(3) Place *at* or *in which* is expressed by **in** and the Ablative, e.g.:
In castrīs mānsit, He remained in the camp.

BUT—With proper names of towns and small islands, with **domus** and **rūs,** place *at which* is expressed by the Locative Case which—

(*a*) in singular nouns of 1st and 2nd declensions ends like genitive;

(*b*) in other singular nouns ends in **-ī;**

(*c*) in all plural nouns ends like ablative; e.g.:

Rōmae	at Rome.
Brundisiī . . .	at Brundisium.
domī	at home.
rūrī	in the country.
Carthāginī . . .	at Carthage.
Athēnīs	at Athens.

(4) Place *near* or *close to which,* **ad** and Accusative, e.g.:
Ad iānuam stābat, He was standing at the door.

EXERCISE 44

A

Such was Augustus

[*After Actium,* Octavius, *under the name* Augustus, *bestowed on him by the Senate, founded the Roman Empire and ushered in the Roman Peace. The following deals with the appearance and personality of this extraordinary man.*]

Augustus per tōtam vītam fōrmā fuit īnsignī. Vultū semper erat tam tranquillō ut prīnceps quīdam Gallicus inter suōs dīcere solēret eō sē prohibitum esse cum ōlim in ascēnsū Alpium dē rūpe praecipitī Augustum dēiectūrus esset. Oculōs habuit clārissimōs, gaudēbatque magnopere sī quis in

OLEUM ET OPERAM PERDIDI

cōnspectum prōgressus vultum, quasi (*as if*) ad sōlis ful-
gōrem, dēmīserat.

Domus ēius modica fuit neque ūllō modō īnsignis. Plūs
quadrāgintā annōs in eōdem cubīculō hieme et aestāte
dormiit. Vestīmentīs ūtēbātur quae uxor, soror, fīlia eī
fēcērunt. Paulum cibī sūmēbat, neque umquam plūs
septem hōrās dormiēbat. Ut corpus exercēret, pilā saepe
lūdēbat ; nē longīs negōtiīs multīsque labōribus animus
frangerētur, nonnumquam aut āleā sē dēlectābat aut rūs
profectus hāmō piscābātur.

Augustus amīcōs nōn facile comparābat, sed comparātōs
per tōtam vītam retinēbat. Ante omnēs Maecēnātem
amābat, equitem Rōmānum, quī bonīs eum cōnsiliīs magnopere adiuvābat. Scrīptōrēs quoque in numerō amīcōrum
Augustus habēbat, Titum Līvium, Pūblium Vergilium

Marōnem, Quīntum Horātium Flaccum, ā quibus rēs gestae populī Rōmānī maximā cum glōriā celebrantur.

Pedibus saepe per urbem Augustus ambulābat et omnēs cīvēs benignō sermōne aut etiam iocō accipiēbat. Itaque cum homō quīdam libellum eī dare vellet sed propter metum nunc manum porrigeret, nunc retraheret, rīdēns Augustus, " Quid ? " inquit, " Putāsne tē assem elephantō dare ? " Pācuviō Taurō praemium petentī et affirmantī multōs hominēs pecūniam sibi ab eō datam esse dīcere, Augustus, " Sed tū," inquit, " nōlī crēdere." Vēnit ōlim ad eum in viā homō quīdam corvum tenēns quem haec dīcere docuerat : " Salvē, Caesar, victor, imperātor ! " Augustus avem magnō pretiō ēmit. Quā rē audītā, sūtor quīdam corvum comparāvit et eadem verba eum docēre coepit. Difficilis rēs fuit ; saepe enim corvus dīcere nōlēbat, et sūtor īrātus exclāmābat, " Oleum et operam perdidī." [1] Sed tandem corvus salūtātiōnem bene et celeriter dīcere coepit. Quae cum ita essent, laetissimus sūtor avem ad Augustum tulit. Quī cum corvī salūtātiōnem audīvisset, " Satis," inquit, " domī tālium salūtātōrum habeō." Quibus audītīs, statim corvus, " Ēheu ! " inquit, " Oleum et operam perdidī." Rīsit Augustus pretiōque maximō avem emī iūssit.

[1] I've lost my time and trouble (*literally*, I have wasted my oil and work). The proverb is derived from burning the midnight oil and toiling to no purpose.

A ROMAN LAMP

B

1. Ten days ago ; after five years ; in nineteen days ; he lived forty-five years ; a few days after ; a few days before ; on the sixteenth day ; Marcus is twenty-three years old ; twenty-seven days before.
2. (a) Let us set out for the country.
   (b) Do not leave home, my friend.
   (c) We shall sail from Brundisium.
   (d) We crossed to Carthage.
   (e) I shall remain in the country.
   (f) Do you (s.) not live in the city ?
   (g) Yes, indeed, I live at Rome.
   (h) Is Quintus at home ?   No, he is at Athens.
3. We had resolved to sail from Brundisium to Greece.
4. But our fear of pirates was so great that we remained at home.
5. Do you (pl.) remember how many years we stayed in Rome ?
6. It is said that Augustus was a man of distinguished appearance.
7. Horace has begun to write about the achievements of Augustus.
8. The storm will not prevent me from going to Sicily.
9. Writers say that Augustus kept his friends for many years.
10. Augustus has spared his enemies.   This is a great honour to him.
11. Many nations used to obey the rule (*imperium*) of the Roman people.
12. After a few years the young man went to Athens to study.

ABOUT THE ROMAN FORUM

If you could see the Forum, probably your first feeling would be one of amazement that a spot so small should have been so important.   For, after all, the Forum was only about one hundred yards long and roughly half as broad at its maximum.

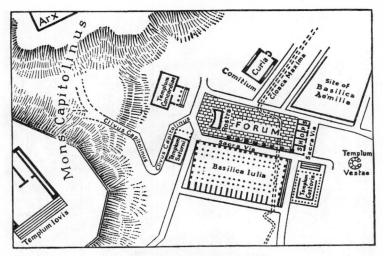

PLAN OF THE ROMAN FORUM

Its importance was due in the first place to its position. In the early city it was the natural and convenient centre for meetings and for markets. As the city grew, important temples and buildings naturally sought to be near this central point. The Forum thus became the hub of the city, and when the city became the capital of a great empire the Forum became the very centre of the Roman dominions. Imagine that in London the Houses of Parliament, Westminster Abbey, St. Paul's, the Law Courts, the Stock Exchange, were all grouped closely round a small rectangular space. That space would be decidedly prominent in our talk and thoughts. Well, something like that was the case with the Roman Forum. Look at your plan and notice some of the buildings that crowded closely round it. To the West you see the Capitoline Hill towering above it, bearing on its summit the Temple of Jupiter and on its slope the Temple of Concord. To the South you see the Temple of Saturn, the great Basilica Julia where the Law Courts met, the Temple of Castor and the

RUINS IN THE ROMAN FORUM   *Anderson.*

Temple of Vesta. On the North side notice the Curia, the Basilica Aemilia. Inside the Forum proper note the Comitium or place of assembly of the citizens and the Rostra. You see now that, small though it is in itself, the Forum was the centre of the religious, legal and political life of Rome. It was also the centre of the business world of ancient Rome. Thus the citizen going to a political assembly, the senator going to the Senate, the lawyer or advocate going to the Courts, the merchant or banker going to his office, all gravitated towards the Forum. And it was not only in business hours that the Forum was thronged. In the evenings it was the haunt of an eager, interested and ever interesting crowd, meeting with and talking to one another, discussing all the events of the day, finding amusement in the fortune tellers and dealers who hawked their wares amid the throng. It must have presented a wonderful spectacle when thronged with citizens on the occasion of an assembly or an election or when some speaker addressed the people from the Rostra.

The Forum was also the centre of much of the city's pageantry. Triumphal processions passed up the Sacred Way to the Capitol. Public amusements, as for instance gladiatorial combats, were sometimes given in the Forum.

Then the Forum was the great centre of news, always filled with people eager to hear the latest about a war or expedition or the newest developments in politics. The Forum was the place in which to learn all that. The Romans had no cables, no telegraph and no newspapers. From all over Italy and the empire news was constantly brought in to the government by special couriers. Some idea of what was going on was imparted to the people, first by announcements and, from the time of Caesar, by the posting up in the Forum of what was called the *Ācta diurna pūblica*. This was a sheet giving a summary of the acts of the Senate and people, items of news from Italy and the provinces. It was renewed daily. People not only made a point of reading the *Ācta diurna* but made or procured copies to send to friends in distant parts of the empire. In time the *Ācta* came to contain not only notices of new laws, decrees of the senate, appointments, magistrates, campaigns, but also more personal items, e.g. announcements of births, marriages and deaths, notices of fires, festivals, processions and sacrifices—even mention of divorces.

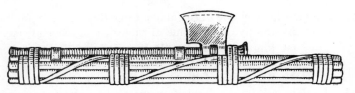

THE FASCES
The symbol of authority carried by the lictors.

XLV

THE ROMAN CALENDAR

60. The names of the months in Latin are used as adjectives.
They are—

Iānuārius	Iūlius (Quīntīlis)
Februārius	Augustus (Sextīlis)
Mārtius	September
Aprīlis	Octōber
Maius	November
Iūnius	December

Of the above, those in **-us** are declined like **bonus** ;
those in **-is** like **trīstis** ; those in **-er** like **ācer.**

Quīntīlis and **Sextīlis** are the older names. The
former was changed to **Iūlius** in honour of Julius Caesar,
the latter to **Augustus** in honour of the Emperor
Augustus.

61. In each month there are three special days from which the
others are reckoned. These are the Kalends (**Kalendae,
-ārum,** *f.*), the Nones (**Nōnae, -ārum,** *f.*), the Ides
(**Idūs, -uum,** *f.*).

The Kalends invariably fall on the 1st of a month.

The Nones fall on the 5th $\left\{\begin{array}{l}\text{except in March, July, Octo-}\\\text{ber, May, when Nones fall on}\\\text{the 7th day, and Ides on the}\\\text{15th.}\end{array}\right.$
The Ides fall on the 13th

62. If a date falls on one of the above three days, it is expressed
by the ablative with name of month in agreement, e.g. :

1st January,	**Kalendīs Iānuāriīs.**
13th December,	**Īdibus Decembribus.**
15th March,	**Īdibus Mārtiīs.**

63. If a date falls on the day before one of these three days, it is
expressed by **prīdiē** and the accusative, e.g. :

30th September, **Prīdiē Kalendās Octōbrēs.**

64. Any other date is expressed as the " so-many-eth " day before the next Kalends, Nones or Ides ; and in reckoning the number of days the Romans included both the day they started from and the day they were counting to (*inclusive reckoning*), e.g. :

To express " 19th May " in Latin.

We see that Kalends, Nones and Ides of May are all past ; the next landmark in the Calendar is the Kalends (i.e. 1st) of June. By inclusive reckoning 19th May is the 14th day before the Kalends of June. This is expressed in Latin—**Ante diem quārtum decimum Kalendās Iūniās.**

Notice the peculiarity of this expression : you would expect **diē quārtō decimō ante Kalendās Iūniās ;** but **ante** is placed first and everything following is thrown into the accusative case.

EXERCISE 45

A

GRAVEN IN STONE

[*In* 1555 *A.D. there was found on the walls of a ruined temple at Ancyra, the modern Angora, a long Latin inscription which proved to be a copy of the list of his achievements which* AUGUSTUS *drew up in* 14 *A.D., the last year of his life. The following is based upon extracts from the Monumentum Ancyranum as this famous inscription is called.*]

Annōs ūndēvīgintī nātus exercitum prīvātō cōnsiliō comparāvī. Quī parentem meum interfēcērunt eōs in exsilium expulī et posteā bellum īnferentēs reī pūblicae vīcī bis aciē. Bella terrā et marī cīvīlia externaque tōtō in orbe

E.N.A.

THE MONUMENTUM ANCYRANUM

terrārum saepe gessī, victorque omnibus veniam petentibus cīvibus pepercī.

Iānum Quirīnum (*The "temple" of Janus*), quem clausum esse maiōrēs nostrī voluērunt cum per tōtum imperium populī Rōmānī terrā marīque esset facta victōriīs pāx, cum ante mē ā conditā urbe (*from the foundation of the city*) bis omnīnō (*in all*) clausus fuisse dīcātur, ter mē prīncipe senātus claudī iūssit.

Mare pācāvī ā praedōnibus. Galliās et Hispāniās prōvinciās et Germāniam ā Gādibus ad ōstium Albis flūminis pācāvī. Clāssis mea per Ōceanum ab ōstiō Rhēnī ad sōlis orientis regiōnem ūsque ad fīnēs Cimbrōrum nāvigāvit, quō neque terrā neque marī quisquam Rōmānus ante id tempus īverat, Cimbrīque et Charydēs et Semnōnēs et aliī Germānōrum populī per lēgātōs amīcitiam meam et populī Rōmānī petiērunt. Meō iūssū ductī sunt duo exercitūs eōdem fere tempore in Aethiopiam et in Arabiam, maximaeque hostium cōpiae caesae sunt in aciē et complūra oppida capta. Aegyptum imperiō populī Rōmānī addidī.

Ad mē ex Indiā rēgum lēgātiōnēs saepe missae sunt, nōn vīsae ante id tempus apud quemquam Rōmānōrum ducem. Nostram amīcitiam petiērunt per lēgātōs Bastarnae Scythaeque et Sarmatōrum quī sunt circā flūmen Tanaim.

In cōnsulātū sextō et septimō, bella ubi cīvīlia extinxeram, rem pūblicam ex meā potestāte in senātūs populīque Rōmānī arbitrium trānstulī. Quam ob rem senātūs cōnsultō Augustus appellātus sum. Post id tempus auctōritāte omnibus praestitī ; potestātis tamen• nihil amplius habuī quam cēterī quī mihi in magistrātū collēgae fuērunt.

B

1. (a) Write down your birthday in Latin.
   (b) Express to-day's date in Latin.
   (c) Give Latin for : 1st January ; 14th March ; 4th April ; 4th May ; 15th June ; 15th July ; 7th December ; 7th October ; 13th September ; 26th November.
2. Come (s.) to Rome on the 6th of April and stay for a few days.
3. The war began to be waged on the 4th of August.
4. We read that embassies were sent to Rome from many lands.
5. The games had begun to be celebrated a few days before.
6. The great orator was born on the 3rd of January.
7. We know that Caesar was killed on the 15th of March.
8. I do not know why you (s.) refuse to come home on the 1st of April.
9. Do you (s.) know why those men hated Caesar ?
10. Octavius was in command of an army (when) nineteen years old.
11. For many years Augustus excelled all in authority.
12. Look, Sextus ! The temple of Janus is closed. There is peace in the whole world.

C

1. A bedroom.
8. Governs acc. or abl.
10. Cicero made many of these.
12. Preceded by 13 across and followed by another word makes a familiar phrase.
13. Abl. sing. of a one-syllable noun which in sing. has only nom., acc., abl.
14. In the country.
16. Twice ten.
18. Of snow.
20. Throw !
21. Introduces final and consecutive clauses.
23. Fiercely.
25. For an old man.
27. A field.
30. Future indic. of *sum*.

32. Very nearly a Latin word used in English and meaning " for nothing."
33. A horse.
36. Foreign.
37. By movement.
39. This had to be favourable for Caesar's crossing of the Channel (*dat.*).
40. Safety.
42. This might well have been no. 51.
45. Nor is sometimes rendered by this word.
47. You (*sing.*).
48. They will turn.
49. Very pleasant after work (*abl.*).
50. This plus 39 down takes us back to the Rubicon.
51. A groan (*acc.*).

Clues Down

1. A talking bird.
2. The senators killed **by** the Gauls had long ones.
3. It goes.
4. A citizen (*dat.*).
5. Read ! (*pl.*).
6. To use.
7. Fortify ! (*sing.*).
8. For mother (*reversed*).
9. Territory.
11. Nominative of **14** across.
13. A conqueror.
15. With **23** across is advice for a horseman in a hurry.
17. Perf. indic. of **46** down.
19. Reflexive pronoun.
22. Not once nor twice.
24. Prisoner at the bar (*acc.*).
26. If he gets into deep water let him do this.
27. Three reversed.
28. Part of the human body (*pl.*).
29. Same as 11 down.
31. Having exhausted.
32. Singular of 28 down.
34. O Quintus !
35. He has paid.
38. In safety.
39. One of Augustus's amusements.
41. Either, or.
43. He goes.
44. My (*fem.*).
46. 1st person of 43 down.
48. By force.

REVISION EXERCISES

A

1. We are not able ; he refuses ; let them prefer ; we shall go ; they will become ; we shall have preferred ; let them go ; may you (*pl.*) refuse ; let us be willing ; you (*pl.*) will wish ; you (*s.*) might go ; to have gone.
2. Let us go to Rome to sell the corn.
3. Having left Rome we began to make a journey to Brundisium.
4. Not daring to set out late we resolved to stay at home all night.
5. Since no one is willing to come to our help, we shall resist the enemy alone.
6. Persuade (*s.*) your friend to obey the laws.
7. I do not think that the master is angry with us.
8. Tell (*pl.*) me who is in command of the legion.
9. I hope that you will pardon us, master.
10. We cannot bear the pride of the king.

B

1. Nōlīte fīdere lēgātīs ; cūr dīvitī invidētis ? ; cūr māvultis
   ōtiōsī esse ? ; dīcō litterās ad mē lātās esse ; equitēs
   praesidiō sunt castrīs ; quō nāvis ventō fertur ? ; quis
   mēcum ībit ? ; nesciō quid fīat ; dīc mihi quō īverīs ;
   ferrī nōn potest.
2. Rēx tam superbus est ut ferrī nōn possit.
3. Nōlī fīdere huic hominī nē ab eō dēcipiāris.
4. Imperā puerīs nē in vīcīs lūdant.
5. Tantus fulgor sōlis fuit ut oculōs dēmitterem.
6. Gaudeō nōs hodiē ōtiōsōs esse.
7. Post merīdiem enim ad lūdōs īre poterimus.
8. Herī enim tanta multitūdō convēnerat ut nihil vidēre possēmus.
9. Tantus est clāmor ut amīcōrum vōcēs audīre nōn possim.
10. Ventō et aestū nāvēs in saxa ferēbantur. Nautae dē vītā
    iam dēspērābant.

C

1. Who can tell me why Marcus has not yet arrived ?
2. We know that he left for home before midday.
3. I have been informed that he was seen on the road three
   hours ago.
4. He is a man of such great courage that no one will dare to
   attack him.
5. Perhaps he has fallen from his horse.
6. Do you (*s.*) think he has fallen into the ditch ?
7. Since we do not know where he is, let us set out to find him.
8. Look ! don't you (*s.*) see Marcus walking towards us ?
9. How do you do, Marcus ? Where is your horse ?
10. Hang it all, I don't know. You (*pl.*) haven't seen it, have
    you ?

D

1. How do you do, Sextus ?   When did you begin to work ?
2. Do you (*s.*) not remember that I began to work on the 26th of December ?
3. That huge sword is a burden to Lentulus.
4. The plan which you (*s.*) have adopted will be a great help to us.
5. Do you (*pl.*) know how long Quintus has been in command of the legion ?
6. It is late, Marcus.   Don't you think you ought to go to your bedroom now ?
7. Set out in the morning so that no one may see you (*s.*).
8. When I was a boy of ten (i.e. of ten *years*), my father took me to Rome.
9. The raven is able to speak, a thing which (*quae rēs*) is a source of wonder to all.
10. I hope that the new laws will be a source of safety to the state.

E

1. Tell me when I ought to set out.
2. I do not know why food is lacking.
3. Our master's wisdom is wonderful.   He knows when there will be an eclipse of the moon.
4. Ask grandfather why he has a long beard.
5. I do not know if he will answer kindly.
6. Do you (*pl.*) know why swallows fly away to other lands ?
7. The poor man told me why he had no enemies.
8. Ask (*s.*) the little girl why she is weeping.
9. I do not know whether my father will come home to-day or not.
10. Tell (*pl.*) me whether you prefer to live in the city in winter or in summer.

EPILOGUE

Rome's Mission

There could be no better expression of the majesty of Rome and of her mission than the magnificent lines from Virgil's Aeneid which are given below. Study them ; compare the Latin with the translations which follow ; get at the meaning with your teacher's help if necessary ; above all, learn the lines by heart.

Excūdent aliī spīrantia mollius aera
(crēdō equidem), vīvōs dūcent dē marmore vultūs,
ōrābunt causās melius, caelīque meātūs
dēscrībent radiō et surgentia sīdera dīcent :
tū regere imperiō populōs, Rōmāne, mementō
(hae tibi erunt artēs), pācisque impōnere mōrem,
parcere subiectīs et dēbellāre superbōs.

Others will forge statues of bronze breathing with more grace (I for my part believe it), they will portray living faces in marble, they will plead lawsuits better, and will trace the courses of heaven with the astronomer's rod and tell of rising stars : you, O Roman, remember to rule peoples with imperial sway (these will be your arts), and to impose the habit of peace, to spare the subdued and to war down the proud.

Or, as Lord Bowen has translated it in English verse :
Others will mould their bronzes to breathe with a tenderer grace,
Draw, I doubt not, from marble a vivid life to the face,
Plead at the bar more deftly, with sapient wands of the wise
Trace heaven's courses and changes, predict us stars to arise.
Thine, O Roman, remember, to reign over every race !
These be thine arts, thy glories, the ways of peace to proclaim,
Mercy to show to the fallen, the proud with battle to tame !

APPENDIX I

A MACARONIC

Once upon a time it was a favourite diversion of more or less learned people to compose Macaronics, i.e. poems in a mixture of Latin and modern words. Macaronics are, for the most part, burlesque or humorous in tone. Some of them are very comical indeed. Here is one which has been specially written for you. Any unfamiliar words in it, as in the songs which follow, are given in the general vocabulary at the end of the book. After you have read it, why not attempt a Macaronic of your own?

A " Peel " of Laughter

Relinquunt librōs all *dīscipulī.*
Ex portā volant happy to be free-;
But some, *priusquam abeunt domum,*
Agree *certāmen* would be quite *bonum.*
Clāmant " A race! *Quis est celerrimus?*
Is will be *victor celeberrimus!*
Magnō tumultū omnēs gather round,
As when *rosās pulchrās apēs* have found.
Mox stant parātī: volunt forth to dart,
Sed Tubby—*valdē pinguis*—gets a start.
The pace is *calidus. Lentus sed* sure
Nōn currit Tubby, simply *volvitur.*
Tum cito Tom the Sprinter *práevolat:*
But lo! *Fortūna pinguēs adiuvat.*
Nam like *sagitta missa* from a bow,
Or *fulmen* which *corūscat ē caelō,*
So, *lābens* on a soft banana skin,
Propulsus Tubby *praecurrit,* to win.
Some *rīdent: plaudunt aliī*; some hiss;
Then *eum captum portant humerīs.*
Haec docet fābula—as you may guess—
" Eat more fruit, *sī vīs lābī ad* success! "

APPENDIX II

SONGS IN LATIN

Sodalis enim est Gratus

Tune : "For he's a Jolly Good Fellow"

Sodālis enim est grātus,
Sodālis enim est grātus,
Sodālis enim est grātus.
Num quis illud negat ?
Num tū ? num tū ? num tū ?
Num tū ? num tū ? num tū ?

Sodālis enim est grātus,
Sodālis enim est grātus,
Sodālis enim est grātus.
Num quis illud negat ?

Puellula mea abivit

Tune : "My Bonnie is over the Ocean"

Puellula mea abīvit :
Trāns undās abīvit ā mē.
Puellula mea abīvit :
Domum reportētur ad mē.
Illam, illam domum remitte ad mē, ad mē ;
Illam, illam, ō domum remitte ad mē.

Per undās perflāte, procellae,
Et tendite vēla, Notī.
Per undās perflāte, procellae,
Illamque portāte mihī.
Illam, illam iam reportāte mihī, mihī ;
Illam, illam, ō iam reportāte mihī.

In Caverna dum Metalla

Tune : " Clementine "

1. In cavernā, dum metalla
    Quaerit fossor aurea,
    Habitābat et iuvābat
    Clementīna fīlia.

Chorus : O divīna Clementīna,
          O meae deliciae !
          Periistī ; occidistī ;
          Inde meae lacrimae.

2. Matutīna Clementīna
    Anaticulās agit,
    Assulāque supplantāta
    En, in spūmam incidit !

    Chorus

3. At labella haec puella
    Bullāns exserit aquā.
    Heu, amātor nōn natātor,
    Orbus sum puellulā.

    Chorus

4. Tum angōre, tum dolōre,
    Clementīnam maeruī.
    Sed sorōre ex amōre
    Bāsiātā, valuī.

    Chorus

SUMMARY OF GRAMMAR

I. NOUNS

1. THE FIRST DECLENSION

mēnsă, mēnsae, *f.,* a table

	SINGULAR	PLURAL
Nom.	mēns-ă	mēns-ae
Voc.	mēns-ă	mēns-ae
Acc.	mēns-am	mēns-ās
Gen.	mēns-ae	mēns-ārum
Dat.	mēns-ae	mēns-īs
Abl.	mēns-ā	mēns-īs

Notes.—(1) Nouns of the First Declension are feminine, except names of males and nouns denoting male occupations, as **nauta**, a sailor ; **agricola**, a farmer ; **poēta**, a poet.
   (2) The dative and ablative plural of **dea**, a goddess, and of **fīlia**, a daughter, are **deābus, fīliābus.**

2. THE SECOND DECLENSION

	dominus, -ī, *m.,* master	**ager, -rī,** *m.,* field	**puer, -ī,** *m.,* boy	**bellum, -ī,** *n.,* war
Nom.	domin-us	ager	puer	bell-um
Voc.	domin-ĕ	ager	puer	bell-um
Acc.	domin-um	agr-um	puer-um	bell-um
Gen.	domin-ī	agr-ī	puer-ī	bell-ī
Dat.	domin-ō	agr-ō	puer-ō	bell-ō
Abl.	domin-ō	agr-ō	puer-ō	bell-ō
Nom.	domin-ī	agr-ī	puer-ī	bell-ă
Voc.	domin-ī	agr-ī	puer-ī	bell-ă
Acc.	domin-ōs	agr-ōs	puer-ōs	bell-ă
Gen.	domin-ōrum	agr-ōrum	puer-ōrum	bell-ōrum
Dat.	domin-īs	agr-īs	puer-īs	bell-īs
Abl.	domin-īs	agr-īs	puer-īs	bell-īs

Notes.—(1) Nouns ending in **-us** and **-er** are mostly masculine ; nouns ending in **-um** are neuter.
   (2) **Fīlius**, a son, has vocative sing. **fīlī**, and gen. sing. **fīliī** or **fīlī.**
   (3) Proper names ending in **-ius** are declined like **fīlius.**
   (4) **Deus**, a god, has vocative **deus** ; nom. and voc. plural **dī** or **dĕī** ; dat. and abl. plural **dīs** or **dĕīs.**
   (5) **Vir, virī,** *m.* a man, is declined like **puer.**

3. The Third Declension

(a) Increasing nouns, masculine, feminine, neuter.

	rēx, rēgĭs, m., king	legiō, -iōnĭs, f., legion	nōmen, -inis, n., name	ŏnus, -erĭs, n., burden
Nom.	rēx	legiō	nōmen	ŏnus
Voc.	rēx	legiō	nōmen	ŏnus
Acc.	rēg-em	legiōn-em	nōmen	ŏnus
Gen.	rēg-is	legiōn-is	nōmin-is	ŏner-ĭs
Dat.	rēg-ī	legiōn-ī	nōmin-ī	ŏner-ī
Abl.	rēg-ĕ	legiōn-ĕ	nōmin-ĕ	ŏner-ĕ
Nom.	rēg-ēs	legiōn-ēs	nōmin-ă	ŏner-ă
Voc.	rēg-ēs	legiōn-ēs	nōmin-ă	ŏner-ă
Acc.	rēg-ēs	legiōn-ēs	nōmin-ă	ŏner-ă
Gen.	rēg-um	legiōn-um	nōmin-um	ŏner-um
Dat.	rēg-ibus	legiōn-ibus	nōmĭn-ibus	ŏnér-ibus
Abl.	rēg-ibus	legiōn-ibus	nōmĭn-ibus	ŏnér-ibus

(b) Non-increasing nouns, masc., fem., neuter.

	cīvĭs, -ĭs, m., citizen	nāvĭs, -ĭs, f., ship	cubīlĕ, -ĭs, n., bed
Nom.	cīvĭs	nāvĭs	cubīlĕ
Voc.	cīvĭs	nāvĭs	cubīlĕ
Acc.	cīv-em	nāv-em	cubīlĕ
Gen.	cīv-ĭs	nāv-ĭs	cubīl-ĭs
Dat.	cīv-ī	nāv-ī	cubīl-ī
Abl.	cīv-ĕ	nāv-ĕ	cubīl-ī
Nom.	cīv-ēs	nāv-ēs	cubīl-ĭă
Voc.	cīv-ēs	nāv-ēs	cubīl-ĭă
Acc.	cīv-ēs	nāv-ēs	cubīl-ĭă
Gen.	cīv-ium	nāv-ium	cubīl-ium
Dat.	cīv-ibus	nāv-ibus	cubīl-ibus
Abl.	cīv-ibus	nāv-ibus	cubīl-ibus

Note.—The genitive plural of non-increasing nouns regularly ends in -ium.

(c) Monosyllabic nouns whose stem ends in two consonants.

urbs, urbĭs, f., a city

	Singular	Plural
Nom.	urbs	urb-ēs
Voc.	urbs	urb-ēs
Acc.	urb-em	urb-ēs
Gen.	urb-ĭs	urb-ium
Dat.	urb-ī	urb-ibus
Abl.	urb-ĕ	urb-ibus

Note.—The genitive plural of nouns of this class ends in -ium.

(d) Exceptional words of the Third Declension.

senex, senĭs, m., old man	bōs, bŏvĭs, c., ox, cow	vīs, f., s., force pl., strength	Iūppiter, Iŏvis, m., Jupiter
Nom. senex	bōs	vīs	Iūppiter
Voc. senex	bōs	—	Iūppiter
Acc. sen-em	bŏv-em	vĭm	Iŏv-em
Gen. sen-ĭs	bŏv-ĭs	—	Iŏv-ĭs
Dat. sen-ī	bŏv-ī	—	Iŏv-ī
Abl. sen-ĕ	bŏv-ĕ	vī	Iŏv-ē
Nom. sen-ēs	bŏv-ēs	vīrēs	
Voc. sen-ēs	bŏv-ēs	vīrēs	
Acc. sen-ēs	bŏv-ēs	vīrēs	
Gen. sen-um	bŏum	vīrium	
Dat. sen-ibus	bōbus (būbus)	vīribus	
Abl. sen-ibus	bōbus (būbus)	vīribus	

Notes.—(1) **Păter, pătrĭs,** m., father; **māter, mātrĭs,** f., mother; **frāter, frātrĭs,** m., brother; **cănĭs, cănĭs,** c., dog; **iuvenĭs, iuvenĭs,** m., young man, have **-um** in the genitive plural.

(2) **Moenia, moenium,** n., city walls, is used in plural only. Decline like plural of **cubīle.**

4. THE FOURTH DECLENSION

exercitus, -ūs, m., army **cornū, -ūs,** n., horn, wing (of army)

	SINGULAR	PLURAL	SINGULAR	PLURAL
Nom.	exercit-us	exercit-ūs	corn-ū	corn-uă
Voc.	exercit-us	exercit-ūs	corn-ū	corn-uă
Acc.	exercit-um	exercit-ūs	corn-ū	corn-uă
Gen.	exercit-ūs	exercit-uum	corn-ūs	corn-uum
Dat.	exercit-uī	exercit-ibus	corn-ū	corn-ibus
Abl.	exercit-ū	exercit-ibus	corn-ū	corn-ibus

5. THE DECLENSION OF **dŏmus, dŏmūs,** f., a house

	SINGULAR	PLURAL
Nom.	dŏm-us	dŏm-ūs
Voc.	dŏm-us	dŏm-ūs
Acc.	dŏm-um	dŏm-ūs or dŏm-ōs
Gen.	dŏm-ūs	dŏm-uum or dŏm-ōrum
Dat.	dŏm-uī	dŏm-ibus
Abl.	dŏmō	dŏm-ibus

6. THE FIFTH DECLENSION

dĭēs, dĭēī, *m.,* a day   **rēs, rĕī,** *f.,* a thing

	SINGULAR	PLURAL	SINGULAR	PLURAL
Nom.	dĭ-ēs	dĭ-ēs	r-ēs	r-ēs
Voc.	dĭ-ēs	dĭ-ēs	r-ēs	r-ēs
Acc.	dĭ-em	dĭ-ēs	r-em	r-ēs
Gen.	dĭ-ēī	dĭ-ērum	r-ĕī	r-ērum
Dat.	dĭ-ēī	dĭ-ēbus	r-ĕī	r-ēbus
Abl.	dĭ-ē	dĭ-ēbus	r-ē	r-ēbus

Notes.—(1) **Fidēs, fĭdĕī,** *f.,* faith ; **spēs, spĕī,** *f.,* hope, are declined like **rēs.**

(2) In the Fifth Declension **dĭēs** and **rēs** have complete plurals. **Aciēs, aciēī,** *f.,* line of battle, and **spēs** have nominative and accusative plural only. Most other nouns of this declension have no plural.

II. ADJECTIVES

1. ADJECTIVES OF FIRST AND SECOND DECLENSIONS

(a) **bŏnus, bŏna, bŏnum,** good

SINGULAR

	Masc.	*Fem.*	*Neuter*
Nom.	bonus	bona	bonum
Voc.	bone	bona	bonum
Acc.	bonum	bonam	bonum
Gen.	bonī	bonae	bonī
Dat.	bonō	bonae	bonō
Abl.	bonō	bonā	bonō

PLURAL

	Masc.	*Fem.*	*Neuter*
Nom.	bonī	bonae	bonă
Voc.	bonī	bonae	bonă
Acc.	bonōs	bonās	bonă
Gen.	bonōrum	bonārum	bonōrum
Dat.	bonīs	bonīs	bonīs
Abl.	bonīs	bonīs	bonīs

(b) pulcher, pulchra, pulchrum, beautiful

SINGULAR

	Masc.	Fem.	Neuter
Nom.	pulcher	pulchra	pulchrum
Voc.	pulcher	pulchra	pulchrum
Acc.	pulchrum	pulchram	pulchrum
Gen.	pulchrī	pulchrae	pulchrī
Dat.	pulchrŏ	pulchrae	pulchrŏ
Abl.	pulchrŏ	pulchrā	pulchrŏ

PLURAL

	Masc.	Fem.	Neuter
Nom.	pulchrī	pulchrae	pulchră
Voc.	pulchrī	pulchrae	pulchră
Acc.	pulchrŏs	pulchrās	pulchră
Gen.	pulchrŏrum	pulchrārum	pulchrŏrum
Dat.	pulchrīs	pulchrīs	pulchrīs
Abl.	pulchrīs	pulchrīs	pulchrīs

(c) tener, tenera, tenerum, tender

SINGULAR

	Masc.	Fem.	Neuter
Nom.	tener	tenera	tenerum
Voc.	tener	tenera	tenerum
Acc.	tenerum	teneram	tenerum
Gen.	tenerī	tenerae	tenerī
Dat.	tenerŏ	tenerae	tenerŏ
Abl.	tenerŏ	tenerā	tenerŏ

PLURAL

	Masc.	Fem.	Neuter
Nom.	tenerī	tenerae	teneră
Voc.	tenerī	tenerae	teneră
Acc.	tenerŏs	tenerās	teneră
Gen.	tenerŏrum	tenerārum	tenerŏrum
Dat.	tenerīs	tenerīs	tenerīs
Abl.	tenerīs	tenerīs	tenerīs

2. ADJECTIVES OF THE THIRD DECLENSION

(a) audāx, audācis, bold

SINGULAR

	Masc.	Fem.	Neuter
Nom.	audāx	audāx	audāx
Voc.	audāx	audāx	audāx
Acc.	audācem	audācem	audāx
Gen.	audācis	audācis	audācis
Dat.	audācī	audācī	audācī
Abl.	audācī	audācī	audācī

PLURAL

	Masc.	Fem.	Neuter
Nom.	audācēs	audācēs	audāciă
Voc.	audācēs	audācēs	audāciă
Acc.	audācēs	audācēs	audāciă
Gen.	audācium	audācium	audācium
Dat.	audācibus	audācibus	audācibus
Abl.	audācibus	audācibus	audācibus

(b) ingēns, ingentis, huge

SINGULAR

	Masc.	Fem.	Neuter
Nom.	ingēns	ingēns	ingēns
Voc.	ingēns	ingēns	ingēns
Acc.	ingentem	ingentem	ingēns
Gen.	ingentis	ingentis	ingentis
Dat.	ingentī	ingentī	ingentī
Abl.	ingentī	ingentī	ingentī

PLURAL

	Masc.	Fem.	Neuter
Nom.	ingentēs	ingentēs	ingentiă
Voc.	ingentēs	ingentēs	ingentiă
Acc.	ingentēs	ingentēs	ingentiă
Gen.	ingentium	ingentium	ingentium
Dat.	ingentibus	ingentibus	ingentibus
Abl.	ingentibus	ingentibus	ingentibus

(c) **fortis, fortis, fortĕ,** brave

SINGULAR

	Masc.	Fem.	Neuter
Nom.	fortis	fortis	fortĕ
Voc.	fortis	fortis	fortĕ
Acc.	fortem	fortem	fortĕ
Gen.	fortis	fortis	fortis
Dat.	fortī	fortī	fortī
Abl.	fortī	fortī	fortī

PLURAL

	Masc.	Fem.	Neuter
Nom.	fortēs	fortēs	fortiă
Voc.	fortēs	fortēs	fortiă
Acc.	fortēs	fortēs	fortiă
Gen.	fortium	fortium	fortium
Dat.	fortibus	fortibus	fortibus
Abl.	fortibus	fortibus	fortibus

(d) **ācer, ācris, ācrĕ,** keen, eager

SINGULAR

	Masc.	Fem.	Neuter
Nom.	ācer	ācris	ācrĕ
Voc.	ācer	ācris	ācrĕ
Acc.	ācrem	ācrem	ācrĕ
Gen.	ācris	ācris	ācris
Dat.	ācrī	ācrī	ācrī
Abl.	ācrī	ācrī	ācrī

PLURAL

	Masc.	Fem.	Neuter
Nom.	ācrēs	ācrēs	ācriă
Voc.	ācrēs	ācrēs	ācriă
Acc.	ācrēs	ācrēs	ācriă
Gen.	ācrium	ācrium	ācrium
Dat.	ācribus	ācribus	ācribus
Abl.	ācribus	ācribus	ācribus

Note.—**Celer, celĕris, celĕrĕ,** swift, is declined like **ācer,** but keeps the **e** throughout.

(e) vetus, vetĕris, old

Singular

	Masc.	Fem.	Neuter
Nom.	vetus	vetus	vetus
Voc.	vetus	vetus	vetus
Acc.	veterem	veterem	vetus
Gen.	veteris	veteris	veteris
Dat.	veterī	veterī	veterī
Abl.	vetere	vetere	vetere

Plural

	Masc.	Fem.	Neuter
Nom.	veterēs	veterēs	veteră
Voc.	veterēs	veterēs	veteră
Acc.	veterēs	veterēs	veteră
Gen.	veterum	veterum	veterum
Dat.	veteribus	veteribus	veteribus
Abl.	veteribus	veteribus	veteribus

(f) dīvĕs, dīvitis, rich
(g) pauper, paupĕris, poor

	Singular Masc. Fem.	Plural Masc. Fem.	Singular Masc. Fem.	Plural Masc. Fem.
Nom.	dīvĕs	dīvitēs	pauper	pauperēs
Voc.	dīves	dīvitēs	pauper	pauperēs
Acc.	dīvitem	dīvitēs	pauperem	pauperēs
Gen.	dīvitis	dīvitum	pauperis	pauperum
Dat.	dīvitī	dīvitibus	pauperī	pauperibus
Abl.	dīvite	dīvitibus	paupere	pauperibus

III. NUMERALS

(a) Cardinal Numbers		(b) Ordinal Numbers	
1 I	ūnus, -a, -um	1st	prīmus, -a, -um
2 II	duŏ, -ae, -ŏ	2nd	secundus, -a, -um
3 III	trēs, trēs, trĭă	3rd	tertius, -a, -um
4 IV	quattuor	4th	quārtus, -a, -um
5 V	quīnque	5th	quīntus, -a, -um
6 VI	sex	6th	sextus, -a, -um
7 VII	septem	7th	septimus, -a, -um
8 VIII	octō	8th	octāvus, -a, -um
9 IX	nŏvem	9th	nōnus, -a, -um
10 X	dĕcem	10th	decimus, -a, -um

9

11 XI	ūndecim	11th	ūndecimus, -a, -um
12 XII	duŏdecim	12th	duŏdecimus, -a, -um
13 XIII	trĕdecim	13th	tertius decimus
14 XIV	quattuordecim	14th	quārtus decimus
15 XV	quīndecim	15th	quīntus decimus
16 XVI	sēdecim	16th	sextus decimus
17 XVII	septendecim	17th	septimus decimus
18 XVIII	duodēvīgintī	18th	duodēvīcēsimus, -a, -um
19 XIX	ūndēvīgintī	19th	ūndēvīcēsimus, -a, -um
20 XX	vīgintī	20th	vīcēsimus, -a, -um
30 XXX	trīgintā	30th	trīcēsimus, -a, -um
40 XL	quadrāgintā	40th	quadrāgēsimus, -a, -um
50 L	quīnquāgintā	50th	quīnquāgēsimus, -a, -um
60 LX	sexāgintā	60th	sexāgēsimus, -a, -um
70 LXX	septuāgintā	70th	septuāgēsimus, -a, -um
80 LXXX	octōgintā	80th	octōgēsimus, -a, -um
90 XC	nōnāgintā	90th	nōnāgēsimus, -a, -um
100 C	centum	100th	centēsimus, -a, -um
200 CC	ducentī, -ae, -a	200th	ducentēsimus, -a, -um
300 CCC	trecentī, -ae, -a	300th	trecentēsimus, -a, -um
400 CCCC	quadringentī, -ae,-a	400th	quadringentēsimus, -a, -um
500 D	quīngentī, -ae, -a	500th	quīngentēsimus, -a, -um
600 DC	sēscentī, -ae, -a	600th	sēscentēsimus, -a, -um
700 DCC	septingentī, -ae, -a	700th	septingentēsimus, -a, -um
800 DCCC	octingentī, -ae, -a	800th	octingentēsimus, -a, -um
900 DCCCC	nōngentī, -ae, -a	900th	nōngentēsimus, -a, -um
1000 M	mīlle	1000th	mīllēsimus, -a, -um
2000 MM	duŏ mīlia	2000th	bis mīllēsimus

(c) Declension of ūnus

	Masc.	Fem.	Neuter
Nom.	ūnus	ūna	ūnum
Acc.	ūnum	ūnam	ūnum
Gen.	ūnīus	ūnīus	ūnīus
Dat.	ūnī	ūnī	ūnī
Abl.	ūnō	ūnā	ūnō

(d) Declension of duŏ

	Masc.	Fem.	Neuter
Nom.	duŏ	duae	duŏ
Acc.	duŏs	duās	duŏ
Gen.	duŏrum	duārum	duŏrum
Dat.	duŏbus	duābus	duŏbus
Abl.	duŏbus	duābus	duŏbus

(e) Declension of **trēs**

	Masc.	*Fem.*	*Neuter*
Nom.	trēs	trēs	trĭă
Acc.	trēs	trēs	trĭă
Gen.	trĭum	trĭum	trĭum
Dat.	trĭbus	trĭbus	trĭbus
Abl.	trĭbus	trĭbus	trĭbus

Notes.—(1) Cardinals from **quattuor** to **centum** are indeclinable.

(2) The hundreds from **ducentī** to **nōngentī** are declined like the plural of **bonus, -a, -um** except that gen. plural ends in -**um**.

(3) Compounds between 20 and 100 are formed by putting first the smaller with **et**, or else the larger without **et**, e.g. twenty-six is **sex et vīgintī**, or **vīgintī sex.**

(4) Compounds above 100 are formed by putting the larger first with or without **et**, e.g. 305 is **trecentī (et) quīnque.**

(5) **Mīlle** is an indeclinable adjective, e.g. 1000 soldiers is **mīlle mīlitēs** ; of 1000 soldiers is **mīlle mīlitum.**

(6) **Mīlia** is a neuter plural noun declined like the plural of **cubīle.**

Hence, 2000 soldiers, **duŏ mīlia mīlitum.**

of   ,, ,,   **duŏrum mīlium mīlitum.**

with ,, ,,   **cum duŏbus mīlibus mīlit-um.**

(7) The ordinals are declined like **bonus, -a, -um.**

(8) The following are declined in the singular like **ūnus** ; their plural is regular,—**sōlus, -a, -um,** alone ; **tōtus, -a, -um,** whole ; **nūllus, -a, -um,** no, none ; **ūllus, -a, -um,** any ; **alius, -a, -ud,** other, another ; **alter, -era, -erum,** the other ; **neuter, -tra, -trum,** neither ; **uter, -tra, -trum ?** which of two ?

IV. COMPARISON OF ADJECTIVES

1. To form the comparative, change -**ī** or -**is** of the genitive singular into -**ior.**

   To form the superlative, change -**ī** or -**is** of the genitive singular into -**issimus.**

   e.g., **altus,** high, deep   **altior**   **altissimus**

2. Adjectives ending in -**er** form their comparative according to the rule, but form the superlative by adding -**rimus** to the nom. sing. masc. of the positive.

e.g. **mĭser**	**mĭserior**	**mĭserrimus**
nĭger	**nĭgrior**	**nĭgerrimus**

3. Six adjectives ending in **-ilis** are compared thus :

facilis, easy	**facilior**	**facillimus**
difficilis, difficult	**difficilior**	**difficillimus**
similis, like	**similior**	**simillimus**
dissimilis, unlike	**dissimilior**	**dissimillimus**
gracilis, thin, slender	**gracilior**	**gracillimus**
humilis, low, humble	**humilior**	**humillimus**

4. Adjectives ending in **-us** preceded by any vowel except **-u** are compared by means of the adverbs **magis**, more, and **maximē**, most.

e.g. **dubius**, doubtful	**magis dubius**	**maximē dubius**
idōneus, suitable	**magis idōneus**	**maximē idōneus**

But **antīquus,** ancient, is compared according to rule.

e.g. **antīquus**	**antīquior**	**antīquissimus**

5. The following are irregular :

bonus, good	**melior**	**optimus**
mălus, bad	**pēior**	**pessimus**
magnus, great	**māior**	**maximus**
parvus, small	**mĭnor**	**mĭnimus**
multus, much	**plūs**	**plūrimus**
multī, many	**plūrēs**	**plūrimī**

6. A comparative adjective is declined thus :

SINGULAR

	Masc.	*Fem.*	*Neuter*
Nom.	**fortior**	**fortior**	**fortius**
Voc.	**fortior**	**fortior**	**fortius**
Acc.	**fortiōrem**	**fortiōrem**	**fortius**
Gen.	**fortiōris**	**fortiōris**	**fortiōris**
Dat.	**fortiōrī**	**fortiōrī**	**fortiōrī**
Abl.	**fortiōre**	**fortiōre**	**fortiōre**

PLURAL

	Masc.	*Fem.*	*Neuter*
Nom.	**fortiōrēs**	**fortiōrēs**	**fortiōră**
Voc.	**fortiōrēs**	**fortiōrēs**	**fortiōră**
Acc.	**fortiōrēs**	**fortiōrēs**	**fortiōră**
Gen.	**fortiōrum**	**fortiōrum**	**fortiōrum**
Dat.	**fortiōribus**	**fortiōribus**	**fortiōribus**
Abl.	**fortiōribus**	**fortiōribus**	**fortiōribus**

V. COMPARISON OF ADVERBS

1. To form the comparative adverb, change **-ior** of the comparative adjective into **-ius**.

   To form the superlative adverb, change **-us** of the superlative adjective into **-ē**.

   e.g. altē, deeply   **altius**   **altissimē**

altē, deeply	**altius**	**altissimē**
pulchrē, beautifully	**pulchrius**	**pulcherrimē**
facilē, easily	**facilius**	**facillimē**
breviter, briefly	**brevius**	**brevissimē**
sapienter, wisely	**sapientius**	**sapientissimē**

2. The following are irregular :

běně, well	**melius**	**optimē**
mălě, badly	**pēius**	**pessimē**
paulum, little	**minus**	**minimē**
multum, much	**plūs**	**plūrimum**
magnŏpere, greatly	**magis**	**maximē**
diū, for a long time	**diūtius**	**diūtissimē**
saepě, often	**saepius**	**saepissimē**

VI. PRONOUNS

1. PERSONAL PRONOUNS

	ego, I		**tū,** you	
	SINGULAR	PLURAL	SINGULAR	PLURAL
Nom.	ego	nōs	tū	vōs
Acc.	mē	nōs	tē	vōs
Gen.	meī	nostrī, nostrum	tuī	vestrī, vestrum
Dat.	mihi	nōbīs	tibi	vōbīs
Abl.	mē	nōbīs	tē	vōbīs

2. DEMONSTRATIVE PRONOUNS

(a) **is, ěǎ, id** (*pron.*), he, she, it ; (*adj.*) that

	SINGULAR			PLURAL		
	Masc.	*Fem.*	*Neuter*	*Masc.*	*Fem.*	*Neuter*
Nom.	is	ěǎ	id	ěī (īī)	ěae	ěǎ
Acc.	ěum	ěam	id	ěōs	ěās	ěǎ
Gen.	eius	eius	eius	ěōrum	ěārum	ěōrum
Dat.	ěī	ěī	ěī	ěīs (īīs)	ěīs (īīs)	ěīs (īīs)
Abl.	ěō	ěā	ěō	ěīs (īīs)	ěīs (īīs)	ěīs (īīs)

(b) hīc, haec, hōc, this

	SINGULAR			PLURAL		
	Masc.	*Fem.*	*Neuter*	*Masc.*	*Fem.*	*Neuter*
Nom.	hic	haec	hoc	hī	hae	haec
Acc.	hunc	hanc	hoc	hōs	hās	haec
Gen.	huius	huius	huius	hōrum	hārum	hōrum
Dat.	huĭc	huĭc	huĭc	hīs	hīs	hīs
Abl.	hōc	hāc	hōc	hīs	hīs	hīs

(c) ille, illa, illud, that

	SINGULAR			PLURAL		
	Masc.	*Fem.*	*Neuter*	*Masc.*	*Fem.*	*Neuter*
Nom.	ille	illa	illud	illī	illae	illă
Acc.	illum	illam	illud	illōs	illās	illă
Gen.	illīus	illīus	illīus	illōrum	illārum	illōrum
Dat.	illī	illī	illī	illīs	illīs	illīs
Abl.	illō	illā	illō	illīs	illīs	illīs

(d) īdem, eădem, ĭdem, the same

SINGULAR

	Masc.	*Fem.*	*Neuter*
Nom.	īdem	eădem	ĭdem
Acc.	eundem	eandem	ĭdem
Gen.	ēiusdem	ēiusdem	ēiusdem
Dat.	eīdem	eīdem	eīdem
Abl.	eōdem	eādem	eōdem

PLURAL

	Masc.	*Fem.*	*Neuter*
Nom.	eīdem	eaedem	eădem
Acc.	eōsdem	eāsdem	eădem
Gen.	eōrundem	eārundem	eōrundem
Dat.	eīsdem	eīsdem	eīsdem
Abl.	eīsdem	eīsdem	eīsdem

3. REFLEXIVE PRONOUNS

(a) **mē,** myself   (b) **tē,** yourself   (c) **sē,** himself, herself, itself, themselves

	SINGULAR	PLURAL	SINGULAR	PLURAL	SINGULAR AND PLURAL
Acc.	mē	nōs	tē	vōs	sē
Gen.	meī	nostrī, nostrum	tuī	vestrī, vestrum	suī
Dat.	mihi	nōbīs	tibi	vōbīs	sibi
Abl.	mē	nōbīs	tē	vōbīs	sē

4. THE EMPHASISING PRONOUN

ipse, ipsa, ipsum, self

SINGULAR

	Masc.	Fem.	Neuter
Nom.	ipse	ipsa	ipsum
Acc.	ipsum	ipsam	ipsum
Gen.	ipsīus	ipsīus	ipsīus
Dat.	ipsī	ipsī	ipsī
Abl.	ipsō	ipsā	ipsō

PLURAL

	Masc.	Fem.	Neuter
Nom.	ipsī	ipsae	ipsă
Acc.	ipsōs	ipsās	ipsă
Gen.	ipsōrum	ipsārum	ipsōrum
Dat.	ipsīs	ipsīs	ipsīs
Abl.	ipsīs	ipsīs	ipsīs

5. THE RELATIVE PRONOUN

quī, quae, quod, who, which

	Masc.	Fem.	Neuter	Masc.	Fem.	Neuter
	SINGULAR			PLURAL		
Nom.	quī	quae	quod	quī	quae	quae
Acc.	quem	quam	quod	quōs	quās	quae
Gen.	cuius	cuius	cuius	quōrum	quārum	quōrum
Dat.	cuī	cuī	cuī	quibus	quibus	quibus
Abl.	quō	quā	quō	quibus	quibus	quibus

6. THE INTERROGATIVE PRONOUN

quis, who? quid, what?

	Masc.	Fem.	Neuter	Masc.	Fem.	Neuter
	SINGULAR			PLURAL		
Nom.	quis	quis	quid	quī	quae	quae
Acc.	quem	quam	quid	quōs	quās	quae
Gen.	cuius	cuius	cuius	quōrum	quārum	quōrum
Dat.	cuī	cuī	cuī	quibus	quibus	quibus
Abl.	quō	quā	quō	quibus	quibus	quibus

Note.—The interrogative adjective **quī, quae, quod,** what? is declined like the relative pronoun.

7. POSSESSIVE ADJECTIVES AND PRONOUNS

1st person **meus, mea, meum,** my, mine (voc. sing. masc., **mī**). **noster, nostra, nostrum,** our, ours.

2nd person **tuus, tua, tuum,** your, yours (belonging to you, *sing.*).
vester, vestra, vestrum, your, yours (belonging to you, *pl.*).

3rd person **eius** (gen. sing. of **is, ea, id**), his, her, its.
eōrum, eārum (gen. pl. of **is, ea, id**), their.
suus, sua, suum, his own, her own, its own, their own (indicating that which belongs to subject of nearest verb).

VII. VERBS

1. THE IRREGULAR VERB **sum, esse, fuī,** to be

INDICATIVE MOOD

Present Tense		*Perfect Tense*	
sum	sumus	fú-ī	fú-imus
es	estis	fu-istī	fu-istis
est	sunt	fú-it	fu-ērunt

Future Tense		*Future Perfect Tense*	
érō	érimus	fú-erō	fu-erimus
éris	éritis	fú-eris	fu-eritis
érit	érunt	fú-erit	fú-erint

Imperfect Tense		*Pluperfect Tense*	
éram	érāmus	fú-eram	fu-erāmus
érās	érātis	fú-erās	fu-erātis
érat	érant	fú-erat	fú-erant

SUBJUNCTIVE MOOD

Present Tense		*Perfect Tense*	
sim	sīmus	fú-erim	fu-erīmus
sīs	sītis	fú-erīs	fu-erītis
sit	sint	fú-erit	fu-erint

Imperfect Tense		*Pluperfect Tense*	
éssem	essēmus	fu-íssem	fu-issēmus
éssēs	essētis	fu-íssēs	fu-issētis
ésset	éssent	fu-ísset	fu-íssent

IMPERATIVE

ĕs, be (thou) ; **éste,** be (ye)

INFINITIVES

Pres. **esse,** to be
Perf. **fuisse,** to have been
Fut. **fore** or **futūrus esse,** to be about to be

PARTICIPLE

Fut. **futūrus, -a, -um,** about to be

2. The Irregular Verb

possum, posse, pŏtuī, to be able

Indicative Mood		Subjunctive Mood	
Present Tense		*Present Tense*	
póssum	póssŭmus	póssim	possīmus
pótes	potéstis	póssīs	possītis
pótest	póssunt	póssit	póssint

Future Tense	
poterō	poterimus
poteris	poteritis
poterit	poterunt

Imperfect Tense		*Imperfect Tense*	
poteram	poterāmus	póssem	possēmus
poterās	poterātis	póssēs	possētis
poterat	poterant	pósset	póssent

Perfect Tense		*Perfect Tense*	
potuī	potuimus	potuerim	potuerīmus
potuistī	potuistis	potuerīs	potuerītis
potuit	potuērunt	potuerit	potuerint

Future Perfect Tense	
potuerō	potuerimus
potueris	potueritis
potuerit	potuerint

Pluperfect Tense		*Pluperfect Tense*	
potueram	potuerāmus	potuissem	potuissēmus
potuerās	potuerātis	potuissēs	potuissētis
potuerat	potuerant	potuisset	potuissent

Infinitives

Pres. **posse**, to be able
Perf. **potuisse**, to have been able

Participle

Pres. **potēns, -ntis** (*used only as adj.* =powerful)

3. REGULAR VERBS

INDICATIVE MOOD

Present Indicative Active

ám-ō	ámā-s	áma-t	amā-mus	amā-tis	áma-nt
mone-ō	monē-s	mone-t	monē-mus	monē-tis	mone-nt
reg-ō	reg-is	reg-it	reg-imus	reg-itis	reg-unt
capi-ō	cap-is	cap-it	cap-imus	cap-itis	capi-unt
audi-ō	audī-s	audi-t	audī-mus	audī-tis	audi-unt

Future Indicative Active

amā-
monē- } bō   -bis   -bit   -bimus   -bitis   -bunt

reg-
capi- } am   -ēs   -et   -ēmus   -ētis   -ent
audi-

Imperfect Indicative Active

amā-
monē- } bam   -bās   -bat   -bāmus   -bātis   -bant

reg-
capi- } ēbam   -ēbās   -ēbat   -ēbāmus   -ēbātis   -ēbant
audi-

Perfect Indicative Active

amāv-
monu-
rēx-   } ī   -istī   -it   -imus   -istis   -ērunt
cēp-
audīv-

Future Perfect Indicative Active

amāv-
monu-
rēx-   } erō   -eris   -erit   -erimus   -eritis   -erint
cēp-
audīv-

Pluperfect Indicative Active

amāv-
monu-
rēx-   } eram   -erās   -erat   -erāmus   -erātis   -erant
cēp-
audīv-

Present Indicative Passive

ám-or	amā-ris	amā-tur	amā-mur	amā-minī	ama-ntur
móne-or	monē-ris	monē-tur	monē-mur	monē-minī	mone-ntur
reg-or	reg-ĕris	reg-ĭtur	reg-ĭmur	reg-ĭminī	reg-untur
capi-or	cap-ĕris	cap-ĭtur	cap-ĭmur	cap-ĭminī	capĭ-untur
audi-or	audī-ris	audī-tur	audī-mur	audī-minī	audĭ-untur

Future Indicative Passive

amā-
monē- } bor   -beris   -bitur   -bimur   -biminī   -buntur

reg-
capi- } ar   -ēris   -ētur   -ēmur   -ēminī   -entur
audi-

Imperfect Indicative Passive

amā-
monē- } bar   -bāris   -bātur   -bāmur   -bāminī   -bantur

reg-
capi- } ēbar   -ēbāris   -ēbātur   -ēbāmur -ēbāminī -ēbantur
audi-

Perfect Indicative Passive

amātus
monitus   amātī
rēctus } sum es   monitī
captus   est   rēctī } sumus estis
audītus   captī   sunt
                   audītī

Future Perfect Indicative Passive

amātus
monitus   amātī
rēctus } erō eris monitī
captus   erit   rēctī } erimus eritis
audītus   captī   erunt
                   audītī

Pluperfect Indicative Passive

amātus
monitus   amātī
rēctus } eram erās monitī
captus   erat   rēctī } erāmus erātis
audītus   captī   erant
                   audītī

Subjunctive Mood

Present Subjunctive Active

| am- | em | -ēs | -et | -ēmus | -ētis | -ent |

| mone-
reg-
capi-
audi- } | am | -ās | -at | -āmus | -ātis | -ant |

Imperfect Subjunctive Active

| amā-
monē-
rege-
cape-
audī- } | rem | -rēs | -ret | -rēmus | -rētis | -rent |

Perfect Subjunctive Active

| amāv-
monu-
rēx-
cēp-
audīv- } | erim | -erīs | -erit | -erīmus | -erītis | -erint |

Pluperfect Subjunctive Active

| amāv-
monu-
rēx-
cēp-
audīv- } | issem | -issēs | -isset | -issēmus | -issētis | -issent |

Present Subjunctive Passive

| am- | er | -ēris | -ētur | -ēmur | -ēminī | -entur |

| mone-
reg-
capi-
audi- } | ar | -āris | -ātur | -āmur | -āminī | -antur |

Imperfect Subjunctive Passive

| amā-
monē-
rege-
cape-
audī- } | rer | -rēris | -rētur | -rēmur | -rēminī | -rentur |

Perfect Subjunctive Passive

| amātus
monitus
rēctus
captus
audītus } | sim sīs
sit | | amātī
monitī
rēctī
captī
audītī } | sīmus sītis
sint |

Pluperfect Subjunctive Passive

| amātus monitus rēctus captus audītus | essem essēs esset | amātī monitī rēctī captī audītī | essēmus essētis essent |

IMPERATIVE MOOD

ACTIVE

amā	amāte
monē	monēte
rege	regite
cape	capite
audī	audīte

PASSIVE

amāre	amāminī
monēre	monēminī
regere	regiminī
capere	capiminī
audīre	audīminī

INFINITIVE MOOD

Pres. Act.	*Perf. Act.*	*Fut. Act.*
amāre monēre regere capere audīre	amāv- monu- rēx- cēp- audīv- }-issc	amāt- monit- rēct- capt- audīt- }-ūrus esse

Pres. Pass.	*Perf. Pass.*	*Fut. Pass.*
amārī monērī regī capī audīrī	amātus monitus rēctus captus audītus }esse	amātum monitum rēctum captum audītum }īrī

PARTICIPLES

Pres. Act.	*Fut. Act.*	*Perf. Pass.*
amāns, -ntis monēns, -ntis regēns, -ntis capiēns, -ntis audiēns, -ntis	amāt- monit- rēct- capt- audīt- }-ūrus, -a, -um	amātus, -a, -um monitus, -a, -um rēctus, -a, -um captus, -a, -um audītus, -a, -um

4. Irregular Verbs

> vŏlō, velle, vŏluī, to wish, to be willing
> nōlō nōlle, nōluī, to be unwilling, to refuse
> mālō, mālle, māluī, to prefer
> eō, īre, īvī, ĭtum, to go
> fīō, fĭĕrī, factus sum, to be made, to become

Indicative Mood

Present Tense

vŏlō	nōlō	mālō	éō	fīō
vīs	nōn vīs	māvīs	īs	fīs
vult	nōn vult	māvult	it	fit
volŭmus	nōlŭmus	mālŭmus	īmus	—
vultis	nōn vultis	māvultis	ītis	—
vŏlunt	nōlunt	mālunt	éunt	fīunt

Future Tense

vŏlam	nōlam	mālam	ībō	fīam
vŏlēs	nōlēs	mālēs	ībis	fīēs
etc.	etc.	etc.	etc.	etc.

Imperfect Tense

vŏlēbam	nōlēbam	mālēbam	ībam	fīēbam
vŏlēbās	nōlēbās	mālēbās	ībās	fīēbās
etc.	etc.	etc.	etc.	etc.

Perfect Tense

vŏluī	nōluī	māluī	īvī	factus sum
vŏluistī	nōluistī	māluistī	īvistī	factus es
etc.	etc.	etc.	etc.	etc.

Future Perfect Tense

vŏluerō	nōluerō	māluerō	īverō	factus erō
vŏlueris	nōlueris	mālueris	īveris	factus eris
etc.	etc.	etc.	etc.	etc.

Pluperfect Tense

vŏlueram	nōlueram	mālueram	īveram	factus eram
vŏluerās	nōluerās	māluerās	īverās	factus erās
etc.	etc.	etc.	etc.	etc.

SUBJUNCTIVE MOOD

Present Tense

vĕlim	nōlim	mālim	eam	fīam
vĕlīs	nōlīs	mālīs	eās	fīās
vĕlit	nōlit	mālit	eat	fīat
vĕlīmus	nōlīmus	mālīmus	eāmus	fīāmus
vĕlītis	nōlītis	mālītis	eātis	fīātis
vĕlint	nōlint	mālint	eant	fīant

Imperfect Tense

vellem	nōllem	māllem	īrem	fīĕrem
vellēs	nōllēs	māllēs	īrēs	fīĕrēs
etc.	etc.	etc.	etc.	etc.

Perfect Tense

vŏluerim	nōluerim	māluerim	īverim	factus sim
vŏluerīs	nōluerīs	māluerīs	īverīs	factus sīs
etc.	etc.	etc.	etc.	etc.

Pluperfect Tense

vŏluissem	nōluissem	māluissem	īvissem	factus essem
vŏluissēs	nōluissēs	māluissēs	īvissēs	factus essēs
etc.	etc.	etc.	etc.	etc.

IMPERATIVE

—	nōlī	—	ī	—
—	nōlīte	—	īte	—

INFINITIVES

Present

vĕlle	nōlle	mālle	īre	fīĕrī

Future

—	—	—	itūrus esse	factum īrī

Perfect

vŏluisse	nōluisse	māluisse	īvisse	factus esse

PARTICIPLES

Present

vŏlēns	nōlēns	—	iēns, euntis	—

Future

—	—	—	itūrus	—

Perfect

—	—	—	—	factus, -a, -um

5. THE IRREGULAR VERB

ferō, ferre, tŭlī, lātum, to bear

INDICATIVE MOOD: ACTIVE AND PASSIVE

ACTIVE		PASSIVE	
Present Tense			
ferō	ferimus	feror	ferimur
fers	fertis	ferris	feriminī
fert	ferunt	fertur	feruntur

Future Tense			
feram	ferēmus	ferar	ferēmur
ferēs	ferētis	ferēris	ferēminī
feret	ferent	ferētur	ferentur

Imperfect Tense			
ferēbam	ferēbāmus	ferēbar	ferēbāmur
ferēbās	ferēbātis	ferēbāris	ferēbāminī
ferēbat	ferēbant	ferēbātur	ferēbantur

Perfect Tense			
tulī	tulimus	lātus sum	lātī sumus
tulistī	tulistis	lātus es	lātī estis
tulit	tulērunt	lātus est	lātī sunt

Future Perfect Tense			
tulerō	tulerimus	lātus erō	lātī erimus
tuleris	tuleritis	lātus eris	lātī eritis
tulerit	tulerint	lātus erit	lātī erunt

Pluperfect Tense			
tuleram	tulerāmus	lātus eram	lātī erāmus
tulerās	tulerātis	lātus erās	lātī erātis
tulerat	tulerant	lātus erat	lātī erant

SUBJUNCTIVE MOOD: ACTIVE AND PASSIVE

ACTIVE   PASSIVE

Present Tense

feram	ferāmus	ferar	ferāmur
ferās	ferātis	ferāris	ferāminī
ferat	ferant	ferātur	ferantur

Imperfect Tense

ferrem	ferrēmus	ferrer	ferrēmur
ferrēs	ferrētis	ferrēris	ferrēminī
ferret	ferrent	ferrētur	ferrentur

Perfect Tense

tulerim	tulerīmus	lātus sim	lātī sīmus
tulerīs	tulerītis	lātus sīs	lātī sītis
tulerit	tulerint	lātus sit	lātī sint

Pluperfect Tense

tulissem	tulissēmus	lātus essem	lātī essēmus
tulissēs	tulissētis	lātus essēs	lātī essētis
tulisset	tulissent	lātus esset	lātī essent

IMPERATIVE: ACTIVE AND PASSIVE

ACTIVE	PASSIVE
2nd Sing. fer	ferre
„ Plur. ferte	feriminī

INFINITIVES: ACTIVE AND PASSIVE

ACTIVE	PASSIVE
Pres. ferre	ferrī
Fut. lātūrus esse	lātum īrī
Perf. tulisse	lātus esse

PARTICIPLES: ACTIVE AND PASSIVE

ACTIVE	PASSIVE
Pres. ferēns, -ntis	—
Fut. lātūrus, -a, -um	—
Perf. —	lātus, -a, -um

6. The Deponent Verb

ūtor, ūtī, ūsus sum, to use

Indicative Mood		Subjunctive Mood	
Present Tense		*Present Tense*	
ūtor	ūtĭmur	ūtar	ūtāmur
ūtĕris	ūtĭminī	ūtāris	ūtāminī
ūtĭtur	ūtuntur	ūtātur	ūtantur
Future Tense			
ūtar	ūtēmur		
ūtēris	ūtēminī		
ūtētur	ūtentur		
Imperfect Tense		*Imperfect Tense*	
ūtēbar	ūtēbāmur	ūtĕrer	ūtĕrēmur
ūtēbāris	ūtēbāminī	ūtĕrēris	ūtĕrēminī
ūtēbātur	ūtēbantur	ūtĕrētur	ūtĕrentur
Perfect Tense		*Perfect Tense*	
ūsus sum	ūsī sumus	ūsus sim	ūsī sīmus
ūsus es	ūsī estis	ūsus sīs	ūsī sītis
ūsus est	ūsī sunt	ūsus sit	ūsī sint
Future Perfect Tense			
ūsus erō	ūsī erimus		
ūsus eris	ūsī eritis		
ūsus erit	ūsī erunt		
Pluperfect Tense		*Pluperfect Tense*	
ūsus eram	ūsī erāmus	ūsus essem	ūsī essēmus
ūsus erās	ūsī erātis	ūsus essēs	ūsī essētis
ūsus erat	ūsī erant	ūsus esset	ūsī essent

Imperative

ūtĕrĕ, use (thou) ; ūtĭminī, use (ye)

Infinitives

Pres. ūtī, to use
Fut. ūsūrus esse, to be about to use
Perf. ūsus esse, to have used

Participles

Pres. ūtēns, -ntis, using
Fut. ūsūrus, -a, -um, about to use
Perf. ūsus, -a, -um, having used

SPECIAL VOCABULARIES

PRELIMINARY EXERCISES

A

aedificium, -iī, *n.*, building
bōs, bǒvis, *c.*, ox, cow
cubīle, -is, *n.*, bed
lūdus, -ī, *m.*, school, game
parēns, -entis, *c.*, parent
rīsus, -ūs, *m.*, smile
stultitia, -ae, *f.*, foolishness, folly
vōx, vōcis, *f.*, voice
vultus, -ūs, *m.*, expression, countenance
castīgō, -āre, -āvī, -ātum, chide, rebuke, scold
dēlectō, -āre, -āvī, -ātum, delight
intrō, -āre, -āvī, -ātum, enter

poenās dō, dare, dedī, datum, to pay the penalty, to be punished
trahō, -ere, trāxī, tractum, to drag, draw
salūtō, -āre, -āvī, -ātum, to greet, salute
īgnāvus, -a, -um, idle, lazy *coward*
trux, trucis, grim
crās (*adv.*), to-morrow
enim (*conj.*, 2nd word in clause), for *(nam — 1st word of sentence — at clause)*
sērō (*adv.*), late, too late
hodiē (*adv.*), to-day
igitur (*conj.*, 2nd word in clause), therefore

B

aurum, -ī, *n.*, gold
cēna, -ae, *f.*, dinner, *supper*
Mārcus, -ī, *m.*, Marcus
moenia, -ium, *n.pl.*, walls (of city)
pila, -ae, *f.*, ball
senex, senis, *m.*, old man
tempus, -oris, *n.*, time
vestīmentum, -ī, *n.*, garment;
pl. clothes
vīcus, -ī, *m.*, street
vīlla, -ae, *f.*, country house
agō, agere, ēgī, āctum (*with* dē *and abl.*), to discuss
coniciō, -ere, -iēcī, -iectum, to throw

reddō, -ere, reddidī, redditum, to restore, give back
sepeliō, -īre, -īvī, sepultum, to bury
tōtus esse in, to be engrossed in
dēfessus, -a, -um, tired, weary
immemor, -oris, forgetful of *+gen.*
īrātus, -a, -um, angry
novus, -a, -um, new
sordidus, -a, -um, dirty
stultus, -a, -um, foolish
extrā (*prep. gov. acc.*), outside
mehercule !, upon my word !
quod, because

① principal meal of Romans, taken about 3.0 or 4.0 p.m.

C

iūstitia, -ae, *f.*, justice

scientia, -ae, *f.*, knowledge

(3) colō, -ere, -uī, cultum, to cultivate

alius, -ia, -iud, other, another

P244 — nōbilis, -is, -e, noble (cf *fortis*)

vīcīnus, -a, -um, neighbouring

vīcīnus, -ī, *m.*, neighbour

fortāsse, perhaps

nisi, unless, if not

ōlim, once, once upon a time, formerly, some day

prō (*prep. gov. abl.*), for, on behalf of

quidem, indeed

umquam, ever

Britannī, -ōrum, *m.pl.*, the Britons

Gallī, -ōrum, *m.pl.*, the Gauls

Graecī, -ōrum, *m.pl.*, the Greeks

Poenī, -ōrum, *m.pl.*, the Carthaginians

D

dolor, -ōris, *m.*, grief, pain

honōs, -ōris, *m.*, honour

īgnāvia, -ae, *f.*, idleness, laziness, cowardice

īra, -ae, *f.*, anger

— līberī, -ōrum, *m.pl.*, children

pondus, -eris, *n.*, mass, weight

pretium, -iī, *n.*, reward

pulvis, -eris, *m.*, dust

rīpa, -ae, *f.*, bank (of a river)

scūtum, -ī, *n.*, shield

signum, -ī, *n.*, standard, *signal*

virgō, -inis, *f.*, maiden

vulnus, -eris, *n.*, wound

collocō, -āre, -āvī, -ātum, to place

custōdiō, -īre, -īvī, -ītum, to guard

inquit (*pl.* inquiunt), says, *or* said he, she, it

inveniō, -īre, -vēnī, -ventum, to find

lūdō, -ere, lūsī, lūsum, to play

aeternus, -a, -um, eternal, everlasting

scelestus, -a, -um, wicked

ubi, when

sine (*prep. gov. abl.*), without

nusquam, nowhere

campus, -ī, *m.*, a plain

Campus Mārtius (*or* Campus), the Campus Martius

E

Cicerō, -ōnis, *m.*, Cicero

sella, -ae, *f.*, seat, chair

uxor, -ōris, *f.*, wife

vir, virī, *m.*, man, husband

comparō, -āre, -āvī, -ātum, to procure

P245 dīves, -itis, rich

iūstus, -a, -um, just

P245 pauper, -eris, poor

sollicitus, -a, -um, anxious, troubled

satis (*indeclinable*), enough

sīcut, just as

F

centuriō, -iōnis, *m.*, centurion
fundus, -ī, *m.*, farm
hōra, -ae, *f.*, hour
mandāta, -ōrum, *n.pl.*, instructions
sacerdōs, -ōtis, *m.*, priest

dēspērō, -āre, -āvī, -ātum, to despair
īgnōrō, -āre, -āvī, -ātum, not to know
rīdeō, -ēre, rīsī, rīsum, to laugh
dūrus, -a, -um, hard, harsh
sapiēns, -entis, wise

G

arx, arcis, *f.*, citadel
forum, -ī, *n.*, forum, market place
exerceō, -ēre, -uī, -itum, to exercise, train
sedeō, -ēre, sēdī, sessum, to sit

deinde, afterwards, then, thereafter
intereā, meanwhile, in the meantime
prīmum, first, in the first place

EXERCISE 1

conveniō, -īre, -vēnī, -ventum, to come together, assemble, gather
vocō, -āre, -āvī, -ātum, to call, invite
īnfēstus, -a, -um, hostile, dangerous
agmen, -inis, *n.*, army (in marching order)
latrō, -ōnis, *m.*, robber
cīvitās, -ātis, *f.*, state
vinculum, -ī, *n.*, bond, fetter ; in vincula conicere, to throw into prison, put in chains

idōneus, -a, -um, suitable
petō, -ere, petīvī, petītum, to seek, ask
agō, -ere, ēgī, āctum, to do, act ; agere dē, to discuss ; grātiās agere, to thank
sī, if
facilis, -is, -e, easy
niger, -ra, -rum, black
perterritus, -a, -um, terrified, thoroughly frightened
ōrātiō, -iōnis, *f.*, speech
Syrus, -ī, *m.*, Syrus (a slave's name)

EXERCISE 2

condō, -ere, -didī, -ditum, to found
lūcus, -ī, *m.*, a grove
asȳlum, -ī, *n.*, a place of refuge
societās, -ātis, *f.*, alliance
cōnūbium, -iī, *n.*, right of marriage *conubium*
benignē (*adv.*), kindly
sīc, thus
spectāculum, -ī, *n.*, spectacle, show

mēns, mentis, *f.*, mind
dēfīgō, -ere, -fīxī, -fīxum, to fix
salvē, salvēte, hail ! good morning ! good day !
quid agis ? how do you do ?
euge ! bravo ! well done !
gaudium, -iī, *n.*, joy
iānua, -ae, *f.*, door
trīstis, -is, -e, sad — *p. 244*
causa, -ae, *f.*, cause

Proper Names

Rōmulus, -ī, *m.*, Romulus.
Mōns Capitōlīnus, the Capitoline Hill.

Sabīnī, -ōrum, *m.pl.*, the Sabines.
Sabīnus, -a, -um, Sabine.
Lūcia, -ae, *f.*, Lucia.

EXERCISE 3

armilla, -ae, *f.*, bracelet
ānulus, -ī, *m.*, ring
sinister, -tra, -trum, left
prōditiō, -iōnis, *f.*, treachery, betrayal
proelium committō, -ere, -mīsī, -missum, to join battle
dirimō, -ere, -ēmī, -ēmptum, break off
aciēs, -iēī, *f.*, line of battle
socer, -erī, *m.*, father-in-law
gener, -erī, *m.*, son-in-law

sanguis, -inis, *m.*, blood
maculō, -āre, -āvī, -ātum, to stain
vertō, -ere, vertī, versum, to turn
moveō, -ēre, mōvī, mōtum, to move
condiciō, -iōnis, *f.*, condition ; *pl.* terms
neglegō, -ere, -lēxī, -lēctum, to neglect
fortāsse, perhaps

Proper Names

Tatius, -iī, *m.*, Tatius.
Tarpēia, -ae, *f.*, Tarpeia.

Tarpēius, -ī, *m.*, Tarpeius.

EXERCISE 4

discēdō, -ere, -cessī, -cessum, to depart
relinquō, -ere, relīquī, relictum, to leave
sepeliō, -īre, -īvī, -ultum, to bury
aperiō, -īre, -uī, apertum, to open
claudō, -ere, clausī, clausum, to shut
ursa, -ae, *f.*, she-bear
Caesar, -aris, *m.*, Caesar
augeō, -ēre, auxī, auctum, to enlarge, increase

paulisper, for a short time
cōgitō, -āre, -āvī, -ātum, to think, ponder
fera, -ae, *f.*, wild beast
ferōx, -ōcis, fierce
colō, -ere, coluī, cultum, to worship
Ō mē miserum !, woe is me !, wretched man that I am !, hang it all !
rīsus, -ūs, *m.*, smile
umquam, ever

EXERCISE 5

dēnsus, -a, -um, thick, dense

nūbēs, -is, *f.*, cloud

tempestās, -ātis, *f.*, storm

posteā, afterwards, after

dēfleō, -ēre, -ēvī, -ētum, to lament, weep over

timor, -ōris, *m.*, fear

ūllus, -a, -um, any

caelum, -ī, *n.*, sky, heaven

ita, thus, so

cultus, -ūs, *m.*, worship

minus, less

prūdentia, -ae, *f.*, prudence, wisdom

fundāmentum, -ī, *n.*, foundation

āra, -ae, *f.*, altar

cōnsecrō, -āre, -āvī, -ātum, to consecrate

ārdeō, -ēre, ārsī, ārsum, to burn, be on fire

nōbilis, -is, -e, noble

creō, -āre, -āvī, -ātum, to appoint, elect

sella curūlis, sellae curūlis, *f.*, the curule chair

indicō, -āre, -āvī, -ātum, to mark, indicate

sermō, -ōnis, *m.*, talk, conversation

adiuvō, -āre, -iūvī, -iūtum, to help

neglegō, -ere, neglēxī, neglēctum, to neglect

PROPER NAMES

Quirīnus, -ī, *m.*, Quirinus, name given to Romulus after he became a god.

Ēgeria, -ae, *f.*, Egeria, a goddess who was supposed to give counsel to Numa.

Vesta, -ae, *f.*, Vesta, the goddess of the hearth.

Vestālis virgō, *f.*, a Vestal virgin. The Vestal virgins were noble maidens dedicated to the service of Vesta.

EXERCISE 6

aut, or ; aut . . . aut, either . . . or

cōgitātiō, -iōnis, *f.*, thought

doctus, -a, -um, learned

māchina, -ae, *f.*, engine

mīrābilis, -is, -e, wonderful

respondeō, -ēre, -ī, -sum, to reply, answer

secundus, -a, -um, second

vincō, -ere, vīcī, victum, to conquer

Syrācūsae, -ārum, *f.pl.*, Syracuse, largest city of Sicily

EXERCISE 7

nesciō, -īre, -īvī (iī), -ītum, I do not know

respōnsum, -ī, *n.*, reply

īnsignis, -is, -e, distinguished

taceō, -ēre, -uī, -itum, to be silent

īgnōrō, -āre, -āvī, -ātum, to be ignorant of

ruīna, -ae, *f.*, ruin

quiēs, -ētis, *f.*, rest

nepōs, -ōtis, *m.*, grandson

avus, -ī, *m.*, grandfather

trēdecim, thirteen

toga praetexta, togae praetextae, *f.*, the toga praetexta—purple bordered toga worn by Roman boys and magistrates

bulla, -ae, *f.*, the bulla—a kind of locket or charm worn by Roman boys

īnsignia, -ium, *n.pl.*, emblems, distinctions, decorations

locus, -ī, *m.*, place (*pl.* is loca)

siccō, -āre, -āvī, -ātum, to dry

nēmō, no one (*gen.* nūllīus ; *abl.*, nūllō)

Alba Longa, *f.,* Alba Longa, ancient town of Latium.

Ancus Mārtius, *m.,* Ancus Martius, fourth king of Rome.

Cloāca Maxima, *f.,* The Cloaca Maxima or great drain, drained the low ground between the Roman hills.

Latīnī, -ōrum, *m.pl.,* The Latini, inhabitants of Latium.

Pōns Sublicius, *m.,* the Pons Sublicius, or Bridge of Piles, most ancient bridge over Tiber, made of wood.

Tullus Hostīlius, *m.,* third king of Rome.

Tiberis, -is, *m.,* the Tiber.

Tarquinius Prīscus, *m.,* Tarquinius Priscus, fifth king of Rome.

EXERCISE 8

rēgia, -ae, *f.,* palace

dormiō, -īre, -īvī, -ītum, to sleep

videor, -ērī, vīsus sum, to seem

flamma, -ae, *f.,* flame.

contendō, -ere, -dī, -tum, to hasten

celeriter *(adv.),* quickly

excitō, -āre, -āvī, -ātum, to arouse, waken

suā sponte, of his own accord

sapienter *(adv.),* wisely

crūdēliter *(adv.),* cruelly

mītis, -is, -e, gentle, mild

pietās, -ātis, *f.,* duty, filial piety

scelus, -eris, *n.,* crime, wickedness

super *(prep. gov. acc.),* over, above

currus, -ūs, *m.,* chariot

scelerātus, -a, -um, accursed

antīquus, -a, -um, ancient

Lūcius Tarquinius, *m.,* Lucius Tarquinius, son of Tarquinius Priscus, and afterwards seventh king of Rome (Lucius Tarquinius Superbus).

Servius Tullius, *m.,* Servius Tullius, sixth king of Rome.

Tullia, -ae, *f.,* Tullia, daughter of Servius Tullius.

EXERCISE 9

audācia, -ae, *f.,* boldness

aditus, -ūs, *m.,* approach

cōnstantia, -ae, *f.,* firmness, resolution, constancy

cohors, -tis, *f.,* cohort

invīsus, -a, -um, hateful

magnopere *(adv.),* greatly

proximus, -a, -um, next, nearest

quīdam, quaedam, quoddam, a certain . . .

sollicitus, -a, -um, anxious, disturbed

statiō, -iōnis, *f.,* outpost

vīs *(acc.* **vim,** *abl.* **vī),** *f.,* force

EXERCISE 10

crūdēlis, -is, -e, cruel
praetereā, besides
superbus, -a, -um, proud
molestus, -a, -um, troublesome
anus, -ūs, *f.,* old woman
ōrāculum, -ī, *n.,* oracle
pretium, -iī, *n.,* price
sānus, -a, -um, sane, sound
tantus, -a, -um, so great
sordidus, -a, -um, dirty
inūtilis, -is, -e, useless

restō, -āre, -stitī, to be left over, remain
dēlīrō, -āre, -āvī, -ātum, to rave, be mad
sērius, -a, -um, serious
attentus, -a, -um, attentive
quid multa ?, to cut a long story short
suspīciō, -iōnis, *f.,* suspicion
convocō, -āre, -āvī, -ātum, to call together
perīculōsus, -a, -um, dangerous

Proper Name

Librī Sibyllīnī, *m.pl.,* the Sibylline books.

EXERCISE 11

cārus, -a, -um, dear
expellō, -ere, -pulī, -pulsum, to expel, banish, drive out
lībertās, -ātis, *f.,* liberty
rēgius, -a, -um, royal
nōn modo . . . sed etiam, not only . . . but also
addō, -ere, -didī, -ditum, to add
beneficium, -iī, *n.,* kindness
removeō, -ēre, -mōvī, -mōtum, to remove
metus, -ūs, *m.,* fear
sē abdicāre *(with abl.)* to resign from
cōnsulātus, -ūs, *m.,* consulship

nē . . . . quidem, not even
epistola, -ae, *f.,* letter
paene, almost
amor, -ōris, *m.,* love
līctor, -ōris, *m.,* lictor (attendant on Roman magistrate)
verberō, -āre, -āvī, -ātum, to beat
praeclārus, -a, -um, famous
ars, artis, *f.,* art
littera, -ae, *f.,* letter (of alphabet)
nunc, now (at present moment)
prūdēns, -entis, wise, prudent
rēs pūblica, reī pūblicae, *f.,* the state

EXERCISE 12

cūrō, -āre, -āvī, -ātum, to look after, to care for

condūcō, -ere, -dūxī, -ductum, to hire

cingō, -ere, cinxī, cinctum, to surround

cibus, -ī, m., food

dēsistō, -ere, -stitī, -stitum (*with* ā *and abl.*), to cease from

dīligēns, -tis, diligent

discō, -ere, didicī, to learn

ēducō, -āre, -āvī, -ātum, to bring up, to educate

fossa, -ae, f., ditch

hīc (*adv.*), here

inquam, I say

mercēs, -ēdis, f., pay, wages

ōtiōsus, -a, -um, at leisure

prandium, -iī, n., breakfast

praeceptor, -ōris, m., teacher

pecūnia, -ae, f., money

Rōstra, -ōrum, n.pl., The Rostra —the speaker's platform in the Forum

studeō, -ēre, -uī, to study

sub (*prep. gov. abl.*), under, beneath

vallum, -ī, n., rampart

valeō, -ēre, -uī, to be well, to be strong

studium, -iī, n., a study, pursuit

EXERCISE 13

plēbs, plēbis, f., the plebs, the common people

plēbēius, -ī, m., a plebeian

hūmānus, -a, -um, human

artus, -ūs, m., limb

venter, -tris, m., belly

medius, -a, -um, middle

ōs, ōris, n., mouth

dēns, dentis, m., tooth

quoque, also

operam dare ut, take pains that

famēs, -is, f., hunger

nūtriō, -īre, -īvī, -ītum, nourish

amīcitia, -ae, f., friendship

quasi, as if

discordia, -ae, f., discord, strife

concordia, -ae, f., concord, harmony

āvertō, -ere, -ī, āversum, turn away

tribūnus plēbis, m., tribune of the plebs

patricius, -iī, m., patrician

superbia, -ae, f., pride

tranquillus, -a, -um, quiet, tranquil

vītam agere, to pass one's life

discō, -ere, didicī, to learn

ibi, there

tenebrae, -ārum, f.pl., darkness

Proper Names

Mōns Sacer, The Sacred Mount, a hill about two miles from Rome.

Menēnius Agrippa, Menēniī Agrippae, m., Menenius Agrippa.

EXERCISE 14

terror, -ōris, *m.,* terror, fear

salūs, -ūtis, *f.,* safety

dictātor, -ōris, *m.,* dictator

nūdus, -a, -um, naked, lightly-clad

togātus, -a, -um, clad in the toga

sūdor, -ōris, *m.,* sweat

abstergeō, -ēre, abstersī, abstersum, to wipe away

postrīdiē, on the next day

iūssū, by command of

sōlis occāsus, -ūs, *m.,* sunset

armātus, -a, -um, armed

media nox, mediae noctis, *f.,* midnight

prīmō, at first

inclūdō, -ere, inclūsī, inclūsum, to shut in, enclose

rem gerō, -ere, gessī, gestum, carry on a fight

(sē) dēdō, -ere, dēdidī, dēditum, to surrender

dīmittō, -ere, -mīsī, -missum, to send away

glōria, -ae, *f.,* glory

ante (*prep. gov. acc.*), before

praemium, -iī, *n.,* reward, prize

dēpōnō, -ere, posuī, -positum, to lay aside

verbum, -ī, *n.,* word

Proper Names

Aequī, -ōrum, *m.pl.,* the Aequi, the Aequians, a people of ancient Italy.

Algidus, -ī, *m.,* Mt. Algidus, a high mountain near Rome.

EXERCISE 15

prīnceps, -cipis, *m.,* chief

interficiō, -ere, -fēcī, -fectum, to kill

īnferior, -iōris, lower, inferior

speciēs, -iēī, *f.,* appearance

abiciō, -ere, -iēcī, -iectum, to throw away

procul, far

dexter, -tra, -trum, right

perveniō, -īre, -vēnī, -ventum, to arrive

praeter (*prep. gov. acc.*), except

adventus, -ūs, *m.,* arrival

crūdēlis, -is, -e, cruel

magistrātus, -ūs, *m.,* magistrate

vestibulum, -ī, *n.,* porch, entrance, vestibule

dīgnitās, -ātis, *f.,* dignity

undique, on all sides

immōtus, -a, -um, motionless, unmoved, still

barba, -ae, *f.,* beard

permulceō, -ēre, -mulsī, -mulsum, to stroke

initium, -iī, *n.,* beginning

caedēs, -is, *f.,* slaughter, bloodshed

cēterī, -ae, -a, the rest

Proper Names

Allia, -ae, *f.,* The Allia, a little river in the Sabine territory, about eleven miles N. of Rome.

Alliēnsis, -is, -e, of, pertaining to, the Allia.

Clūsium, -iī, *n,* Clusium, town in Etruria.

Clūsīnī, -ōrum, *m.pl.,* the Clusini, the people of Clusium.

Capitōlium, -iī, *n.,* The Capitol, great temple of Jupiter at Rome ; also hill upon which it stood.

Gallicus, -a, -um, Gallic.

EXERCISE 16

dēiciō, -ere, dēiēcī, dēiectum, to hurl down, thrust down

exsilium, -iī, n., exile

imperō, -āre, -āvī, -ātum, to command

obsecrō, -āre, -āvī, -ātum, to beseech

ōrō, -āre, -āvī, -ātum, to pray

pānis, -is, m., bread

pōstulō, -āre, -āvī, -ātum, to demand

persuādeō, -ēre, -suāsī, -suāsum, to persuade

revocō, -āre, -āvī, -ātum, to recall

saxum, -ī, n., rock

turpis, -is, -e, base, disgraceful, ugly

vestīgium, -iī, n., trace, track, print, footprint

vetō, -āre, vetuī, vetitum, to forbid

EXERCISE 17

cōnstituō, -ere, -uī, -ūtum, to determine

prīma lūx, dawn

clādēs, -is, f., defeat

dēpellō, -ere, -pulī, -pulsum, to drive down, thrust down, hurl down

itaque, and so

obsidiō, -iōnis, f., siege

ascendō, -ere, ascendī, ascēnsum, to climb, to ascend

silentium, -iī, n., silence

summus, -a, -um, highest; summus mōns, the top of the mountain

ānser, -eris, m., goose

Iūnō, Iūnōnis, f., Juno

sacer, -ra, -rum, sacred

interrogō, -āre, -āvī, -ātum, ask (questions)

inopia, -ae, f., want, scarcity, lack

abstineō, -ēre, -uī, -tentum, to abstain from

clangor, -ōris, m., noise

āla, -ae, f., wing

strepitus, -ūs, m., din

dēturbō, -āre, -āvī, -ātum, throw down

cāsus, -ūs, m., fall

sternō, -ere, strāvī, strātum, to lay low

praeceps, -cipitis, headlong, steep

dictātōrem dīcere, appoint a dictator

iniūria, -ae, f., wrong, injury

inīquus, -a, -um, unfavourable, unfair

ferrum, -ī, n., iron, the sword

omnēs ad ūnum, to a man

PROPER NAMES

Brennus, -ī, m., Brennus, the leader of the Gauls who sacked Rome 390 B.C.

Camillus, -ī, m., Camillus, great Roman hero, captured Veii 396 B.C., exiled, but recalled to cope with Gauls, 390 B.C.

M. Manlius, defender of the Capitol, 390 B.C.

EXERCISE 18

vallis, -is, *f.,* valley

circumveniō, -īre, -vēnī, -ventum, to surround

tribūnus, -ī, *m.,* tribune

quadringentī, -ōrum, four hundred

convertō, -ere, -ī, -versum, to turn

reliquus, -a, -um, remaining, the remaining, the rest of

certus, -a, -um, certain

laus, laudis, *f.,* praise

suscipiō, -ere, -cēpī, -ceptum, to undertake

tūtus, -a, -um, safe

immortālis, -is, -e, immortal

fortūna, -ae, *f.,* fortune

pār, paris, equal

mortuus, -a, -um, dead

cōnfectus, -a, -um, exhausted

convalēscō, -ere, -valuī, grow well

corōna, -ae, *f.,* garland, crown; **corōna obsidiōnālis,** crown given for freeing army from siege, etc.

adhūc, hitherto, as yet

cōnficiō, -ere, -fēcī, -fectum, to complete, finish

quīndecim, fifteen

Proper Names

Atīlius Cālātīnus, Atilius Calatinus, Roman consul, beleaguered in Sicily.

Brundisium, -iī, *n.,* Brundisium, modern Brindisi, important seaport S.E. Italy.

Calpurnius, -iī, *m.,* Calpurnius, tribune of soldiers under Calatinus.

Graecia, -ae, *f.,* Greece.

Ītalia, -ae, *f.,* Italy.

EXERCISE 19

affirmō, -āre, -āvī, -ātum, to declare

comes, -itis, *c.,* companion

frīgus, -oris, *n.,* cold

grātus, -a, -um, popular, pleasing

humī, on the ground

lēgātiō, -iōnis, *f.,* embassy

linter, -tris, *f.,* boat

nūper, recently

opēs, -um, *f.pl.,* wealth, resources

putō, -āre, -āvī, -ātum, to think

tardē, slowly

sacrificō, -āre, -āvī, -ātum, to sacrifice

Proper Name

Carthāgō, -inis, *f.,* Carthage.

EXERCISE 20

iūrō, -āre, -āvī, -ātum, to swear
obtineō, -ēre, -uī, obtentum, to hold
cōnsēnsus, -ūs, *m.*, consent, agreement
calor, -ōris, *m.*, heat
pār, -is, equal
patientia, -ae, *f.*, endurance
sūmō, -ere, sūmpsī, sūmptum, to take
ultimus, -a, -um, last
vitium, -iī, *n.*, fault, failing

aequō, -āre, -āvī, -ātum, to match, equal
inhūmānus, -a, -um, inhuman
crūdēlitās, -ātis, *f.*, cruelty
perfidia, -ae, *f.*, treachery
sinus, -ūs, *m.*, fold
placeō, -ēre, -uī, -itum, to please
clāmō, -āre, -āvī, -ātum, to cry, shout
excutiō, -ere, excussī, excussum, to shake out
viātor, -ōris, *m.*, traveller

PROPER NAMES

Fabius, -iī, *m.*, Fabius.
Hamilcar, -is, *m.*, Hamilcar.
Hannibal, -is, *m.*, Hannibal.

Hasdrubal, -is, *m.*, Hasdrubal.
Hispānia, -ae, *f.*, Spain.
Saguntum, -ī, *n.*, Saguntum.

EXERCISE 21

iugum, -ī, *n.*, ridge
nix, nivis, *f.*, snow
ostendō, -ere, -ī, ostentum, to point out, show
prōmittō, -ere, -mīsī, -missum, to promise
plānus, -a, -um, level
prōclīvis, -is, -e, downhill
potestās, -ātis, *f.*, power
ascēnsus, -ūs, *m.*, ascent
angustus, -a, -um, narrow
lūbricus, -a, -um, slippery
āmittō, -ere, -mīsī, -missum, to lose
cadō, -ere, cecidī, cāsum, to fall
neque quidquam, and nothing

lāpsus, -ūs, *m.*, fall; terrae lāpsus, landslide
rupēs, -is, *f.*, crag, precipice, rock
frangō, -ere, frēgī, frāctum, to break
īnfundō, -ere, īnfūdī, īnfūsum, to pour upon
quīntus decimus, fifteenth
cōpiae, -ārum, *f.pl.*, forces
vīgintī, twenty
pedes, -itis, *m.*, infantryman
eques, -itis, *m.*, cavalryman
trīgintā, thirty
fidēs, -eī, *f.*, faith, loyalty
spērō, -āre, -āvī, -ātum, to hope
cupiō, -ere, -īvī, -ītum, to desire

PROPER NAMES

Alpēs, -ium, *f.pl.*, the Alps.
Āfrica, -ae, *f.*, Africa.
Scīpiō, -iōnis, *m.*, Scipio.

Circumpadānus, -a, -um, around the Po.

EXERCISE 22

effugiō, -ere, effūgī, to escape
fenestra, -ae, *f.*, window
īnsidiae, -ārum, *f.pl.*, ambush
obstō, -āre, -stitī, to stand in the way

saltus, -ūs, *m.*, pass, defile
sentiō, -īre, sēnsī, sēnsum, feel, realise

EXERCISE 23

lacus, -ūs, *m.*, lake
inde, thence
īnsurgō, -ere, īnsurrēxī, īnsur-rēctum, to rise up
aditus, -ūs, *m.*, approach
levis armātūra, *f.*, light-armed troops
circumdūcō, -ere, -dūxī, -ductum, to lead around
nebula, -ae, *f.*, mist
praetor, -ōris, *m.*, praetor
dē (*prep. gov. abl.*), down from

perturbō, -āre, -āvī, -ātum, to confuse
ubīque, everywhere, on all sides
circā (*prep. gov. acc.*), around
victima, -ae, *f.*, victim
Mānēs, -ium, *m.pl.*, spirits (of the dead)
tum vērō, then indeed
praecipitō, -āre, -āvī, -ātum, throw headlong
mātrōna, -ae, *f.*, matron, married woman
laetus, -a, -um, glad, joyful

PROPER NAMES

Cortōnēnsēs, -ium, *m.pl.*, the people of Cortona.
Lacus Trasumēnus, the Trasimene Lake.
M. Pompōnius, Marcus Pomponius.

EXERCISE 24

committō, -ere, -mīsī, -missum to entrust
levis, -is, -e, light
mīlle passūs, a mile ; *plur.* mīlia passuum, miles

vērus, -a, -um, true
ventus, -ī, *m.*, wind
Aenēās, -ae, *m.*, Aeneas

EXERCISE 25

ratiō, -iōnis, *f.,* plan, method

agmen, -inis, *n.,* column, army (in marching order)

prior, -ōris, previous, earlier

excipiō, -ere, -cēpī, -ceptum, to intercept, capture, take

impediō, -īre, -īvī, -ītum, to hinder

cunctātiō, -iōnis, *f.,* delay

quō ūsque tandem ? how far, pray ?

probō, -āre, -āvī, -ātum, to approve

temerārius, -a, -um, rash

instruō, -ere, -strūxī, -strūctum, to draw up

adversus, -a, -um, opposite, against, unfavourable

volvō, -ere, volvī, volūtum, to roll

caedō, -ere, cecīdī, caesum, to cut down, cut, slay

culpa, -ae, *f.,* blame

lacrima, -ae, *f.,* tear

frustrā, in vain

strāgēs, -is, *f.,* slaughter

vix, hardly, scarcely, with difficulty

Proper Names

Aemilius Paulus, Lucius Aemilius Paulus, one of the consuls for 216 B.C. killed in battle of Cannae in that year.

Cannae, -ārum, *f.pl.,* Cannae, village on the river Aufidus in Apulia ; near it Hannibal defeated Romans 216 B.C.

Lentulus, Cn. Cornelius Lentulus, tribune of cavalry at battle of Cannae; tried to assist Aemilius to escape.

Varrō, -ōnis, C. Terentius Varro, colleague of Aemilius in consulship for 216 B.C. ; engaged in battle with Hannibal at Cannae ; utterly defeated.

EXERCISE 26

palam, openly

novae cōpiae, *f.pl.,* reinforcements

retrahō, -ere, -trāxī, -tractum, to drag back

totiēns, so often

fugō, -āre, -āvī, -ātum, to put to flight

dēformitās, -ātis, *f.,* shamefulness

reditus, -ūs, *m.,* return

opprimō, -ere, oppressī, oppressum, to overwhelm

praesidium, -iī, *n.,* garrison, guard

simulō, -āre, -āvī, -ātum, to pretend

rōbur, -oris, *n.,* strength, ' flower of an army

lītus, -oris, *n.,* shore

cruentus, -a, -um, blood-stained

cōnsenēscō, -ere, -senuī, to grow old

accūsō, -āre, -āvī, -ātum, to accuse

dētrahō, -ere, -trāxī, -tractum, to drag away

recipiō, -ere, -cēpī, -ceptum, to take back ; **sē recipere,** to retreat, betake one's self

venēnum, -ī, *n.,* poison

Proper Names

Antiochus, -ī, *m.,* Antiochus, king of Syria; he gave shelter to Hannibal in 195 B.C.

Hannō, -ōnis, *m.,* Hanno, eminent Carthaginian, strongly opposed to Hannibal and the war policy.

Cannēnsis, -is, -e, of, belonging to, Cannae.

Cūmae, -ārum, *f.pl.,* Cumae, ancient city on Bay of Naples.

Nōla, -ae, *f.,* Nola, city in South Italy.

Zama, -ae, *f.,* Zama, near Carthage, scene of great battle 202 B.C., when Hannibal was decisively beaten by Scipio.

EXERCISE 27

caelum, -ī, *n.,* sky, heaven

cōnspectus, -ūs, *m.,* sight

cōnficiō, -ere, -fēcī, -fectum, to complete, finish

bellum indīcō, -ere, -dīxī, -dictum, to declare war upon

lūna, -ae, *f.,* moon

obscūrō, -āre, -āvī, -ātum, to darken

orbis, -is, *m.,* circle

plēnus, -a, -um, full

porrigō, -ere, -rēxī, -rēctum, to stretch out

prōdigium, -iī, *n.,* marvel, portent, prodigy

respōnsum, -ī, *n.,* answer, reply

EXERCISE 28

dēfectiō, -iōnis, *f.,* an eclipse

dēficiō, -ere, -fēcī, -fectum, to be eclipsed

fulgeō, -ēre, fulsī, to shine

umbra, -ae, *f.,* shadow

perterreō, -ēre, -uī, -itum, to frighten

indūtus, -a, -um, clad, dressed

praetōrium, -iī, *n.,* the praetorium, the general's tent

genū, -ūs, *n.,* knee

procumbō, -ere, -cubuī, -cubitum, to fall forward, to sink upon

fleō, -ēre, -ēvī, -ētum, to weep

clēmentia, -ae, *f.,* mercy, pity, clemency

fīdūcia, -ae, *f.,* confidence

praebeō, -ēre, -buī, -bitum, provide, offer

mūtātiō, -iōnis, *f.,* change

debeō, -ēre, -uī, -itum, I ought

crēdō, -ere, -idī, -itum, believe, trust

tractō, -āre, -āvī, -ātum, to treat

Macedō, -ŏnis, *m.,* a Macedonian

Macedonia, -ae, *f.,* Macedonia

EXERCISE 29

cognōscō, -ere, cognōvī, cognitum, to find out, learn, ascertain, get to know

cohors, -tis, *f.,* cohort

fēriae, -ārum, *f.pl.,* holidays

fodiō, -ere, fōdī, fossum, to dig

hortus, -ī, *m.,* garden

nūbēs, -is, *f.,* cloud

vēndō, -ere, vēndidī, vēnditum, to sell

EXERCISE 30

s(alūtem) p(lūrimam) d(īcit), gives heartiest greetings to

agricultūra, -ae, *f.*, agriculture

peccō, -āre, -āvī, -ātum, to sin, do wrong, misbehave, blunder

possum, posse, potuī, to be able

īnspiciō, -ere, -spexī, -spectum, to inspect, examine, superintend

frūctus, -ūs, *m.*, fruit, profit

vīlicus, -ī, *m.*, bailiff, farm steward

vīnum, -ī, *n.*, wine

tempestās, -ātis, *f.*, weather

aufugiō, -ere, -fūgī, run away, flee away

pluvius, -a, -um, rainy

pūrgō, -āre, -āvī, -ātum, to clean

horreum, -ī, *n.*, granary

vetus, -eris, old

reficiō, -ere, -fēcī, -fectum, to repair

mūniō, -īre, -īvī, -ītum, to fortify ; **viam mūnīre,** to make, construct, a road

pūblicus, -a, -um, belonging to the state, public

aegrōtō, -āre, -āvī, -ātum, to be sick

dēsum, -esse, -fuī, to be lacking

sī quis, sī quid, if anyone, if anything

supersum, -esse, -fuī, to be left over, to survive

Fundānus, -ī, *m.*, Fundanus

EXERCISE 31

aestās, -ātis, *f.*, summer

amoenus, -a, -um, lovely, pleasant, beautiful

apud (*prep. gov. acc.*), at the house of

āvolō, -āre, -āvī, -ātum, to fly away

cēnō, -āre, -āvī, -ātum, to dine

cupidus, -a, -um, desirous of, eager for

doctrīna, -ae, *f.*, learning

hiems, -is, *f.*, winter

hirundō, -inis, *f.*, swallow

volō, velle, voluī, to wish, to be willing

EXERCISE 32

ingenium, -iī, *n.*, ability

praesum, -esse, -fuī, to be in command of (*dat. case*)

luxuria, -ae, *f.*, luxury

indulgeō, -ēre, -sī, -tum, to indulge (*dat. case*)

ōtium, -iī, *n.*, ease, leisure, peace

dēdō, -ere, dēdidī, dēditum, give up, surrender ; **sē dēdere,** to give one's self up to

mīlitāris, -is, -e, military

tollō, -ere, sustulī, sublātum, to remove

sūmptus, -ūs, *m.*, expense

mōlēs, -is, *f.*, mass (of masonry)

iniciō, -ere, -iēcī, -iectum, to throw into

fluctus, -ūs, *m.*, wave

sēdēs, -is, *f.*, seat, abode, home

magnificentia, -ae, *f.*, magnificence, grandeur

respondeō, -ēre, -dī, -sum, to answer, to match, correspond to

expendō, -ere, -dī, -sum, to expend

talentum, -ī, *n.*, a talent

ferculum, -ī, *n.*, tray, course

PROPER NAMES

Persa, -ae, *m.,* a Persian.
Pompeius, -iī, *m.,* Pompey, i.e. Cn. Pompeius Magnus, great Roman general.
Pontus, -ī, *m.,* Pontus, kingdom in northern Asia Minor.
Xerxēs, -is, *m.,* Xerxes, famous Persian king, invaded Greece 480 B.C.

EXERCISE 33

cōnfōrmō, -āre, -āvī, -ātum, to shape, mould, fashion
ēlegantia, -ae, *f.,* elegance, good taste
ōrnāmentum, -ī, *n.,* ornament
fībula, -ae, *f.,* brooch
gemma, -ae, *f.,* jewel
pretiōsus, -a, -um, costly, precious
mālō, mālle, māluī, to prefer
incultus, -a, -um, untilled, uncultivated
lēgem rogāre, to propose a law
ager pūblicus, public land, land belonging to the State
dīvidō, -ere, -vīsī, -vīsum, to divide

dīvitiae, -ārum, *f.pl.,* wealth, riches
tumultus, -ūs, *m.,* riot
difficultās, -ātis, *f.,* difficulty
lēgem ferō, ferre, tulī, lātum, to carry a law, get a law passed
posterus, -a, -um, next
violō, -āre, -āvī, -ātum, break, violate
vīlis, -is, -e, cheap ; **vīlī,** at a low price, cheaply, cheap
dēcernō, -ere, -crēvī, -crētum, to decree, decide
dētrīmentum, -ī, *n.,* harm, damage, loss
superior, -is, higher
cervīcēs, -um, *f.pl.,* neck

PROPER NAMES

Mōns Aventīnus, *m.,* The Aventine Mount, one of the seven hills of ancient Rome.
Cornēlia, -ae, *f.,* Cornelia, mother of the Gracchi.
Tiberius Gracchus, *m.,* Tiberius Gracchus, Roman statesman, tribune of plebs, 133 B.C.
Gaius Gracchus, *m.,* Gaius Gracchus, brother of above. tribune of plebs, 123 B.C.
Ītalicī, -ōrum, *m.pl.,* the Italians.
Scīpiō Nāsīca, *m.,* Publius Cornelius Scipio Nasica, leader of the mob of senatorial supporters which killed Tiberius Gracchus.

EXERCISE 34

dictātūra, -ae, *f.,* dictatorship
persequor, -sequī, -secūtus sum to pursue

quotiēns, how often ?
rūs, rūris, *n.,* the country ; **rūrī,** in the country

EXERCISE 35

quam ob rem, wherefore
inimīcus, -ī, *m.* (personal) enemy
victor, -ōris, *m.,* victor, conqueror
prōpōnō, -ere, -posuī, -positum, to set forth
capitis damnāre, to condemn to death
turbulentus, -a, -um, disorderly
castīgō, -āre, -āvī, -ātum, punish, chide
quīngentī, -ae, -a, five hundred
tabula, -ae, *f.,* tablet, notice, list
caedēs, -is, *f.,* bloodshed

prōscrībō, -ere, -scrīpsī, -scrīptum, to proscribe
avāritia, -ae, *f.,* greed, covetousness
prīvātus, -a, -um, private ; *as noun,* a private citizen
adulēscēns, -tis, *m.,* youth
probrum, -ī, *n.,* reproach, insult
aequō animō, calmly
efficiō, -ere, -fēcī, -fectum, to bring to pass; **efficiō ut . . . ,** I bring it to pass that ; **efficiō nē . . . ,** I bring it to pass that . . . not

Proper Names

Albānus, -a, -um, Alban.
Metellus, -ī, *m.,* Metellus

Sulla, -ae, *m.,* Sulla.

EXERCISE 36

cīvīlis, -is, -e, civil
nātus, -a, -um, old (*lit.* born)
cārus, -a, -um, dear
negōtium, -iī, *n.,* business
celeritās, -ātis, *f.,* speed
surgō, -ere, -rēxī, -rēctum, rise
sexāgintā, sixty
redeō, -īre, rediī, reditum, return
incrēdibilis, -is, -e, incredible
obviam īre, to go to meet (*dative case*)

triumphus, -ī, *m.,* triumphal procession, a triumph
significō, -āre, -āvī, -ātum, to mean, signify
intellegō, -ere, -ēxī, -ēctum, to understand
cōnstantia, -ae, *f.,* firmness, resolution
triumphō, -āre, -āvī, -ātum, to triumph, i.e. to hold a triumphal procession
merīdiēs, -iēī, *m.,* midday

EXERCISE 37

varius, -a, -um, varied, various, different
verbera, -um, *n.pl.,* blows, lashes
praedō, -ōnis, *m.,* pirate
portus, -ūs, *m.,* harbour
ineunte vēre, at the beginning of spring
teneō, -ēre, -uī, to hold
cōpiae, -ārum, *f.pl.,* forces
tergum, -ī, *n.,* back ; **ā tergō,** in the rear

ōrdō, -inis, *m.,* rank
pertineō, -ēre, -tinuī, -tentum, to stretch
dēcipiō, -ere, -cēpī, -ceptum, deceive
mittō, -ere, mīsī, missum, hurl, launch (a missile)
compōnō, -ere, -posuī, -positum, to arrange, settle
fūmus, -ī, *m.,* smoke

PROPER NAME

Sertōrius, -iī, *m.,* Sertorius, Roman general who waged war against Sulla in Spain.

EXERCISE 38

subitō, suddenly
ōrātiō, -iōnis, *f.,* speech
certiōrem facere, to inform
certior fierī, to be informed
summus, -a, -um, greatest, highest
mōs, mōris, *m.,* custom, manner ; *in plur.,* character
scrīptor, -ōris, *m.,* writer
facētus, -a, -um, witty
inopia, -ae, *f.,* want, scarcity, lack
dīligentia, -ae, *f.,* diligence
praetor, -ōris, *m.,* praetor
reus, -ī, *m.,* defendant, accused person

damnō, -āre, -āvī, -ātum, to condemn
ēloquentia, -ae, *f.,* eloquence
patefaciō, -ere, -fēcī, -factum, to expose, lay bare, open
restituō, -ere, -uī, -ūtum, to restore
venia, -ae, *f.,* pardon
mediocris, -is, -e, moderate, average, ordinary
bibō, -ere, -ī, bibitum, to drink
aetās, -ātis, *f.,* age
modo, only
perficiō, -ere, -fēcī, -fectum, to complete

PROPER NAMES

Arpīnum, -ī, *n.,* Arpinum.
Volscī, -ōrum, *m.pl.,* the Volsci.
Cicerō, -ōnis, *m.,* Cicero.
Roscius, -iī, *m.,* Roscius.
Ameria, -ae, *f.,* Ameria.

Chrysogonus, -ī, *m.,* Chrysogonus.
Catilīna, -ae, *m.,* Catiline.
Athēnae, -ārum, *f.pl.,* Athens.
Rhodus, -ī, *f.,* Rhodes.
Clōdius, -iī, *m.,* Clodius.

EXERCISE 39

altitūdō, -inis, *f.,* height, depth
cōnsistō, -ere, -stitī, to halt
aquila, -ae, *f.,* eagle, standard
prōdō, -ere, prodidī, prōditum, to betray
nātūra, -ae, *f.,* nature
incitō, -āre, -āvī, -ātum, to spur on
animadvertō, -ere, -ī, -versum, to notice

circiter, about
cōnspiciō, -ere, -spexī, -spectum, to catch sight of, observe, notice, sight
cunctor, -ārī, cunctātus sum, to hesitate
aestus, -ūs, *m.,* tide
secundus, -a, -um, favourable
regiō, -iōnis, *f.,* district, region

EXERCISE 40

contineō, -ēre, -tinuī, -tentum,
to enclose
ancora, -ae, *f.,* anchor
nancīscor, -īscī, nactus sum, to
obtain
apertus, -a, -um, open
plānus, -a, -um, level
cōnstituō, -ere, -uī, -ūtum, to
place, station
praemittō, -ere, -mīsī, -missum
to send ahead
essedārius, -iī, *m.,* chariot-fighter

ob (*prep. gov. acc.*), on account of
magnitūdō, -inis, *f.,* size
altum, -ī, *n.,* deep water
studium, -iī, *n.,* eagerness, zeal
nāvis onerāria, a transport
latus, -eris, *n.,* side
certē, certainly, at least
officium, -iī, *n.,* duty
praestō, -āre, -stitī, -stātum,
perform
inter sē, one another

EXERCISE 41

Druidēs, -um, *m.pl.,* the Druids
dīvīnus, -a, -um, divine
contrōversia, -ae, *f.,* dispute
fīnēs, -ium, *m.,* boundaries
iūdicō, -āre, -āvī, -ātum, to
judge
poena, -ae, *f.,* penalty
cōnstituō, -ere, -uī, -ūtum, to
fix, settle
auctōritās, -ātis, *f.,* authority
dīgnitās, -ātis, *f.,* rank, dignity
pār, paris, equal
suffrāgium, -iī, *n.,* vote
cōnsīdō, -ere, -sēdī, -sessum, to
sit down, be seated, take one's
place, hold session

cōnsecrō, -āre, -āvī, -ātum, to
consecrate
tribūtum, -ī, *n.,* tax, tribute
solvō, -ere, solvī, solūtum, to
pay
versus, -ūs, *m.,* line, verse
mandō, -āre, -āvī, -ātum, to
commit, entrust
etiamsī, even if
anima, -ae, *f.,* soul
sīdus, -eris, *n.,* star, constellation
mōtus, -ūs, *m.,* movement
mundus, -ī, *m.,* world, universe
capillus, -ī, *m.,* a hair
statūra, -ae, *f.,* height, stature

EXERCISE 42

fessus, -a, -um, tired, weary
integer, -ra, -rum, fresh
vertō, -ere, -ī, versum, to turn
dēlīrō, -āre, -āvī, -ātum, to rave,
be mad

praedīcō, -ere, -dīxī, -dictum,
to foretell
gemitus, -ūs, *m.,* groan

PROPER NAMES

Thessalia, -ae, *f.,* Thessaly.
Patāvium, -iī, *n.,* Patavium.
Cornēlius, -iī, *m.,* Cornelius.

Pompeiānī, -ōrum, *m.pl.,* Pom-
peians, followers of Pompey.

EXERCISE 43

eques, -itis, *m.*, knight (i.e. member of equestrian order or class, ranking next below senatorial class in the social scale)

genus, -eris, *n.*, family

adoptō, -āre, -āvī, -ātum, to adopt

hērēs, -ēdis, *c.*, heir

obiciō, -ere, -iēcī, -iectum, to expose

appropinquō, -āre, -āvī, -ātum, to approach

trādō, -ere, -didī, -ditum, to hand over, to hand down, relate

dēfleō, -ēre, -ēvī, -ētum, to weep over

trānsfīgō, -ere, -fīxī, -fīxum, to transfix, pierce, stab

aspis, -idis, *f.*, asp, viper

admoveō, -ēre, -mōvī, -mōtum, to apply

piscor, -ārī, piscātus sum, to fish

Proper Names

Brūtus, -ī, *m.*, M. Brutus, friend of Caesar who joined the conspiracy against him.

Cassius, -iī, *m.*, C. Cassius, one of the murderers of Caesar, who afterwards aided Brutus against Antony and Octavius.

Cāsca, -ae, *m.*, Servilius Casca, one of the murderers of Caesar.

Philippī, -ōrum, *m.pl.*, Philippi, town in Macedonia.

Antōnius, -iī, *m.*, Mark Antony, friend and avenger of Caesar.

Octāvius, -iī, *m.*, nephew and adopted son of Caesar.

Cleopātra, -ae, *f.*, Cleopatra, the beautiful queen of Egypt.

Actium, -iī, *n.*, Actium, promontory in W. Greece, scene of defeat of fleets of Antony and Cleopatra by Octavius in 31 B.C.

EXERCISE 44

fōrma, -ae, *f.*, shape, appearance, beauty

prohibeō, -ēre, -uī, -itum, to prevent, hinder

rupēs, -is, *f.*, rock, cliff

clārus, -a, -um, bright

cōnspectus, -ūs, *m.*, sight

fulgor, -ōris, *m.*, brightness, radiance

dēmittō, -ere, -mīsī, -missum, to lower

modicus, -a, -um, small, moderate

modus, -ī, *m.*, way, manner

cubīculum, -ī, *n.*, bedroom

ālea, -ae, *f.*, game of dice

hāmus, -ī, *m.*, hook

retineō, -ēre, -uī, -tentum, retain

celebrō, -āre, -āvī, -ātum, to celebrate

benignus, -a, -um, kindly

iocus, -ī, *m.*, jest

as, assis, *n.*, an as, Roman coin worth about ½d.

corvus, -ī, *m.*, raven

avis, -is, *f.*, bird

sūtor, -ōris, *m.*, shoemaker

salūtātiō, -iōnis, *f.*, greeting, salutation

salūtātor, -ōris, *m.*, a greeter, saluter

PROPER NAMES

Maecēnās, -ātis, *m.,* Maecenas, friend and adviser of Augustus.
Līvius, -iī, *m.,* Titus Livius,—Livy, great Roman historian.
Vergilius, -iī, *m.,* Publius Vergilius Maro, greatest of Roman poets.
His works comprise *Eclogues,* series of pastoral poems ; *Georgics,*
a long poem on agriculture ; *Aeneid,* an epic poem telling of fall of
Troy, wanderings of Aeneas to Italy and his settlement there.
Horātius, -iī, *m.,* Quintus Horatius Flaccus, great poet.   Horace's
works include *Odes,* lyric poems ; *Satires* ; *Epistles.*

EXERCISE 45

bellum īnferre, to make war upon
bis, twice
externus, -a, -um, foreign, external
maiōrēs, -um, *m.pl.,* ancestors
condō, -ere, -didī, -ditum, to found ; **ā conditā urbe, ab urbe conditā,** from the foundation of the city
ter, thrice
pācō, -āre, -āvī, -ātum, to pacify
ōstium, -iī, *n.,* mouth (of river)
ūsque ad, right up to, as far as

complūrēs, -es, -a, several
lēgātiō, -iōnis, *f.,* embassy
extinguō, -ere, -tinxī, -tinctum, to extinguish
arbitrium, -iī, *n.,* control, power
trānsferō, -ferre, -tulī, -lātum, to transfer
senātūs cōnsultum, decree of the senate
praestō, -āre, -stitī, -stātum, to excel
amplior, -ior, -ius, more
collēga, -ae, *m.,* colleague

PROPER NAMES

Albis, -is, *m.,* the Elbe (German river).
Gādēs, -ium *f.pl.,* Gades (town in Spain, modern Cadiz).
Ōceanus, -ī, *m.,* the ocean, the Atlantic
Cimbrī, -rōrum, *m.pl.,* the Cimbri, German tribe inhabiting what is now Denmark
Charydēs, -um, *m.pl.,* the Charydes, a German tribe.
Semnonēs, -um, *m.pl.,* The Semnones, a German tribe living between Elbe and Oder.

Aethiopia, -ae, *f.,* Ethiopia.
Arabia, -ae, *f.,* Arabia.
India, -ae, *f.,* India
Bastarnae, -ārum, *m.pl.,* the Bastarnae, German tribe whose lands lay along the Danube.
Scythae, -ārum, *m.pl.,* the Scythians, tribes of nomads who lived around Black Sea.
Sarmatae, -ārum, *m.pl.,* the Sarmatians, a people dwelling between Vistula and Don.
Tanais, -is, *m.,* the Don.

GENERAL VOCABULARIES

A. LATIN-ENGLISH

A., abbreviation for **Aulus**, a Roman praenomen

ā, ab (*prep. gov. abl.*), from, by ; **ā latere**, on the flank ; **ā fronte**, in front ; **ā tergō**, in the rear

abdicō, -āre, -āvī, -ātum, give up ; **sē abdicāre**, (*with abl.*), to resign from

abeō, -īre, -iī, -itum, go away, depart

abiciō, -ere, -iēcī, -iectum, throw away

abūtor, -ūtī, abūsus sum, use up, exhaust

accipiō, -ere, -cēpī, -ceptum, receive, accept ; **clādem accipere**, to sustain a disaster

accūsō, -āre, -āvī, -ātum, to accuse

ācer, ācris, ācre, fierce, keen, spirited

acētum, -ī, *n.*, vinegar

aciēs, -iēī, *f.*, line of battle

Actium, -iī, *n.*, Actium

ad (*prep. gov. acc.*), to, towards, at, near

addō, -ere, -didī, -ditum, to add

adeō (*adv.*), so, to such an extent

adeō, -īre, -iī, -itum, to go to, come to, approach

adhūc (*adv.*), as yet, up to this time

adipīscor, -ī, adeptus sum, to obtain

aditus, -ūs, *m.*, approach, entrance

adiuvō, -āre, -iūvī, -iūtum, to help, assist

admīrātiō, -iōnis, *f.*, wonder, surprise, admiration

admoveō, -ēre, -mōvī, -mōtum, to move to, to apply

adoptō, -āre, -āvī, -ātum, to adopt

adulēscēns, -entis, *m.*, youth, young man

adversus, -a, -um, opposite, unfavourable

aedificium, -iī, *n.*, building

aedificō, -āre, -āvī, -ātum, to build

aeger, aegra, aegrum, sick

aegrōtō, -āre, -āvī, -ātum, to be ill, be sick

Aegyptus, -ī, *f.*, Egypt

Aenēās, -ae, *m.*, Aeneas

Aequī, -ōrum, *m.pl.*, the Aequi

aequō, -āre, -āvī, -ātum, to match, to equal

aequus, -a, -um, equal, fair, level ; **in aequō locō**, on level ground, on favourable ground ; **aequō animō**, calmly

aestās, -ātis, *f.*, summer

aestus, -ūs, *m.*, tide

aetās, -ātis, *f.*, age, time (of life)

aeternus, -a, -um, eternal, everlasting

Aethiopia, -ae, f., Ethiopia

affirmō, -āre, -āvī, -ātum, declare, assert

Āfrica, -ae, f., Africa

age ! agite !, come !

ager, -rī, m., field, land ; ager pūblicus, public land, land owned by the State

agmen, -inis, n., army (in marching order), column of march, band

agō, -ere, ēgī, āctum, do, act, drive, lead ; agere dē, to discuss ; grātiās agere, to thank ; vītam agere, to spend or pass one's life

agricola, -ae, m., farmer

agricultūra, -ae, f., agriculture

āla, -ae, f., wing

Alba Longa, Albae Longae, f., Alba Longa

Albānus, -a, -um, Alban

Albis, -is, m., the Elbe

albus, -a, -um, white

ālea, -ae, f., dice

aliquantō (adv.), considerably, somewhat

alius, -a, -ud, other, another ; aliī . . . aliī, some . . . others

Allia, -ae, f., the Allia

Alliēnsis, -is, -e, belonging to the Allia

Alpēs, -ium, f.pl., the Alps

alter, -era, -erum, the other (of two) ; the one (of two)

altitūdō, -inis, f., height, depth

altus, -a, -um, deep, high ; as noun, altum, -ī, n., deep water

amātor, -ōris, m., lover

ambulō, -āre, -āvī, -ātum, to walk

Ameria, -ae, f., Ameria

amīcitia, -ae, f., friendship

amīcus, -ī, m., friend

āmittō, -ere, -mīsī, -missum, lose, let go, send away

amō, -āre, -āvī, -ātum, to love

amoenus, -a, -um, beautiful, pleasant

amor, -ōris, m., love

amplius (adj. and adv.), more, besides, further

anaticula, -ae, f., duckling

ancora, -ae, f., anchor

Ancus Mārtius, Ancī Mārtiī, m., Ancus Martius

angor, -ōris, m., pain, anguish

angustus, -a, -um, narrow

anima, -ae, f., soul

animadvertō, -ere, -vertī, -versum, notice

animus, -ī, m., mind, spirit

annus, -ī, m., year

ānser, -eris, m., goose

ante (adv. and prep. gov. acc.), before

Antiochus, -ī, m., Antiochus

antīquus, -a, -um, ancient

ānulus, -ī, m., ring

anus, -ūs, f., old woman

aperiō, -īre, -uī, -tum, to open

apertus, -a, -um, open

apis, -is, f., bee

appellō, -āre, -āvī, -ātum, to call

appropinquō, -āre, -āvī, -ātum, approach

apud (prep. gov. acc.), among, at house of

aqua, -ae, f., water

aquila, -ae, f., eagle, standard

āra, -ae, f., altar

Arabia, -ae, f., Arabia

arbitrium, -iī, n., decision, sway, power

Archimēdēs, -is, m., Archimedes

dextra, -ae, *f.,* the right hand ;
  ā dextrā, on the right
dīcō, -ere, dīxī, dictum, to say,
  tell, nominate
dictātor, -ōris, *m.,* dictator
dictātūra, -ae, *f.,* dictatorship
diēs, diēī, *m.,* day
difficilis, -is, -e, hard, difficult
difficultās, -ātis, *f.,* difficulty
diffīdō, -ere, diffīsus sum, to
  distrust
dīgnitās, -ātis, *f.,* rank, position,
  dignity
dīgnus, -a, -um, worthy
dīligēns, -entis, diligent, hard-
  working
dīligenter (*adv.*), diligently
dīligentia, -ae, *f.,* diligence
dīmittō, -ere, -mīsī, -missum,
  send away
dirimō, -ere, -ēmī, -emptum,
  break off, stop
discēdō, -ere, -cessī, -cessum,
  depart, go away
discipulus, -ī, *m.,* pupil
discō, -ere, didicī, to learn
discordia, -ae, *f.,* strife, discord
diū (*adv.*), for a long time
dīves, -itis, rich
dīvidō, -ere, -vīsī, -vīsum, to
  divide
dīvīnus, -a, -um, divine
dō, dare, dedī, datum, to give
doceō, -ēre, -uī, doctum, to
  teach
doctrīna, -ae, *f.,* learning
doctus, -a, -um, learned
dolor, -ōris, *m.,* grief, pain
dominus, -ī, *m.,* master, owner,
  lord
domus, -ūs, *f.,* home, house
dōnum, -ī, *n.,* gift
dormiō, -īre, -īvī, -ītum, to
  sleep

Druidēs, -um, *m.pl.,* Druids
dūcō, -ere, dūxī, ductum, to
  lead, marry (*man the subj.*)
dulcis, -is, -e, sweet
dum (*conj.*), while, until
duo, duae, duo, two
dūrus, -a, -um, hard, harsh
dux, ducis, *m.,* leader

ē, ex, (*prep. gov. abl.*), out of, from
ecce !, lo !, behold !, see !, look !
edepol !, upon my word !, goodness gracious !
ēducō, -āre, -āvī, -ātum, bring
  up, train, educate
efficiō, -ere, -fēcī, -fectum,
  bring about, bring to pass, cause
effugiō, -ere, -fūgī, escape
ego, meī, I
ēheu, alas !
ēlegantia, -ae, *f.,* good taste,
  elegance
elephantus, -ī, *m.,* elephant
ēloquentia, -ae, *f.,* eloquence
enim, for
eō (*adv.*), thither, to that place
eō, īre, īvī (iī), itum, to go
epistola, -ae, *f.,* letter
eques, equitis, *m.,* cavalryman,
  knight
equus, -ī, *m.,* horse
errō, -āre, -āvī, -ātum, to err,
  wander
essedārius, -iī, *m.,* chariot fighter
et (*conj.*), and ; **et . . . et,** both
  . . . and
etiam, even, also
etiamsī, even if
euge !, well done ! bravo ! hurrah !
ex, ē, out of, from
excipiō, -ere, cēpī, -ceptum, to
  cut off, catch
excitō, -āre, -āvī, -ātum, rouse,
  arouse, waken

exclāmō, -āre, -āvī, -ātum, shout aloud, exclaim

excutiō, -ere, -cussī, -cussum, shake out

exemplum, -ī, n., example

exerceō, -ēre, -uī, -itum, train, exercise

exercitus, -ūs, m., army

exitium, -iī, n., destruction

expellō, -ere, -pulī, -pulsum, drive out, expel

expendō, -ere, -ī, -pēnsum, to spend

experior, -īrī, expertus sum, to experience, make trial of, try, test

exserō, -ere, -seruī, -sertum, to thrust out, raise forth

exsilium, -iī, n., exile

exspectō, -āre, -āvī, -ātum, to await

exstinguō, -ere, -tinxī, -tinctum, to put out, extinguish

externus, -a, -um, foreign, external

extrā (prep. gov. acc.), outside

fābula, -ae, f., story

facētus, -a, -um, witty

facile (adv.), easily

facilis, -is, -e, easy

faciō, -ere, fēcī, factum, make, do

famēs, -is, f., hunger

fēlīx, -īcis, fortunate, happy

fēmina, -ae, f., woman

fenestra, -ae, f., window

fera, -ae, f., wild beast

ferculum, -ī, n., tray

fēriae, -ārum, f.pl., holidays

ferō, ferre, tulī, lātum, to bear, carry ; lēgem ferre, to get a law passed

ferōciter (adv.), fiercely

ferōx, -ōcis, fierce

ferrum, -ī, n., iron, the sword

fessus, -a, -um, tired, weary

festīnō, -āre, -āvī, -ātum, to hasten, hurry

fībula, -ae, f., brooch

fidēlis, -is, -e, loyal, faithful

fidēs, -eī, f., faith, good faith, trust, loyalty

fīdō, -ere, fīsus sum, to trust

fīdūcia, -ae, f., confidence

fīlia, -ae, f., daughter

fīlius, -iī, m., son

fīnis, -is, m., end, boundary ; fīnēs, -ium, territory

fīō, fierī, factus sum, be made, become

flamma, -ae, f., flame

fleō, flēre, flēvī, flētum, weep

fluctus, -ūs, m., wave

flūmen, -inis, n., river

fodiō, -ere, fōdī, fossum, to dig

fōrma, -ae, f., shape, form, beauty

fortāsse, perhaps

forte, by chance

fortis, -is, -e, brave

fortiter (adv.), bravely

fortūna, -ae, f., fortune

forum, -ī, n., forum

fossa, -ae, f., ditch

fossor, -ōris, m., miner, digger

frangō, -ere, frēgī, frāctum, to break

frāter, -ris, m., brother

frīgus, -oris, n., cold ; frīgora, frosts

frūctus, -ūs, m., fruit, gain, profit

frūmentum, -ī, n., corn, grain

frūstrā (adv.), in vain

fuga, -ae, f., flight

fugiō, -ere, fūgī, fugitum, to flee

fugō, -āre, -āvī, -ātum, put to flight

fulgeō, -ēre, fulsī, to shine
fulgor, -ōris, m., radiance, gleam
fulmen, -inis, n., lightning
fūmus, -ī, m., smoke
fundāmentum, -ī, n., foundation
fundus, -ī, m., farm

Gallicus, -a, -um, Gallic, of or belonging to Gaul
gaudeō, -ēre, gāvisus sum, to rejoice, be glad
gaudium, -iī, n., joy, gladness
gemitus, -ūs, m., groan
gemma, -ae, f., jewel, precious stone
gener, -erī, m., son-in-law
gēns, gentis, f., race, family
genū, -ūs, n., knee
genus, -eris, n., race
gerō, -ere, gessī, gestum, to wage, carry on
gladius, -iī, m., sword
glōria, -ae, f., glory
grātiae, -ārum, f.pl., thanks; grātiās agere, to thank
grātus, -a, -um, pleasing, welcome, grateful
gravis, -is, -e, heavy, serious, important

habeō, -ēre, -uī, -itum, to have, hold
habitātiō, -iōnis, f., lodging, dwelling
habitō, -āre, -āvī, -ātum, dwell, live
Hamilcar, -caris, m., Hamilcar
hāmus, -ī, m., hook
Hannibal, -alis, m., Hannibal
Hannō, -ōnis, m., Hanno
Hasdrubal, -alis, m., Hasdrubal
hasta, -ae, f., spear
hērēs, -ēdis, c., heir
herī (adv.), yesterday

hīc, haec, hōc, this; as pron., he, she, it
hīc (adv.), here
hiems, -emis, f., winter
hirundō, -inis, f., swallow
Hispānia, -ae, f., Spain
hodiē (adv.), to-day
homō, -inis, m., man
honestus, -a, -um, honourable
honōs, -ōris, m., honour, distinction, public office
hōra, -ae, f., hour
Horātius, Q. Flaccus, Horace (the poet)
horreum, -ī, n., granary, barn
hortor, -ārī, hortātus sum, to exhort, encourage
hortus, -ī, m., garden
hostis, -is, m., enemy
hūmānus, -a, -um, human
humerus, -ī, m., shoulder
humī (locative case of humus), on the ground
humilis, -is, -e, low, humble, lowly

iam (adv.), now, already, by this time
iānua, -ae, f., door, gate
Iānus, -ī, m., Janus
ibi (adv.), there, in that place
idōneus, -a, -um, suitable
igitur (second word in clause), therefore
īgnāvia, -ae, f., laziness, sloth, idleness, cowardice
īgnāvus, -a, -um, lazy, slothful, idle, cowardly
īgnis, -is, m., fire
īgnōrō, -āre, -āvī, -ātum, not to know, be ignorant of
īgnōscō, -ere, īgnōvī, īgnōtum, to pardon
ille, illa, illud, that; as pron., he, she, it

illinc (*adv.*), thence, from there

immemor, **-oris**, forgetful, unmindful of

immortālis, **-is**, **-e**, immortal

immōtus, **-a**, **-um**, motionless, still, unmoved

impediō, **-īre**, **-īvī**, **-ītum**, to hinder

imperātor, **-ŏris**, *m.*, general

imperium, **-iī**, *n.*, power, command, authority

imperō, **-āre**, **-āvī**, **-ātum**, to command

impetus, **-ūs**, *m.*, attack

impōnō, **-ere**, **-posuī**, **-positum**, to place upon, impose

in (*prep. gov. abl.*), in

in (*prep. gov. acc.*), into

incendō, **-ere**, **-ī**, **-cēnsum**, set on fire, kindle, burn

incidō, **-ere**, **-cidī**, **-cāsum**, fall into

incipiō, **-ere**, **-cēpī**, **-ceptum**, begin

incitō, **-āre**, **-āvī**, **-ātum**, urge on

inclūdō, **-ere**, **-clūsī**, **-clūsum**, to include, enclose, shut in

incrēdibilis, **-is**, **-e**, incredible

incultus, **-a**, **-um**, uncultivated

inde (*adv.*), thence, from there, thereafter

indicō, **-āre**, **-āvī**, **-ātum**, point out, indicate

indīcō, **-ere**, **-dīxī**, **-dictum**, to declare (war)

indulgeō, **-ere**, **-dulsī**, **-dultum**, indulge, favour

indūtus, **-a**, **-um**, clad in, dressed in

ineō, **-īre**, **-iī**, **-itum**, to enter ; **ineunte vēre**, at the beginning of spring

īnferior, **-iŏris**, lower, weaker, inferior

īnferō, **-ferre**, **-tulī**, **-lātum**, to carry in, carry into, bear against ; **bellum īnferre**, to make war on

īnfēstus, **-a**, **-um**, hostile

īnfundō, **-ere**, **-fūdī**, **-fūsum**, to pour upon

ingenium, **-iī**, *n.*, ability, talent

ingēns, **-tis**, huge, enormous

inhūmānus, **-a**, **-um**, inhuman

iniciō, **-ere**, **-iēcī**, **-iectum**, hurl against

inimīcus, **-ī**, *m.* (private) enemy

inīquus, **-a**, **-um**, unfavourable, unjust

initium, **-iī**, *n.*, beginning

iniūria, **-ae**, *f.*, wrong, injury

innocēns, **-entis**, innocent

inopia, **-ae**, *f.*, lack

inquam, I say, said I ; **inquit**, says, said, he, she, it ; **inquiunt**, they say, they said

īnsidiae, **-ārum**, *f.pl.*, ambush

īnsīgnis, **-is**, **-e**, remarkable, outstanding, conspicuous, distinguished ; **īnsīgnia**, *n.pl.*, distinguishing marks, emblems, distinctions

īnspiciō, **-ere**, **-spexī**, **-spectum**, look into, examine, inspect, supervise

īnstruō, **-ere**, **-strūxī**, **-strūctum**, draw up

īnsula, **-ae**, *f.*, island

īnsurgō, **-ere**, **-surrēxī**, **-surrēctum**, rise up.

integer, **-ra**, **-rum**, fresh

intellegō, **-ere**, **-ēxī**, **-ēctum**, understand

inter (*prep. gov. acc.*), between, among

intereā (*adv.*), meanwhile

interficiō, **-ere**, **-fēcī**, **-fectum**, to kill

interrogō, -āre, -āvī, -ātum, ask, question

intersum, -esse, -fuī, take part in, attend

intrā (*prep. gov. acc.*), within

intrō, -āre, -āvī, -ātum, enter

inūtilis, -is, -e, useless

inveniō, -īre, -vēnī, -ventum, to find

invideō, -ēre, -vīdī, -vīsum, to envy

invīsus, -a, -um, hateful

iocus, -ī, *m.*, jest

ipse, ipsa, ipsum, self

īra, -ae, *f.*, anger

īrāscor, -ī, īrātus sum, grow angry

īrātus, -a, -um, angry

is, ea, id, that ; he, she, it

ita, thus, so, in such a way ; ita vērō, yes indeed

Ītalia, -ae, *f.*, Italy

Ītalicus, -a, -um, Italian ; Ītalicī, -ōrum, *m.pl.*, the Italians

itaque, and so, therefore, accordingly

iter, itineris, *n.*, journey, march, route ; iter facere, to march, to journey, to travel

iterum (*adv.*), again, for a second time

iubeō, -ēre, iūssī, iūssum, order

iūcundus, -a, -um, pleasant

iūdicō, -āre, -āvī, -ātum, judge

iugum, -ī, *n.*, ridge

iungō, -ere, iūnxī, iūnctum, join

Iūnō, Iūnōnis, *f.*, Juno

Iuppiter, Iovis, *m.*, Jupiter

iūrō, -āre, -āvī, -ātum, swear

iūs, iūris, *n.*, right

iūssū, by command of

iūstitia, -ae, *f.*, justice

iūstus, -a, -um, just

iuvenis, -is, *m.*, youth, young man

L., abbreviation for Lūcius

labellum, -ī, *n.*, lip

labor, -ōris, *m.*, work, labour

lābor, -ī, lāpsus sum, to slip

labōrō, -āre, -āvī, -ātum, to work

lacrima, -ae, *f.*, tear

lacus, -ūs, *m.*, lake

laetus, -a, -um, glad

lāpsus, -ūs, *m.*, fall ; lāpsus terrae, landslide

Larēs, -um (-ium), the Lares, household gods

Latīnī, -ōrum, *m.pl.*, the Latini, the Latins

latrō, -ōnis, *m.*, robber

lātus, -ā, -um, wide, broad

latus, -eris, *n.*, side

laudō, -āre, -āvī, -ātum, to praise

laus, laudis, *f.*, praise, glory

lēgātiō, -ionis, *f.*, embassy

lēgātus, -ī, *m.*, ambassador, lieutenant

legiō, -iōnis, *f.*, legion

legō, -ere, lēgī, lēctum, read

lentus, -a, -um, slow

levis, -is, -e, light ; levis armātūra, light-armed troops ; leve proelium, skirmish

lēx, lēgis, *f.*, law ; lēgem ferre, to get a law passed ; lēgem rogāre, to propose a law

libellus, -ī, *m.*, pamphlet

liber, librī, *m.*, book

līber, lībera, līberum, free

līberī, -ōrum, *m.pl.*, children

līberō, -āre, -āvī, -ātum, to set free, to free

lībertās, -ātis, *f.*, liberty

lībertus, -ī, *m.*, freedman
līctor, -ōris, *m.*, lictor
linter, -ris, *f.*, boat
līttera, -ae, *f.*, letter (of alphabet)
lītus, -oris, *n.*, shore
locus, -ī, *m.*, place, position
longē (*adv.*), far, by far
longus, -a, -um, long
loquor, loquī, locūtus sum, say, talk
lūbricus, -a, -um, slippery
lūcus, -ī, *m.*, grove
lūdō, -ere, lūsī, lūsum, play
lūdus, -ī, *m.*, school, game
lūna, -ae, *f.*, moon
lupus, -ī, *m.*, wolf
lūx, lūcis, *f.*, light
luxuria, -ae, *f.*, luxury

M., abbreviation for **Marcus**
Macedō, -onis, *m.*, a Macedonian
Macedonia, -ae, *f.*, Macedonia
māchina, -ae, *f.*, engine
maculō, -āre, -āvī, -ātum, to stain
maereō, -ēre, mourn
magis (*adv.*), more
magister, -trī, *m.*, master (of a school)
magistrātus, -ūs, *m.*, magistrate, magistracy
magnificentia, -ae, *f.*, magnificence
magnitūdō, -inis, *f.*, greatness
magnopere (*adv.*), greatly
magnus, -a, -um, great, big, loud
maiōrēs, -um, *m.pl.*, ancestors
male (*adv.*), badly
mālō, mālle, māluī, to prefer
malus, -a, -um, bad
mandāta, -ōrum, *n.pl.*, instructions
mandō, -āre, -āvī, -ātum, to entrust

maneō, -ēre, mānsī, mānsum, to remain, stay
mānēs, -ium, spirits (of the dead)
manus, -ūs, *f.*, hand
mare, -is, *n.*, sea ; **terrā marīque,** by land and sea
māter, -tris, *f.*, mother
mātrōna, -ae, *f.*, matron, married woman
mātūtīnus, -a, -um, in the morning
medicus, -ī, *m.*, doctor
mediocris, -is, -e, ordinary
Mediolānum, -ī, *n.*, Milan
medius, -a, -um, middle ; **media nox,** midnight
mehercule, upon my word !
meminī, -isse, to remember
mēns, mentis, *f.*, mind
mēnsa, -ae, *f.*, table
mercēs, -ēdis, *f.*, wages
merīdiēs, -iēī, *m.*, midday
metallum, -ī, *n.*, a mine
metus, -ūs, *m.*, fear
meus, -a, -um, my, mine
mīles, -itis, *m.*, soldier
mīlitāris, -is, -e, military
mīlle (*indeclinable adj.*), thousand
minimē (*adv.*), very little, least ; **minimē vērō,** no indeed, not at all
minor, -ōris, less, younger
minus (*adv.*), less
mīrābilis, -is, -e, wonderful
mīrāculum, -ī, *n.*, a marvel, miracle, wonderful happening
mīror, -ārī, mīrātus sum, to wonder, wonder at
miser, misera, miserum, wretched, unhappy ; **ō mē miserum !,** woe is me ! hang it all !
mītis, -is, -e, gentle, mild

mittō, -ere, mīsī, missum, send, launch (a weapon)

modicus, -a, -um, moderate

modo, only; nōn modo . . . sed etiam, not only . . . but also

modus, -ī, m., manner, fashion, method, size

moenia, -ium, n.pl., walls (of a city)

mōlēs, -is, f., mass, pile

molestus, -a, -um, troublesome

moneō, -ēre, -uī, -itum, warn, advise

mōns, -tis, m., mountain

morior, morī, mortuus sum, to die

mors, mortis, f., death

mortālis, -is, -e, mortal

mortuus, -a, -um, dead

mōs, mōris, m., custom; mōrēs, -um, character

mōtus, -ūs, m., movement

moveō, -ēre, mōvī, mōtum, to move

mox, soon, presently

multitūdō, -inis, f., multitude, crowd

multus, -a, -um, much; multī, -ae, -a, many; quid multa ?, to cut a long story short

mundus, -ī, m., world

mūniō, -īre, -īvī, -ītum, to fortify

mūrus, -ī, m., wall

mūtātiō, -iōnis, f., change

mūtō, -āre, -āvī, -ātum, to change

nancīscor, -ī, nactus sum, obtain

nārrō, -āre, -āvī, -ātum, to tell (a story), to relate

nāsus, -ī, m., nose

natātor, -ōris, m., swimmer

natō, -āre, -āvī, -ātum, to swim

nātūra, -ae, f., nature

nātus, -a, -um, old (in expressions of age)

nauta, -ae, m., sailor

nāvālis, -is, -e, naval

nē, lest, that . . . not

nebula, -ae, f., mist

nec, and not, nor; nec mīrum, no wonder

necō, -āre, -āvī, -ātum, to kill

neglegō, -ere, -lēxī, -lēctum, neglect

negō, -āre, -āvī, -ātum, deny, say . . . not

negōtium, -iī, n., business

nēmo, nūllīus, no one

nepōs, -ōtis, m., grandson

neque, and not, nor; neque . . . neque, neither . . . nor

nē . . . quidem, not even

nesciō, -īre, -īvī (-iī), not to know

neuter, -ra, -rum, neither

nēve, and not (after nē)

niger, -ra, -rum, black

nihil, nothing

nimis (adv.), too much

nisi, if not, unless

nix, nivis, f., snow

nōbilis, -is, -e, noble

noceō, -ere, -uī, to hurt

nōlō, nōlle, nōluī, be unwilling, refuse

nōmen, -inis, n., name

nōn, no, not; nōndum, not yet; nōn . . . modo . . . sed etiam, not only . . . but also; nōn-numquam, sometimes

nōnus, -a, -um, ninth

noster, -tra, -trum, our, ours

nostrī, -ōrum, m.pl., our men

Notus, -ī, m., South wind

novus, -a, -um, new, strange; novae cōpiae, reinforcements

nox, noctis, *f.,* night
noxa, -ae, *f.,* harm
nūbēs, -is, *f.,* cloud
nūbō, -ere, nūpsī, nūptum, marry (woman subject)
nūdus, -a, -um, naked, lightly-clad
nūllus, -a, -um, no, none
numquam, never
nunc, now
nūntiō, -āre, -āvī, -ātum, announce
nūntius, -iī, *m.,* messenger
nūper, recently
nusquam, nowhere
nūtriō, -īre, -īvī, -ītum, nourish

obiciō, -ere, -iēcī, -iectum, throw in the way of, throw against
obscūrō, -āre, -āvī, -ātum, to darken
obsecrō, -āre, -āvī, -ātum, to beseech
obsideō, -ēre, -sēdī, -sessum, besiege
obsidiō, -iōnis, *f.,* siege
obstō, -stare, -stitī, oppose, withstand
obtineō, -ēre, -uī, -tentum, hold
obviam īre, to go to meet
occāsiō, -iōnis, *f.,* opportunity
occidō, -ere, -cidī, -cāsum, to perish, set ; **sōl occidēns,** the setting sun, the West
occupō, -āre, -āvī, -ātum, to seize
oculus, -ī, *m.,* eye
ōdī, -isse, to hate
odium, -iī, *n.,* hatred
officium, -iī, *n.,* duty
ōlim, once, once upon a time, some day

omnis, -is, -e, all, every ; **omnēs ad ūnum,** all to a man
onus, -eris, *n.,* burden
operam dare, to take pains
opēs, -um, *f.pl.,* wealth, resources
oppidum, -ī, *n.,* town
opprimō, -ere, -pressī, -pressum, to overwhelm
oppugnō, -āre, -āvī, -ātum, to attack
optimus, -a, -um, best
opus, -eris, *n.,* work, task
ōrāculum, -ī, *n.,* oracle
ōrātiō, -iōnis, *f.,* speech
ōrātor, -ōris, *m.,* orator
orbis, -is, *m.,* ring, circle ; **orbis terrārum,** the world
ōrdō, -inis, *m.,* rank
oriēns, -ientis, rising ; **sōl oriēns,** the rising sun, the East
ōrnāmentum, -ī, *n.,* ornament, adornment
ōrnō, -āre, -āvī, -ātum, to adorn
ōrō, -āre, -āvī, -ātum, to pray
ōs, ōris, *n.,* mouth, face
os, ossis, *n.,* bone
ostendō, -ere, -ī, ostentum, to show, point out
ōstium, -iī, *n.,* river mouth
ōtiōsus, -a, -um, at ease, leisured
ōtium, -iī, *n.,* ease, leisure, peace

P., abbreviation for **Pūblius**
pācō, -āre, -āvī, -ātum, to pacify
paene, almost
palam, openly
pānis, -is, *m.,* bread
pār, paris, equal
parātus, -a, -um, ready, prepared
parcō, -ere, pepercī, parsum, to spare
parēns, -tis, *c.,* parent
pāreō, -ēre, -uī, to obey

parŏ, -āre, -āvī, -ātum, to prepare

pars, partis, f., part; in omnēs partēs, in all directions

parvus, -a, -um, small, little

passus, -ūs, m., step; mīlle passūs, a mile; mīlia passuum, miles

pāstor, -ōris, m., shepherd

Patāvium, -iī. n., Patavium, Padua

patefaciŏ, -ere, -fēcī, -factum, to lay open, bare, expose

pater, -ris, m., father

patientia, -ae, f., patience, endurance

patior, patī, passus sum, to suffer, allow

patrēs, -um, m.pl., senators

patria, -ae, f., native land, fatherland

patriciī, -ōrum, m.pl., patricians

paucī, -ae, -a, few

paulisper, for a short time

paulō, by a little, a little, somewhat

pauper, -is, poor

pāx, pācis, f., peace

peccō, -āre, -āvī, -ātum, do wrong, offend, sin

pecūnia, -ae, f., money

pedes, -itis, m., infantryman, foot soldier

per (prep. gov. acc.), through, over

pereŏ, -īre, -iī, -itum, to perish

perficiŏ, -ere, -fēcī, -fectum, to complete, finish

perfidia, -ae, f., treachery

perflŏ, -āre, -āvī, -ātum, to blow over

perīculōsus, -a, -um, dangerous

perīculum, -ī, n., danger

permulceŏ, -ēre, -mulsī, -mulsum, to stroke

permūtātiŏ, -iōnis, f., change

Persa, -ae, m., a Persian

persequor, -sequī, -secūtus sum, to pursue

persuādeŏ, -ēre, -suāsī, -suāsum, to persuade

perterreŏ, -ēre, -terruī, -territum, to frighten thoroughly; perterritus, -a, -um, thoroughly frightened, alarmed

pertineŏ, -ēre, -tinuī, to extend to

perveniŏ, -īre, -vēnī, -ventum, to arrive, reach

pēs, pedis, m., foot

petŏ, -ere, petīvī, petītum, to seek, ask, make for

Philippī, -ōrum, m.pl., Philippi

pietās, -ātis, f., loyalty, dutifulness, piety, affection, devotion

pila, -ae, f., ball

pinguis, -is, -e, fat

piscor, -ārī, piscātus sum, to fish

placet, it pleases

plānus, -a, -um, level

plaudŏ, -ere, -sī, -sum, to applaud

plēbēiī, -ōrum, m.pl., plebeians

plēbs, -is, f., the plebs, common people

plēnus, -a, -um, full

pluvius, -a, -um, rainy

poena, -ae, f., penalty, punishment; poenās dare, to be punished, pay the penalty.

Poenus, -ī, m., a Carthaginian

poēta, -ae, m., poet

Pompēius, -ī, m., Pompey

pondus, -eris, n., mass, weight

pōnŏ, -ere, posuī, positum, to put, place; castra pōnere, to pitch camp

pōns, pontis, m., bridge

populus, -ī, m., people

porrigō, -ere, -rēxī, -rēctum, stretch out

porta, -ae, *f.,* gate

portō, -āre, -āvī, -ātum, to carry

portus, -ūs, *m.,* harbour

possum, posse, potuī, I can, I am able

post (*prep. gov. acc.*), after ; *as adv.,* after, afterwards

posteā, afterwards

posterus, -a, -um, next

posthāc, after this

postrīdiē, on the next day

pōstulō, -āre, -āvī, -ātum, to demand

potestās, -ātis, *f.,* power

potior, -īrī, potītus sum, gain possession of

praebeō, -ēre, -uī, -itum, show, afford ; provide ; **sē praebēre,** to show one's self

praeceps, -cipitis, steep, headlong

praeceptor, -ōris, *m.,* teacher

praecipitō, -āre, -āvī, -ātum, to throw headlong

praeclārus, -a, -um, famous, distinguished

praecurrō, -ere, -cucurrī, -cursum, run ahead

praeda, -ae, *f.,* booty

praedīcō, -dīcere, -dīxī, -dictum, to foretell

praedō, -ōnis, *m.,* pirate, brigand

praemittō, -ere, -mīsī, -missum, to send ahead

praemium, -iī, *n.,* reward

praesidium, -iī, *n.,* garrison, protection

praestō, -āre, -stitī, -stātum, show, make good ; **fidem praestāre,** keep one's word

praesum, -esse, -fuī, be in command of

praeter (*prep. gov. acc.*), except, past

praytereā, besides

praetor, -ōris, *m.,* praetor

praetōrium, -iī, *n.,* general's tent

praevolō, -āre, -āvī, -ātum, fly ahead

prandium, -iī, *n.,* lunch

pretiōsus, -a, -um, costly, precious

pretium, -iī, *n.,* price, recompense

prīmus, -a, -um, first ; **prīma lūx,** dawn ; **prīmō,** at first ; **prīmum,** first

prīnceps, -ipis, *m.,* chief

prior, -is, earlier, former

priusquam, before

prīvātus, -a, -um, private ; *as noun,* a private citizen

prō (*prep. gov. abl.*), for, on behalf of

probō, -āre, -āvī, -ātum, to approve

probrum, -ī, *n.,* reproach, insult

procella, -ae, *f.,* storm

proclīvis, -is, -e, steep, sloping downhill

procul, far, far off

procumbō, -ere, -cubuī, -cubitum, fall forward, sink down

prōdigium, -iī, *n.,* portent, prodigy

prōditiō, -iōnis, *f.,* treason, betrayal, treachery

prōdō, -ere, -didī, -ditum, to betray

proelium, -iī, *n.,* battle

proficīscor, -ī, profectus sum, to set out

prōgredior, -ī, prōgressus sum, to advance

prohibeō, -ēre, -uī, -itum, prevent, hinder

prōmittō, -ere, -mīsī, -missum, to promise

prope, near, nearly

prōpellō, -ere, -pulī, -pulsum, drive forward

prōpōnō, -ere, -posuī, -positum, set before

propter (*prep. gov. acc.*), owing to, on account of

prōscrībō, -ere, -scrīpsī, -scriptum, to proscribe

prōvincia, -ae, *f.*, province

proximus, -a, -um, nearest, next

prūdēns, -entis, wise, sensible, prudent

prūdentia, -ae, *f.*, wisdom, good sense, prudence

pūblicus, -a, -um, belonging to the State, public

puella, -ae, *f.*, girl

puellula, -ae, *f.*, little girl, dear girl

puer, -ī, *m.*, boy

pugna, -ae, *f.*, fight, battle

pugnō, -āre, -āvī, -ātum, to fight

pulcher, -ra, -rum, beautiful

pulvis, -eris, *m.*, dust

Pūnicus, -a, -um, Carthaginian

pūrgō, -āre, -āvī, -ātum, to clean

putō, -āre, -āvī, -ātum, to think

Q., abbreviation for Quīntus

quadringentī, -ae, -a, four hundred

quaerō, -ere, quaesīvī, quaesītum, seek

quaestor, -ōris, *m.*, quaestor

~~~~~~~is, -e ?, of what kind ? ~~~~~~~s interrog.,~~ how ? ; *in com-* ~~~~~~sons,~~ than, as ; *with super-* ~~~~ives,~~ as . . . as possible ; *as exclamation,* how ! what a ! ; quamdiū ?, how long ?

quandō ?, when ?

quantus, -a, -um ?, how great ? how big ?

quārtus, -a, -um, fourth

quasi, as if

quattuor, four

quī ?, quae ?, quod ?, *interrog, adj.,* what ?, which ? ; quam ob rem ?, why ?, wherefore ?

quī, quae, quod, *rel. pron.,* who, which

quidam, quaedam, quiddam, a certain

quidem, indeed

quiēs, -iētis, *f.,* rest

quīndecim, fifteen

quīngentī, -ae, -a, five hundred

quīnque, five

quīntus, -a, -um, fifth

quīntus decimus, fifteenth

quis ?, quis ?, quid ?, who ?, which ?, what ? ; quid agis ?, how do you do ? ; quid multa ?, to cut a long story short ; quid novī ?, what news ?

quis, quis, quid, *indefinite pron.,* anyone, anything (after sī, nisi, nē, num)

quisquam, quaequam, quicquam, *indefinite pron.,* anyone, anything (after nōn, neque, negō)

quō ?, whither ?, where . . . to ?

quō, in order that (in final clauses containing a comparative)

quō ūsque tandem ?, how far, pray ? ; how long, pray ?

quod, because

quoque, also

quot ?, how many ?

rārō, seldom

ratiō, -iōnis, *f.,* plan, method

recipiō, -ere, -cēpī, -ceptum, take back, recover ; sē recipere, to retreat

reddō, -ere, -didī, -ditum, give back, restore

redeō, -īre, -iī, -itum, return

reditus, -ūs, *m.,* a return

reficiō, -ere, -fēcī, -fectum, repair, renew

rēgia, -ae, *f.,* palace

rēgīna, -ae, *f.,* queen

regiō, -iōnis, *f.,* region, district

rēgius, -a, -um, royal

rēgnum, -ī, *n.,* kingdom

regō, -ere, rēxī, rēctum, to rule

relinquō, -ere, relīquī, relictum, to leave

reliquus, -a, -um, remaining

remittō, -ere, -mīsī, -missum, send back

removeō, -ēre, -mōvī, -mōtum, remove

reportō, -āre, -āvī, -ātum, carry back; **victōriam reportāre,** to win a victory

rēs, reī, *f.,* thing, matter, affair, business; **rem gerere,** carry on operations; **bellum gerere,** wage war; **rēs gestae,** exploits; **rēs pūblica,** the commonwealth, the republic, the State

resistō, -ere, -stitī, to resist

respondeō, -ēre, -ī, respōnsum, to answer, reply

respōnsum, -ī, *n.,* a reply, answer

restituō, -ere, -uī, -ūtum, to restore

restō, -āre, restitī, to be left over, remain

retineō, -ēre, -uī, -tentum, hold back, retain, keep

retrahō, -ere, -trāxī, -tractum, drag back

reus, -ī, *m.,* defendant; **reum facere,** to impeach, bring to trial

revocō, -āre, -āvī, -ātum, call back

rēx, rēgis, *m.,* king

Rhodus, -ī, *f.,* Rhodes

rīdeō, -ēre, rīsī, rīsum, laugh, laugh at

rīpa, -ae, *f.,* bank (of a river)

rīsus, -ūs, *m.,* smile, laugh, laughter

robur, -oris, *n.,* strength, best part of army

rogō, -āre, -āvī, -ātum, to ask, beg; **lēgem rogāre,** to propose a law

Rōma, -ae, *f.,* Rome

Rōmānus, -a, -um, Roman

Rōmānus, -ī, *m.,* a Roman

rosa, -ae, *f.,* rose

Rōstra, -ōrum, *n.pl.,* the Rostra (speaker's platform in the Forum)

ruīna, -ae, *f.,* downfall, ruin

rupēs, -is, *f.,* rock, crag

rūs, rūris, *n.,* the country; **rūrī,** in the country; **rūre,** from the country

Sabīnī, -ōrum, *m.pl.,* the Sabines

Sabīnus, -a, -um, Sabine

sacer, -ra, -rum, sacred

sacerdōs, -ōtis, *m.,* priest

sacrificium, iī, *n.,* sacrifice

sacrificō, -āre, -āvī, -ātum, to sacrifice

saepe, often

saltus, -ūs, *m.,* defile, pass

salūs, -ūtis, *f.,* safety

salūtātiō, -iōnis, *f.,* greeting, salutation

salūtātor, -ōris, saluter, greeter

salūtō, -āre, -āvī, -ātum, to greet

salvē, salvēte, good day !, hail !

sanguis, -inis, *m.,* blood

sānus, -a, -um, sound, healthy, sane

sapiēns, -tis, wise

sapienter, wisely
sapientia, -ae, *f.,* wisdom
satis, enough
saxum, -ī, *n.,* stone, rock, boulder
scelerātus, -a, -um, wicked, accursed
scelestus, -a, -um, wicked
scelus, -eris, *n.,* crime, wickedness
scientia, -ae, *f.,* knowledge
sciō, -īre, scīvī, scītum, to know
scrībō, -ere, scrīpsī, scrīptum, write
scrīptor, -ōris, *m.,* writer
scūtum, -ī, *n.,* shield
Scytha, -ae, *m.,* a Scythian
secundus, -a, -um, second, favourable
secūris, -is, *f.,* axe
sed, but
sedeō, -ēre, sēdī, sessum, to sit
sēdēs, -is, *f.,* seat
sella, -ae, *f.,* seat, chair ; **sella curūlis,** chair of office
semper, always
senātor, -ōris, *m.,* senator
senātus, -ūs, *m.,* senate ; **senātūs cōnsultum,** decree of the senate
senex, senis, *m.,* old man
sententia, -ae, *f.,* opinion
sentiō, -īre, sēnsī, sēnsum, feel, perceive
sepeliō, -īre, -īvī, sepultum, bury
septimus, -a, -um, seventh
sequor, sequī, secūtus sum, follow
serius, -a, -um, serious
sermō, -ōnis, *m.,* conversation, talk, speech
sērō, late, too late
servō, -āre, -āvī, -ātum, save, protect, keep
servus, -ī, *m.,* slave
sexāgintā, sixty
sī, if

sīc, so, thus, in this way
siccō, -āre, -āvī, -ātum, drain
Sicilia, -ae, *f.,* Sicily
sīcut, just as, as
sīdus, -eris, *n.,* star, constellation
significō, -āre, -āvī, -ātum, mean
signum, -ī, *n.,* signal, standard
silentium, -iī, *n.,* silence
similis, -is, -e, like
simplex, -icis, simple
simulō, -āre, -āvī, -ātum, to pretend
sine (*prep. gov. abl.*), without
sinister, -tra, -trum, left ; **sinistra, -ae,** the left hand ; **ā sinistrā,** on the left
sinus, -ūs, *m.,* fold
socer, socerī, *m.,* father-in-law
societās, -ātis, *f.,* alliance
socius, -iī, *m.,* ally
sodālis, -is, *m.,* boon companion
sōl, sōlis, *m.,* sun ; **sōlis occāsus,** sunset
soleō, -ēre, solitus sum, be accustomed
sollicitus, -a, -um, anxious, troubled
sōlus, -a, -um, alone
solvō, -ere, solvī, solūtum, to loose, set sail
somnus, -ī, *m.,* sleep
sordidus, -a, -um, dirty
speciēs, -iēī, *f.,* appearance
spectāculum, -ī, *n.,* show, spectacle, sight
spērō, -āre, -āvī, -ātum, to hope
spēs, speī, *f.,* hope
sponte, of one's own accord
spūma, -ae, *f.,* foam
statim, immediately
statiō, -iōnis, *f.,* picket, outpost ; **in statiōne esse,** to be on picket duty
statūra, -ae, *f.,* size, stature

sternō, -ere, strāvī, strātum, to lay low

stō, stāre, stetī, statum, to stand

strāgēs, -is, *f.*, slaughter, destruction

strenuus, -a, -um, active, energetic

strepitus, -ūs, *m.*, noise

studeō, -ēre, -uī, to study

studium, -iī, *n.*, study, zeal, enthusiasm

stultitia, -ae, *f.*, stupidity, folly

stultus, -a, -um, stupid, foolish

sub, under

subitō, suddenly

subveniō, -īre, -vēnī, -ventum, help, come to help of

sūdor, -ōris, *m.*, sweat

suffrāgium, -iī, *n.*, vote

sum, esse, fuī, to be

summus, -a, -um, highest, greatest ; **summus mōns,** the top of the mountain ; **ad summum,** to the top

sūmō, -ere, sūmpsī, sūmptum, to take, choose

sūmptus, -ūs, *m.*, expense

super, above

superbia, -ae, *f.*, pride, arrogance

superbus, -a, -um, proud, haughty, arrogant

superior, -iōris, higher, upper, preceding

superō, -āre, -āvī, -ātum, to overcome, surmount

supersum, -esse, -fuī, to survive

supplantō, -āre, -āvī, -ātum, to trip

surgō, -ere, -rēxī, -rēctum, to rise

suscipiō, -ere, -cēpī, -ceptum, to undertake

suspīciō, -iōnis, *f.*, suspicion

sustineō, -ēre, -tinuī, -tentum, to withstand

sūtor, -ōris, *m.*, shoemaker

suus, -a, -um, his, her, its own

Syrācūsae, -ārum, *f.pl.*, Syracuse

T., abbreviation for **Titus**

taberna, -ae, *f.*, inn, shop

tabula, -ae, *f.*, tablet, notice

taceō, -ēre, -uī -itum, to be silent

talentum, -ī, *n.*, talent

tālis, -is, -e, such

tam, so

tamen, however, nevertheless

tandem, at length

tantus, -a, -um, so great

tardē, slowly

tēlum, -ī, *n.*, weapon, dart

temerārius, -a, -um, rash

tempestās, -ātis, *f.*, storm, weather

templum, -ī, *n.*, temple

tempus, -oris, *n.*, time

tendō, -ere, tetendī, to stretch

tenebrae, -ārum, *f.pl.*, darkness

teneō, -ēre, -uī, to hold

ter, thrice

tergum, -ī, *n.*, back

terra, -ae, *f.*, land ; **terrā marīque,** by land and sea ; **orbis terrārum,** the world

terreō, -ēre, -uī, -itum, to frighten

terror, -ōris, *m.*, terror

tertius, -a, -um, third

Tiberis, -is, *m.*, the Tiber

timeō, -ēre, -uī, to fear, be afraid

timor, -ōris, *m.*, fear

Thessalia, -ae, *f.*, Thessaly

toga, -ae, *f.*, toga ; **toga praetexta,** the purple-bordered toga ; **toga virīlis,** the toga of manhood

togātus, -a, -um, clad in the toga

tollō, -ere, sustulī, sublātum, raise, lift, remove

tot, so many

totiēns, so often

tōtus, -a, -um, whole ; tōtus esse in, to be engrossed in

trāctō, -āre, -āvī, -ātum, to treat

trādō, -ere, -didī, -ditum, to hand over

trahō, -ere, trāxī, tractum, to draw, drag

tranquillus, -a, -um, calm, quiet

trāns (*prep. gov. acc.*), across

trānseō, -īre, -iī, -itum, to cross

trānsferō, -ferre, -tulī, -lātum, to carry across, carry over, transfer

trānsfīgō, -ere, -fīxī, -fīxum, to pierce, run through, transfix

trecentī, -ae, -a, three hundred

tredecim, thirteen

trēs, trēs, tria, three

tribūnus, -ī, *m.*, tribune ; tribūnus mīlitum, tribune of the soldiers ; tribūnus plēbis, tribune of the plebs

tribūtum, -ī, *n.*, tribute

triclīnium, -iī, *n.*, dining-room

trīstis, -is, -e, sad

triumphō, -āre, -āvī, -ātum, to celebrate a triumph, hold a triumphal procession, triumph

triumphus, -ī, *m.*, triumph, triumphal procession

trux, trucis, grim, stern

tū, tuī, you (*s.*)

tum, then ; tum vērō, then indeed

tumultus, -ūs, *m.*, riot, rising, tumult

tunica, -ae, *f.*, tunic

turbulentus, -a, -um, disorderly

turpis, -is, -e, base, ugly, shameful

tūtus, -a, -um, safe

tuus, -a, -um, your, yours

ubi ?, where ?

ubi, when

ubīque, everywhere

ūllus, -a, -um, any

ūltimus, -a, -um, last

umbra, -ae, *f.*, shadow

umquam, ever

unde ?, whence ?, from where ?

undique, on all sides

ūnus, -a, -um, one

urbs, urbis, *f.*, city

ursa, -ae, *f.*, she-bear

ūsque ad, right up to

ut, that, in order that

uter, utra, utrum ?, which (of two) ?

ūtilis, -is, -e, useful

ūtor, ūtī, ūsus sum, to use

utrum . . . an, whether . . . or

uxor, -ōris, *f.*, wife

vae !, woe !

valdē, exceedingly

valē, valēte, farewell, good day, good-bye

valeō, -ēre, -uī, to be well ; be strong

vallis, -is, *f.*, valley

vallum, -ī, *n.*, rampart

varius, -a, -um, varied, different

vāstō, -āre, -āvī, -ātum, to lay waste

vēlum, -ī, *n.*, sail

vēndō, -ere, -didī, -ditum, to sell

venēnum, -ī, *n.*, poison

venia, -ae, *f.*, pardon, forgiveness, quarter

veniō, -īre, vēnī, ventum, to come

venter, -tris, *m.*, belly

ventus, -ī, *m.,* wind

verber, -eris, *n.,* blow

verberō, -āre, -āvī, -ātum, to beat

verbum, -ī, *n.,* word

vereor, -ērī, veritus sum, to fear

Vergilius, -iī, *m.,* Virgil

versus, -ūs, *m.,* verse

vertō, -ere, vertī, versum, to turn ; **sē vertere,** to turn one's self, turn (*intrans.*)

vērus, -a, -um, true

vescor, vescī, to feed upon

vester, -tra, -trum, your, yours

vestibulum, -ī, *n.,* entrance-hall, porch

vestīgium, -iī, *n.,* track, trace, footprint

vestīmentum, -ī, *n.,* garment ; **vestīmenta, -ōrum,** garments, clothes

vetō, -āre, -uī, -itum, to forbid

vetus, -eris, old

via, ae, *f.,* way, road ; **Via Appia,** the Appian Way ; **viam mūnīre,** to build a road

viātor, -ōris, *m.,* traveller

vīcīnus, -a, -um, neighbouring ; **vīcīnus, -ī,** *m.,* a neighbour

victima, -ae, *f.,* victim

victor, -ōris, *m.,* victor, conqueror ; *as adj.,* victorious

victōria, -ae, *f.,* victory

vīcus, -ī, *m.,* street

videō, -ēre, -ī, vīsum, to see ; **videor, vidērī, vīsus sum,** to seem

vīgintī, twenty

vīlicus, -ī, *m.,* bailiff, overseer (of farm)

vīlis, -is, -e, cheap ; **vīlī,** at a low price, cheap, cheaply

vīlla, -ae, *f.,* country-house

vincō, -ere, vīcī, victum, to conquer

vinculum, -ī, *n.,* bond ; **in vincula conicere,** throw into prison

vīnum, -ī, *n.,* wine

violō, -āre, -āvī, -ātum, violate, harm, break (a law)

vir, virī, *m.,* man, husband

virga, -ae, *f.,* rod

virgō, -inis, *f.,* maiden

virtūs, -ūtis, *f.,* courage, bravery, valour

vīs, *f.* (*sing.*), force, violence ; (*pl.*), strength

vīta, -ae, *f.,* life ; **vītam agere,** to pass, spend (one's life)

vitium, -iī, *n.,* fault, failing

vītō, -āre, -āvī, -ātum, to avoid

vīvō, -ere, vīxī, vīctum, to live

vīvus, -a, -um, alive

vix, hardly, scarcely

vocō, -āre, -āvī, -ātum, call, invite

volō, -āre, -āvī, -ātum, to fly

volō, velle, voluī, to wish, be willing

Volscī, -ōrum, *m.pl.,* the Volscians

volvō, -ere, volvī, volūtum, to roll

vōs, vestrum (-ī), you (*pl.*)

vōx, vōcis, *f.,* voice

vulnerō, -āre, -āvī, -ātum, to wound

vulnus, -eris, *n.,* a wound

vultus, -ūs, *m.,* expression, countenance

Xerxēs, -is, *m.,* Xerxes

Zama, -ae, *f.,* Zama

B. ENGLISH-LATIN

able, to be, possum, posse, potuī
about, dē (*with abl.*)
abuse, male ūtor, ūtī, ūsus sum
accept, accipiō, -ere, -cēpī, -ceptum
accord, of one's own, suā sponte
account, on a. of, propter (*with acc.*)
accustomed, to be, soleō, -ēre, solitus sum
achievements, rēs gestae, rērum gestārum, *f.pl.*
across, trāns (*with acc.*)
add, addō, -ere, -didī, -ditum
adopt a plan, cōnsilium capere
advance, prōgredior, -gredī, -gressus sum
advice, cōnsilium, -iī, *n.*
advise, moneō, -ēre, -uī, -itum
affair, rēs, reī, *f.*
afraid, to be, timeō, -ēre, -uī
after, post (*with acc.*)
again, iterum, rursus
age, . . . years of age, nātus, -a, -um
ago, abhinc
alas, ēheu
alive, vīvus, -a, -um
all, omnis, -is, -e
alliance, societās, -ātis, *f.*
allow, patior, -ī, passus sum
ally, socius, -iī, *m.*
alone, sōlus, -a, -um
already, iam
always, semper
anchor, ancora, -ae, *f.*
and, et
anger, īra, -ae, *f.*

angry, īrātus, -a, -um
another, alius, -a, -ud
answer, respondeō, -ēre, -ī, respōnsum
anxious, sollicitus, -a, -um
anywhere, ūsquam
appearance, fōrma, -ae, *f.*
arise, coorior, -orīrī, coortus sum
army, exercitus, -ūs, *m.*
arrival, adventus, -ūs, *m.*
ascertain, cognōscō, -ere, cognōvī, cognitum
ask, rogō, -āre, -āvī, -ātum
assemble, conveniō, -īre, -vēnī, -ventum
astounded, attonitus, -a, -um
at, ad (*with acc.*)
at once, statim
attack, impetus, -ūs, *m.*
attack, oppugnō, -āre, -āvī, -ātum
attentive, attentus, -a, -um
authority, imperium, -iī, *n.*
avoid, vītō, -āre, -āvī, -ātum
await, exspectō, -āre, -āvī, -ātum
axe, secūris, -is, *f.*

bailiff, vīlicus, -ī, *m.*
ball, pila, -ae, *f.*
bank, rīpa, -ae, *f.*
barbarous, barbarus, -a, -um
battle, pugna, -ae, *f.* ; proelium, -iī, *n.*
be, sum, esse, fuī
bear, ursa, -ae, *f.*
beard, barba, -ae, *f.*
beast, wild beast, fera, -ae, *f.*
beat, verberō, -āre, -āvī, -ātum
beautiful, pulcher, -ra, -rum

because, quod
become, fīō, fierī, factus sum
bed, cubīle, -is, *n.*
bedroom, cubīculum, -ī, *n.*
before, ante (*with acc.*)
beg, ōrō, -āre, āvī, -ātum ; petō -ere, -īvī, -ītum (*with a, ab, and abl.*)
begin, incipiō, -ere, -cēpī, -ceptum ; **I began, I have begun,** coepī, coepisse
beseech, ōrō, -āre, -āvī, -ātum ; implōrō, -āre, -āvī, -ātum
best, optimus, -a, -um
betray, prōdō, -ere, -didī, -ditum
better, melior, melius
big, magnus, -a, -um
blame, culpō, -āre, -āvī, -ātum
blood, sanguis, sanguinis, *m.*
boat, linter, -ris, *f.*
bold, audāx, -ācis
boldness, audācia, -ae, *f.*
book, liber, -rī, *m.*
booty, praeda, -ae, *f.*
born, to be, nāscor, nāscī, nātus sum
both . . . and, et . . . et
boy, puer, puerī, *m.*
brave, fortis, -is, -e
bread, pānis, -is, *m.*
break, frangō, -ere, frēgī, frāctum
break (law), violō, -āre, -āvī, -ātum
break off, dirimō, -ere, -ēmī, -emptum
bridge, pōns, pontis, *m.*
brother, frāter, -ris, *m.*
build, aedificō, -āre, -āvī, -ātum
building, aedificium, -iī, *n.*
burden, onus, -eris, *n.*
burn, incendō, -ere, -ī, incēnsum
bury, sepeliō, -īre, -īvī, sepultum
but, sed
by, a, ab, (*with abl.*)

call, appellō, -āre, -āvī, -ātum ; vocō, -are, -āvī, -ātum
call together, convocō, -āre, -āvī, -ātum
camp, castra, -ōrum, *n.pl.*
carefully, dīligenter
carry, portō, -āre, -āvī, -ātum
case, this being the c., quae cum ita sint *or* essent
catch sight of, cōnspiciō, -ere, spexī, -spectum
cavalry, equitēs, -um, *m.pl.* ; equitātus, -ūs, *m.*
cease, dēsistō, -ere, -stitī, -stitum
celebrate, celebrō, -āre, -āvī, -ātum
centurion, centuriō, -iōnis, *m.*
certain, certus, -a, -um
certain, a, quīdam, quaedam, quiddam
chariot, currus, -ūs, *m.*
cheap, vīlis, -is, -e ; **cheap, cheaply, at a low price,** vīlī
cheer, be of good, bonō animō esse
chide, castīgō, -āre, -āvī, -ātum
chief, prīnceps, -ipis, *m.*
children, līberī, -ōrum, *m.pl.*
citadel, arx, arcis, *f.*
citizen, cīvis, -is, *m.*
citizenship, cīvitās, -ātis, *f.*
city, urbs, urbis, *f.*
clean, pūrgō, -āre, -āvī, -ātum
climb, ascendō, -ere, -ī, ascēnsum
close, claudō, -ere, clausī, clausum
clothes, clothing, vestīmenta, -ōrum, *n.pl.*
cloud, nubēs, -is, *f.*
cold, frīgus, -oris, *n.*
colleague, collēga, -ae, *m.*
come, veniō, -īre, vēnī, ventum
command, imperium, -iī, *n.*
command, to be in c., praesum, -esse, -fuī
companion, comes, -itis, *m.*

complete, cōnficiō, -ere, -fēcī, -fectum ; perficiō, -ere, -fēcī, -fectum

condition, condiciō, -iōnis, *f.*

conquer, vincō, -ere, vīcī, victum

considerably, aliquantō

construct (road), mūniō, -īre, -īvī, -ītum

consul, cōnsul, -is, *m.*

consulship, cōnsulātus, -ūs, *m.*

cook, coquus, -ī, *m.*

corn, frūmentum, -ī, *n.*

count, numerō, -āre, -āvī, -ātum

country, rūs, rūris, *n.* ;
    in the country, rūrī

country-house, vīlla, -ae, *f.*

courage, virtūs, -ūtis, *f.*

cowardice, īgnāvia, -ae, *f.*

crag, rupēs, -is, *f.*

cross, trānseō, -īre, -iī, -itum

crowd, multitūdō, -inis, *f.*

crown, corōna, -ae, *f.*

cruel, crūdēlis, -is, -e

cruelty, crūdēlitās, -ātis, *f.*

cultivate, colō, -ere, coluī, cultum

danger, perīculum, -ī, *n.*

dangerous, perīculōsus, -a, -um

dare, audeō, -ēre, ausus sum

dark, in the, in tenebrīs

darkness, tenebrae, -ārum, *f.pl.*

dawn, prīma lūx

day, diēs, diēī, *m.*

dead, mortuus, -a, -um

death, mors, mortis, *f.*

deceive, dēcipiō, -ere, -cēpī, -ceptum

decide, cōnstituō, -ere, -uī, -ūtum

declare, affirmō, -āre, -āvī, -ātum

declare (war), bellum indīcere

defeat, cladēs, -is, *f.*

defeat, superō, -āre, -āvī, -ātum

defend, dēfendō, -ere, -ī, dēfēnsum

delight, dēlectō, -āre, -āvī, -ātum

demand, pōstulō, -āre, -āvī, -ātum

depart, discēdō, -ere, -cessī, -cessum

depth, altitūdō, -inis, *f.*

desire, cupiō, -ere, -īvī (-iī), -ītum

desirous, cupidus, -a, -um

desist from, dēsistere ā *or* ab (*with abl.*)

despair, dēspērō, -āre, -āvī, -ātum

despair of, dēspērāre dē (*with abl.*)

destroy, dēleō, -ēre, -ēvī, -ētum

determine, cōnstituō, -ere, -uī, -ūtum

dictator, dictātor, -ōris, *m.*

dictatorship, dictātūra, -ae, *f.*

die, morior, morī, mortuus sum

difficulty, difficultās, -ātis, *f.*

dig, fodiō, -ere, fōdī, fossum

dignity, dīgnitās, -ātis, *f.*

diligence, dīligentia, -ae,*f.*

diligent, dīligēns, -entis

diligently, dīligenter

dine, cēnō, -āre, -āvī, -ātum

dirty, sordidus, -a, -um

discuss, agere dē (*with abl.*)

disgraceful, turpis, -is, -e

dispute, contrōversia, -ae, *f.*

distinction, decus, -oris, *n.* ;
    to be a *d.* to, decorī esse

distinguished, īnsignis, -is, -e

distrust, diffīdō, -ere, diffīsus sum

disturb, perturbō, -āre, -āvī, -ātum

ditch, fossa, -ae, *f.*

divide, dīvidō, -ere, -vīsī, -vīsum

do, faciō, -ere, fēcī, factum

dog, canis, -is, *c.*

door, iānua, -ae, *f.*

drag, draw, trahō, -ere, trāxī, tractum

draw up, īnstruō, -ere, -strūxī, -strūctum

dust, pulvis, -eris, *m.*

duty, officium, -iī, *n.*

eagle, aquila, -ae, *f.*
ease, ōtium, -iī, *n.*
easy, facilis, -is, -e
eclipse, dēfectiō, -iōnis, *f.*
eclipsed, to be, dēficiō, -ere, -fēcī, -fectum
educate, ēducō, -āre, -āvī, -ātum
either . . . or, aut . . . aut
elect, creō, -āre, -āvī, -ātum
embassy, lēgātiō -iōnis, *f.*
emblems, īnsignia, -ium, *n.pl.*
employ, ūtor, ūtī, ūsus sum
encourage, hortor, -ārī, hortātus sum
endure, ferō, ferre, tulī, lātum
enemy, hostis, -is, *m.* ; inimīcus, -ī, *m.*
engine, māchina, -ae, *f.*
engrossed in, tōtus in (*with abl.*)
enlarge, augeō, -ēre, auxī, auctum
enough, satis
enter, intrō, -āre, -āvī, -ātum
entrust, committō, -ere, -mīsī, -missum
equal, pār, paris
escape, effugiō, -ere, -fūgī
eternal, aeternus, -a, -um
ever, umquam
everlasting, aeternus, -a, -um
everything, omnia, -ium, *n.pl.*
everywhere, ubīque
examine, īnspiciō, -ere, -spexī, -spectum
example, exemplum, -ī, *n.*
excel, praestō, -āre, -stitī, -stātum
exclaim, exclāmō, -āre, -āvī, -ātum
exhaust, abūtor, abūtī, abūsus sum
exile, exsilium, -iī, *n.*
expel, expellō, -ere, -pulī, -pulsum
expense, sūmptus, -ūs, *m.*
experience, experior, -īrī, expertus sum
expose, patefaciō, -ere, -fēcī, -factum

face, vultus, -ūs, *m.*
fall, cadō, -ere, cecidī, cāsum
famine, famēs, -is, *f.*
famous, praeclārus, -a, -um
farm, fundus, -ī, *m.*
farmer, agricola, -ae, *m.*
father, pater, patris, *m.*
father-in-law, socer, socerī, *m.*
fatherland, patria, -ae, *f.*
favourable, secundus, -a, -um
fear, timeō, -ēre, -uī ; vereor, -ērī, veritus sum
fear, timor, -ōris, *m.* ; metus, -ūs, *m.*
fellow, homō, -inis, *m.*
few, paucī, -ae, -a
field, ager, agrī, *m.*
fierce, ācer, ācris, ācre ; ferōx, -ōcis
fight, pugnō, -āre, -āvī, -ātum
fight, pugna, -ae, *f.*
find, inveniō, -īre, -vēnī, -ventum
finish, cōnficiō, -ere, -fēcī, -fectum ; perficiō, -ere, -fēcī, -fectum
fire, īgnis, -is, *m.*
first (*adj.*), prīmus, -a, -um ; (*adv.*), prīmum ; **at first,** prīmō
fish, pīscor, -ārī, pīscātus sum
flee, fugiō, -ere, fūgī, fugitum
fleet, classis, -is, *f.*
fly away, āvolō, -āre, -āvī, -ātum
follow, sequor, sequī, secūtus sum
folly, stultitia, -ae, *f.*
food, cibus, -ī, *m.*
foolish, stultus, -a, -um
foot, pēs, pedis, *m.*
footstep, vestīgium, -iī, *n.*
for, enim
forbid, vetō, -āre, -uī, -itum
foretell, praedīcō, -ere, -dīxī, -dictum
forgetful, immemor, -oris
fortify, mūniō, -īre, -īvī, -ītum
forum, forum, -ī, *n.*

found, condō, -ere, -didī, -ditum
foundation, fundāmentum, -ī, *n.*
friend, amīcus, -ī, *m.*
frighten, terreō, -ēre, -uī, -itum
from, ā, ab ; ex, ē (*with abl.*)
full, plēnus, -a, -um

gain possession of, potior, potīrī, potītus sum
game, lūdus, -ī, *m.*
garden, hortus, -ī, *m.*
garrison, praesidium, -iī, *n.*
gate, porta, -ae, *f.*
general, imperātor, -ōris, *m.*
gift, dōnum, -ī, *n.*
girl, puella, -ae, *f.*
give, dō, dare, dedī, datum
give back, reddō, -ere, -didī, -ditum
glad, laetus, -a, -um
glad, to be, gaudeō, -ēre, gāvisus sum
go, eō, īre, īvī, itum
go away, abeō, -īre, -iī, -itum
god, deus, -ī, *m.*
goddess, dea, -ae, *f.*
gold, aurum, -ī, *n.*
good, bonus, -a, -um
good-day, salvē, salvēte
goose, ānser, -eris, *m.*
granary, horreum, -ī, *n.*
grandfather, avus, -ī, *m.*
greet, salūtō, -āre, -āvī, -ātum
ground, humus, -ī, *f.* ; **on the ground**, humī
grow well, convalēscō, -ere, -valuī
guard, custōs, -ōdis, *m.*
guard, custōdiō, -īre, -īvī, -ītum

hair, capillus, -ī, *m.*
halt, cōnsistō, -ere, -stitī
hand, manus, -ūs, *f.*
hang it all, ō mē miserum !
happen, fīō, fierī, factus sum

harbour, portus, -ūs, *m.*
hard (*adv.*), dīligenter
hasten, festīnō, -āre, -āvī, -ātum
hate, odium, -iī, *n.*
hate, ōdī, ōdisse
hateful, invīsus, -a, -um
hateful, to be, odiō esse
have, habeō, -ēre, -uī, -itum
he, she, it, is, ea, id
hear, audiō, -īre, -īvī, -ītum
heat, calor, -ōris, *m.*
heavy, gravis, -is, -e
height, altitūdō, -inis, *f.*
help, auxilium, -iī, *n.*
help, adiuvō, -āre, -iūvī, -iūtum
hesitate, cunctor, -ārī, -ātus sum
hide, cēlō, -āre, -āvī, -ātum
high, altus, -a, -um
hinder, impediō, -īre, -īvī, -ītum
hire, condūcō, -ere, -dūxī, -ductum
holidays, fēriae, -ārum, *f.pl.*
home, domus, -ūs, *f.* ; **at home**, domī
honour, honōs, -ōris, *m.*, honestās, -ātis
honour, to be an, honōrī esse
hope, spēs, speī, *f.*
hope, spērō, -āre, -āvī, -ātum
horn, cornū, -ūs, *n.*
horse, equus, -ī, *m.*
horseman, eques, -itis, *m.*
hour, hōra, -ae, *f.*
house, domus, -ūs, *f.*
house, at the h. of, apud (*with acc.*)
how ? quomodo ?
how ? quam ?
how big ? quantus, -a, -um ?
how do you do ? quid agis ?
how long ? quamdiū ?
how often ? quotiēns ?
huge, ingēns, -tis
husband, vir, virī, *m.*
hurry, festīnō, -āre, -āvī, -ātum

idle, īgnāvus, -a, -um
ignorant, to be i. of, īgnōrō, -āre, -āvī, -ātum (*with acc.*)
ill, to be, aegrōtō, -āre, -āvī, -ātum
implore, obsecrō, -āre, -āvi, -ātum
in, in (*with abl.*)
increase, augeō, -ēre, auxī, auctum
infantry, peditēs, -um, *m.pl.*
inform, certiōrem facere
innocent, innocēns, -entis
inspect, īnspiciō, -ere, -spexī, -spectum
instructions, mandāta, -ōrum, *n. pl.*
into, in (*with acc.*)
invite, vocō, -āre, -āvī, -ātum
island, īnsula, -ae, *f.*

join battle, proelium committere
journey, iter, itineris, *n.*;
  to journey, iter facere
joy, gaudium, -iī, *n.*
just, iūstus, -a, -um
just as, sīcut
justice, iūstitia, -ae, *f.*

keep, servō, -āre, -āvī, -ātum
kill, necō, -āre, -āvī, -ātum ;
  interficiō, -ere, -fēcī, -fectum
kindly, benignē
king, rēx, rēgis, *m.*
know, sciō, scīre, scīvī, scītum
know, not to, nesciō, -īre, -īvī ;
  īgnōrō, -āre, -āvī, -ātum

labour, labor, -ōris, *m.*
lacking, to be, desum, -esse, -fuī
land, terra, -ae, *f.*
large, magnus, -a, -um
late, too late, sērō
laugh, laugh at, rīdeō, -ēre, rīsī, rīsum (*with acc.*)
law, lēx, lēgis, *f.*

lay down, dēpōnō, -ere, -posuī, -positum
lazy, īgnāvus, -a, -um
lead, dūcō, -ere, dūxī, ductum
leap down, dēsiliō, -īre, -siluī, -sultum
learn, discō, -ere, didicī
learned, doctus, -a, -um
learning, doctrīna, -ae, *f.*
leave, relinquō, -ere, relīquī, relictum
leave, go away from, discēdō, -ere, -cessī, -cessum
left, sinister, -tra, -trum ;
  the left hand, sinistra, -ae, *f.* ;
  on the left, ā sinistrā
legion, legiō, -iōnis, *f.*
leisured, at leisure, ōtiōsus, -a, -um
letter, epistola, -ae, *f.* ; litterae, ārum, *f.pl.*
liberty, lībertās, -ātis, *f.*
lictor, līctor, -ōris, *m.*
light (*adj.*), levis, -is, -e
light (*noun*), lūx, lūcis, *f.*
like, similis, -is, -e
like, to, amō, -āre, -āvī, -ātum
line (of battle), aciēs, -iēī, *f.*
list, tabula, -ae, *f.*
little, parvus, -a, -um
live, vīvō, -ere, vīxī, vīctum
live on, vescor, vescī
long, longus, -a, -um
long, for a l. time, diū ; *comp.*, diūtius
look !, ecce !
lose, āmittō, -ere, -mīsī, -missum
love, amō, -āre, -āvī, -ātum
low, humilis, -is, -e
lucky, fēlīx, -īcis
lunch, prandium, -iī, *n.*

maiden, virgō, -inis, *f.*
make, faciō, -ere, fēcī, factum

man, homŏ, -inis, *m.* ; vir, -ī, *m.*
man, all to a, omnēs ad ūnum
many, multī, -ae, -a
march, iter, itineris, *n.* ; to march, iter facere
marry, dūcō, -ere, dūxī, ductum ; nūbō, -ere, nūpsī, nūptum
mass, pondus, -eris, *n.*
master, dominus, -ī, *m.* ; magister, -rī, *m.*
matter, rēs, reī, *f.*
means, ratiō, -iōnis, *f.*
meanwhile, intereā
meet, assemble, conveniō, -īre, -vēnī, -ventum
meet, go to meet, obviam īre
midday, merīdiēs, -iēī, *m.*
midnight, media nox
mile, mīlle passūs; *pl.,* mīlia passuum
money, pecūnia, -ae, *f.*
moon, lūna, -ae, *f.*
morning, in the, māne
motionless, immōtus, -a, -um
mother, māter, -ris, *f.*
mountain, mōns, montis, *m.*
much, multus, -a, -um
multitude, multitūdō, -inis, *f.*
my, meus, -a, -um

name, nōmen, -inis, *n.*
nation, gēns, gentis, *f.*
native, barbarus, -ī, *m.*
native land, patria, -ae, *f.*
nature, nātūra, -ae, *f.*
neglect, neglegō, -ere, -lēxī, -lēctum
neither . . . nor, neque . . . neque, nec . . . nec
never, numquam
new, novus, -a, -um,
no (*adj.*), nūllus, -a, -um
no, no indeed, minimē vērō
no one, nēmo, nūllīus
noise, strepitus, -ūs, *m.*

not, nōn
not even, nē . . . quidem
not yet, nōndum
nothing, nihil
notice, animadvertō, -ere, -ī, animadversum
now, iam, nunc
nowhere, nusquam

obey, pāreō, -ēre, -uī
obtain, adipīscor, -ī, adeptus sum ; nancīscor, -ī, nactus sum
often, saepe ; so often, totiēns
old, vetus, -eris
old (*in expressions of age*), nātus, -a, -um
old man, senex, -is, *m.*
old woman, anus, -ūs, *f.*
on, in (*with abl.*)
once, at, statim
one, ūnus, -a, -um ; one (of two), alter, -a, -um ; one . . . another, alius . . . alius; the one . . . the other (of two), alter . . . alter
open, apertus, -a, -um
open, aperiō, -īre, -uī, -tum
orator, ōrātor, -ōris, *m.*
order, imperō, -āre, -āvī, -ātum ; iubeō, -ēre, iūssī, iūssum
other, alius ; other (of two), alter
ought, dēbeō, -ēre, -uī, -itum
our, noster, -tra, -trum
our men, nostrī, -ōrum, *m.pl.*
ourselves, nōs, nostrum (-trī)
outside, extrā (*with acc.*)
ox, bōs, bovis, *m.*

pardon, īgnōscō, -ere, īgnōvī, īgnōtum
parent, parēns, -entis, *c.*
pass, saltus, -ūs, *m.*
pass (a law), lēgem ferre

patience, patientia, -ae, *f.*
pay, solvō, -ere, solvī, solūtum
pay the penalty, poenās dare
peace, pāx, pācis, *f.*
perform, perficiō, -ere, -fēcī, -fectum
perhaps, fortāsse
perish, pereō, -īre, -iī, -itum
persuade, persuādeō -ēre, -suāsī, -suāsum
pirate, praedō, -ōnis, *m.*
pitch (camp), castra pōnere
plan, cōnsilium, -iī, *n.*
play, lūdō, -ere, lūsī, lūsum
pleasant, amoenus, -a, -um
poet, poēta, -ae, *m.*
poor, pauper, -eris
possession, to gain, potior, -īrī, potītus sum
post, collocō, -āre, -āvī, -ātum
pour into, pour upon, infundō, -ere, -fūdī, -fūsum
power, potestās, -ātis, *f.*
praise, laudō, -āre, -āvī, -ātum
prefer, mālō, mālle, māluī
prepare, parō, -āre, -āvī, -ātum
pretend, simulō, -āre, -āvī, -ātum
prevent, prohibeō, -ēre, -uī, -itum
pride, superbia, -ae, *f.*
priest, sacerdōs, -ōtis, *m.*
prison, carcer, -eris, *m.* ; **to throw into prison,** in vincula conicere
prisoner, captīvus, -ī, *m.*
procure, comparō, -āre, -āvī, -ātum
prodigy, prōdigium, -iī, *n.*
promise, prōmittō, -ere, -mīsī, -missum
protect, servō, -āre, -āvī, -ātum
protection, praesidium, -iī, *n.*
province, prōvincia, -ae, *f.*
prudence, prūdentia, -ae, *f.*
prudent, prūdēns, -entis
punish, pūniō, -īre, -īvī, -ītum ; **to be punished,** poenās dare

pupil, discipulus, -ī, *m.*
pursue, persequor, -sequī, -secūtus sum

question, interrogō, -āre, -āvī, -ātum
quickly, celeriter

race, gēns, gentis, *f.*
raise, tollō, -ere, sustulī, sublātum
rampart, vāllum, -ī, *n.*
raven, corvus, -ī, *m.*
reach, perveniō, -īre, -vēnī, -ventum (*with* ad *and acc.*)
read, legō, -ere, lēgī, lēctum
ready, parātus, -a, -um
realise, intellegō, -ere, -ēxī, -ēctum
receive, accipiō, -ere, -cēpī, -ceptum
recover, convalēscō, -ere, -valuī
refuse, nōlō, nōlle, nōluī
reinforcements, novae cōpiae, novārum cōpiārum, *f.pl.*
rejoice, gaudeō, -ēre, gāvisus sum
remain, maneō, -ēre, mānsī, mānsum
remember, meminī, -isse
remove, removeō, -ēre, -mōvī, -mōtum
repair, reficiō, -ere, -fēcī, -fectum
resign, sē abdicāre (*with abl.*)
resist, resistō, -ere, -stitī
resolve, cōnstituō, -ere, -uī, -ūtum
retreat, sē recipere
return, redeō, -īre, -iī, -itum
reward, praemium, -iī, *n.*
rich, dīves, -itis
ring, ānulus, -ī, *m.*
rise, surgō, -ere, surrēxī, surrēctum
river, flūmen, -inis, *n.*
road, via, -ae, *f.*
robber, latrō, -ōnis, *m.*

rouse, excitō, -āre, -āvī, -ātum
royal, rēgius, -a, -um
rule, imperium, -iī, *n.*
rule, regō, -ere, rēxī, rēctum

sacred, sacer, -ra, -rum
sacrifice, sacrificō, -āre, -āvī, -ātum
safe, tūtus, -a, -um
sailor, nauta, -ae, *m.*
same, īdem, eadem, idem
say, inquam ; dīcō, -ere, dīxī, dictum
sea, mare, -is, *n.*
seat, sella, -ae, *f.*
see, videō, -ēre, vīdī, vīsum
see !, ecce !
seek, petō, -ere, -īvī, -ītum
seem, videor, -ērī, vīsus sum
self, ipse, -a, -um
sell, vēndō, -ere, -didī, -ditum
senate, senātus, -ūs, *m.*
senate-house, cūria, -ae, *f.*
senator, senātor, -ōris, *m.*
send, mittō, -ere, mīsī, missum
set out, proficīscor, -ī, profectus sum
settle (dispute), cōnstituō, -ere, -uī, -ūtum
severe, gravis, -is, -e
sight, catch sight of, cōnspiciō, -ere, -spexī, -spectum
silent, to be, taceō, -ēre, -uī, -itum
since, cum
sit, sedeō, -ēre, sēdī, sessum
sixty, sexāgintā
size, magnitūdō, -inis, *f.*
she-bear, ursa, -ae, *f.*
shepherd, pāstor, -ōris, *m.*
shield, scūtum, -ī, *n.*
ship, nāvis, -is, *f.*
shoe, calceus, -ī, *m.*
shoemaker, sūtor, -ōris, *m.*

shop, taberna, -ae, *f.*
shore, lītus, -oris, *n.*
short time, for a, paulisper
shout, clāmor, -ōris, *m.*
shout, clāmō, -āre, -āvī, -ātum
show, ostendō, -ere, -ī, ostentum
sky, caelum, -ī, *n.*
slaughter, caedēs, -is, *f.*
slave, servus, -ī, *m.*
sleep, dormiō, -īre, -īvī, -ītum
sleep, somnus, -ī, *m.*
slowly, tardē
smoke, fūmus, -ī, *m.*
snow, nix, nivis, *f.*
so, tam
so great, tantus, -a, -um
so long, tamdiū
so many, tot
so often, totiēns
soldier, mīles, -itis, *m.*
some . . . others, aliī . . . aliī
son, fīlius, -iī, *m.*
son-in-law, gener, -ī, *m.*
soon, mox
sort, of what ?, quālis, -is, -e ?
source of safety, to be a, salūt esse
spare, parcō, -ere, pepercī, parsum
speak, loquor, loquī, locūtus sum
spectacle, spectāculum, -ī, *n.*
speech, ōrātiō, -iōnis, *f.*
spend (money), expendō, -ere, -ī, -pēnsum
spend (time), agō, -ere, ēgī, āctum
spur on, incitō, -āre, -āvī, -ātum
stain, maculō, -āre, -āvī, -ātum
stand, stō, stāre, stetī, statum
standard, signum, -ī, *n.*
star, sīdus, -eris, *n.*
state, cīvitās, -ātis, *f.* ; rēs pūblica, reī pūblicae, *f.*
stature, statūra, -ae, *f.*

stay, maneō, -ēre, mānsī, mānsum
storm, tempestās, -ātis, *f.*
story, fābula, -ae, *f.*
street, vīcus, -ī, *m.*
strength, vīrēs, -ium, *f.pl.*
study, studeō, -ēre, -uī
study, studium, -iī, *n.*
such, tālis, -is, -e
suddenly, subitō
suffer, patior, patī, passus sum
suitable, idōneus, -a, -um
summer, aestās, -ātis, *f.*
sun, sōl, sōlis, *m.*
sunset, sōlis occāsus, -ūs, *m.*
superintend, cūrō, -āre, -āvī, -ātum ; īnspiciō, -ere, -spexī, -spectum
surround, cingō, -ere, cinxī, cinctum
suspicion, sūspīciō, -iōnis, *f.*
swallow, hirundō, -inis, *f.*
swim, natō, -āre, -āvī, -ātum
sword, gladius, -iī, *m.*

take, capiō, -ere, cēpī, captum ; dūcō, -ere, dūxī, ductum
talent, talentum, -ī, *n.*
task, opus, -eris, *n.*
teach, doceō, -ēre, -uī, doctum
teacher, praeceptor, -ōris, *m.*
tell, dīcō, -ere, dīxī, dictum ; certiōrem facere
tell (*order*), imperō, -āre, -āvi, -ātum ; iubeō, -ēre, iūssī, iūssum
temple, templum, -ī, *n.*
terrify, terreō, -ēre, -uī, -itum
than, quam
thank, grātiās agō, -ere, ēgī, āctum
thanks to, propter (*with acc.*)
that, is, ea, id ; ille, illa, illud
that, in order that, ut
then, tum, deinde
there, ibi

therefore, igitur
thick, dēnsus, -a, -um
thing, rēs, reī, *f.*
think, putō, -āre, -āvī, -ātum ; cōgitō, -āre, -āvī, -ātum
this, hīc, haec, hōc
thither, eō
thoroughly frightened, perterritus, -a, -um
three, trēs, trēs, tria
through, per (*with acc.*)
throw, iaciō, -ere, iēcī, iactum
throw away, abiciō, -ere, -iēcī, -iectum
throw down, deiciō, -ere, -iēcī, -iectum
tide, aestus, -ūs, *m.*
time, tempus, -oris, *n.*
tired, dēfessus, -a, -um
to, ad (*with acc.*)
to-day, hodiē
toga, toga, -ae, *f.*
to-morrow, crās
to-morrow morning, crās māne
top of, summus, -a, -um
towards, ad (*with acc.*)
town, oppidum, -ī, *n.*
track, vestīgium, -iī, *n.*
train, exerceō, -ēre, -uī, -itum
travel, iter facere
treachery, prōditiō, -iōnis, *f.* ; perfidia, -ae, *f.*
tribute, tribūtum, -ī, *n.*
triumph, triumphus, -ī, *m.*
triumph, triumphō, -āre, -āvī, -ātum
troublesome, molestus, -a, -um
trust, fīdō, -ere, fīsus sum ; confīdō, -ere, confīsus sum
truth, to tell the, vēra dīcere ; vēra loquī
try, cōnor, -ārī, cōnātus sum
tumult, tumultus, -ūs, *m.*
turn, vertō, -ere, vertī, versum

unhappy, miser, misera, miserum
unmindful, immemor, -oris
understand, intellegō, -ere, -lēxī, -lēctum
undertake, sūscipiō, -ere, -cēpī, -ceptum
unwilling, to be, nōlō, nōlle, nōluī
upon my word !, edepol !, mehercule !
use, ūtor, ūtī, ūsus sum
useful, ūtilis, -is, -e

vain, in, frustrā
verse, versus, -ūs, *m.*
very, the, ipse, -a, -um
victory, victōria, -ae, *f.*
violence, vīs, *f.*
voice, vōx, vōcis, *f.*

wage (war), gerō, -ere, gessī, gestum
wait for, exspectō, -āre, -āvī, -ātum
waken, excitō, -āre, -āvī, -ātum
walk, ambulō, -āre, -āvī, -ātum
wall, mūrus, -ī, *m.*
walls (of a city), moenia, -ium, *n.pl.*
war, bellum, -ī, *n.*
warn, moneō, -ēre, -uī, -itum
warship, nāvis longa, *f.*
water, aqua, -ae, *f.*
wave, unda, -ae, *f.*
wealth, dīvitiae, -ārum, *f.pl.* ; opēs, -um, *f.pl.*
weather, tempestās, -ātis, *f.*
weep, fleō, flēre, flēvī, flētum ; dēfleō, -ēre, -flēvī, -flētum
well, bene
well, to be, valeō, -ēre, -uī
well, to grow, convalēscō, -ere, -uī
what sort of ?, quālis, -is, -e ?
when ?, quandō ?

when, ubi, cum
where ?, ubi ?
where from ?, whence ?, unde ?
where to ?, whither ?, quō ?
whether . . . or, utrum . . . an
which ?, quī, quae, quod ?
which, quī, quae, quod
which (of two) ?, uter, utra, utrum ?
whither ?, quō ?
who ?, what ?, quis, quis, quid ?
who, which, quī, quae, quod
whole, tōtus, -a, -um
why ?, cūr ?
wicked, scelestus, -a, -um
wife, uxor, -ōris, *f.*
wild beast, fera, -ae, *f.*
willing, to be, volō, velle, voluī
wind, ventus, -ī, *m.*
window, fenestra, -ae, *f.*
wine, vīnum, -ī, *n.*
winter, hiems, -is, *f.*
wisdom, sapientia, -ae, *f.*
wise, sapiēns, -entis
wish, volō, velle, voluī
with, cum (*with abl.*)
without, sine (*with abl.*)
wolf, lupus, -ī, *m.*
woman, fēmina, -ae, *f.* ; old woman, anus, -ūs, *f.*
wonder, to be an object of, admīrātiōnī esse
wonderful, mīrābilis, -is, -e
wood, silva, -ae, *f.*
word, verbum, -ī, *n.*
work, labor, -ōris, *m.*
work, labōrō, -āre, -āvī, -ātum
worship, cultus, -ūs, *m.*
worship, colō, -ere, coluī, cultum
wound, vulnus, -eris, *n.*
wound, vulnerō, -āre, -āvī, -ātum
wreck, frangō, -ere, frēgī, frāctum
wretched, miser, misera, miserum

write, scrībō, -ere, scrīpsī, scrīptum

writer, scrīptor, -ōris, *m.*

wrong, to do, peccō, -āre, -āvī, -ātum

year, annus, -ī, *m.*

yes indeed, ita vērō

yesterday, herī

young man, iuvenis, -is, *m.*

A SELECTION OF
OLIVER & BOYD'S
LATIN BOOKS

A NEW APPROACH TO LATIN
By E. G. Macnaughton and T. W. McDougall

A course in two books covering two or three years' work. It is not merely a revised version of *The Approach to Latin*, but is completely different in style and method, the emphasis being placed on continuous Latin reading with the consequent need for a much wider vocabulary (which need not be memorised, however, as the words are kept 'alive' by frequent repetition). Latin grammar is fully dealt with, but in a fairly informal way.

In *Part 1* the reading passages deal with the Roman way of life—the family, education, houses, travel, entertainment and so on. In *Part 2* they provide a sketch of the history and life of the Roman Empire up to the barbarian invasions with, for good measure, a glance at the Middle Ages.

As many teachers still regard a certain amount of English-Latin composition as a useful teaching instrument, a limited number of such exercises have been included.

ECCE ROMANI
By the Scottish Classics Group

A Latin reading course for beginners, consisting of six course books, two reference books and two teacher's guides. The reading material is grouped around a Roman family in A.D. 80 and vivid drawings assist understanding of the text as well as illustrating Roman background. There is a carefully controlled input of forms, sentence patterns and vocabulary, and the use of small booklets (64 or 80 pages) gives the pupil a feeling of progress and a sense of achievement.

The teacher's handbooks suggest classroom methods and exercises as well as giving a detailed bibliography of sources for background material and a list of appropriate visual aids.

Versiculi—A Companion in Verse

The Scottish Classics Group believe that Latin verse is a natural form of the language and that if it is introduced carefully and gradually from an early stage its difficulties will not loom so large and pupils will easily become accustomed to its conventions. To this end they have planned this little book, closely linking it as regards vocabulary and morphology with the first four books of the *Ecce Romani* course. It consists of 27 passages of verse, the first 21 of which have been specially composed to suit the contents of the course. Help is given with vocabulary, the notes being placed opposite the verse for ease of reference.

A booklet of teacher's notes is also available.

PER SAECULA

By G. Suggitt and H. M. McArdle

The three books in this series have a twofold aim—to provide a wide range of reading material for pupils and to help them to read Latin with understanding and interest. They attempt to bridge the gap between the 'made-up' or adapted Latin of the course book and the complete text of a Latin author. A book of passages for unseen translation and comprehension is included, and this, together with the prose book, contains the bulk of the work required for the O level examination.

Per Saecula—Prose

This book contains a selection of prose passages drawn from a long range of Latin literature from Caesar to George Buchanan. There are sections on history, biography, letters and oratory. For ease of reference the explanatory notes are placed on the page opposite the Latin text. The book is illustrated with photographs. 160 pp.

Per Saecula—Verse

Extracts from the works of both Classical and Medieval authors are included in this book, which is also illustrated.

Per Saecula—Passages for Comprehension and Unseen Translation

This book contains some 40 comprehension passages, with questions, and about 40 passages for useen translation, thus providing useful practice in these types of exercise.